From Economics to Political Economy

T0291428

The discipline of economics has been increasingly criticised for its inability to illuminate the workings of the real world and to provide reliable policy guidance for the major economic and social challenges of our time.

A central problem in contemporary economics, and a problem from which many of its other failings flow, is its lack of plurality. By a lack of plurality it is meant that contemporary economics lacks diversity in its methods, theories, epistemology and methodology. It is also meant that economics has become far less interdisciplinary. *From Economics to Political Economy* offers an explanation as to why economics has become so determinedly non-pluralistic, and also gives considerable attention to exploring and evaluating promising strategies for reform. These strategies include developing a pluralist economics under the label of 'political economy' within other social science departments (such as departments of politics). Along the way the reader will learn about the worldwide student movement seeking greater pluralism in economics, encounter some dramatic case studies in intellectual suppression, gain a fuller sense of the nature of contemporary economics and explore the relationship between economics and other social sciences.

This book is of interest to any social scientist, particularly those with interests in economics and politics.

Tim B. Thornton is a lecturer in the Department of Politics and Philosophy, and the Institute of Human Security and Social Change at La Trobe University, Australia, where he teaches political economy and convenes La Trobe's Bachelor of Politics, Philosophy and Economics and Master of International Development degrees. Tim has a PhD in economics from La Trobe University and a Master of Arts (International Development) from Monash University, Australia. He has published regularly on the topic of pluralism in economics, the nature and direction of contemporary economics and the relationship between economics and other social sciences.

New Political Economy
Richard McIntyre, General Editor

From Economics to Political Economy

The problems, promises and solutions of pluralist economics

Tim B. Thornton

LONDON AND NEW YORK

First published 2017
by Routledge
2 Park Square, Milton Park, Abingdon, Oxon OX14 4RN

and by Routledge
711 Third Avenue, New York, NY 10017

First issued in paperback 2018

Routledge is an imprint of the Taylor & Francis Group, an informa business

British Library Cataloguing in Publication Data
A catalogue record for this book is available from the British Library

Library of Congress Cataloging in Publication Data
Names: Thornton, Tim B., author.
Title: From economics to political economy : the problems, promises and
solutions of pluralist economics / Tim B. Thornton.
Description: New York : Routledge, 2016.
Identifiers: LCCN 2016005699| ISBN 9781138933101 (hardback) |
ISBN 9781315678740 (ebook)
Subjects: LCSH: Economics.
Classification: LCC HB171.5 T477 2016 | DDC 330--dc23
LC record available at https://lccn.loc.gov/2016005699

ISBN 13: 978-1-138-59932-1 (pbk)
ISBN 13: 978-1-138-93310-1 (hbk)

Typeset in Times New Roman
by Saxon Graphics Ltd, Derby

[I]f reforms to economics depend on the tolerance, good will and liberalism of mainstream economists I wouldn't have too much confidence of success. There is nearly always a resident dissident or two. They may try and do innovative things, teach in a way that's engaging to students and put on different types of courses, but they come and go. The courses come and go with them and the mainstream flows on forever. That is why I think it is important to have a separate institutional base. In an ideal world you wouldn't have to separate groups in this way, but in a less than ideal world this is probably the optimal situation.

(Frank Stilwell, in telephone interview with Tim B. Thornton,

29 September 2008)

Contents

Illustrations

Figure

Tables

Acknowledgements

I would like to thank my colleagues, friends, and current and former students. Particular thanks are owed to Professor Richard McIntyre for suggesting that I submit a proposal to Routledge. Andrew Humphries, Laura Johnson, Daniel Bourner and all the team at Routledge UK are also thanked for support, advice and professionalism. Dave Wright was project manager for the book and Nigel Hope was the copy-editor. I thank them both for all their work, expertise and professionalism. This book is based on my PhD thesis, though many of the ideas have been further developed here. Given this, I would like to again thank Professor John King for his supervision of the thesis. I also thank Dr Miriam Bankovsky, Professor Rod O'Donnell, Professor Frank Stilwell and Dr George Argyrous for their support. Professor Marika Vicziany and Associate Professor Ian Ward are also to be thanked for the encouragement and help they gave me early in my career. Of course, none of these people bear any responsibility for any errors within this book, nor should it be assumed that all views expressed in the book are necessarily views that they share. Thanks are owed to my family, particularly my mother Margaret Thornton, my father Bruce Thornton, my daughters Tallulah and Isabella, and most of all, my wife Amanda.

Several of the chapters draw on material that has been published in academic journals:

- Chapter 3 includes material published in T. B. Thornton, 'The Changing Face of Mainstream Economics?', *Journal of Australian Political Economy*, no. 75, Winter (2015), and T. Thornton, 'The "Complexity Revolution" Seen from a Historical and Heterodox Perspective', in J. Courvisanos, A. Millmow and J. Doughney (eds), *Reclaiming Pluralism*, Routledge, London, 2016, pp. 238–50.
- Chapter 8 includes material published in T. B. Thornton, 'The Economics Curriculum in Australian Universities', *Economic Papers*, vol. 31, no. 1 (2012), pp. 103–13, and T. B. Thornton, 'The Narrowing of the Australian Economics Curriculum: An Analysis of the Problem and a Proposed Solution', *The Economic Record*, vol. 89, Supplement S1 June (2013), pp. 106-14.
- Chapter 12 draws on material from published in T. Thornton, 'Are Employers Currently Interested in a Reformed Economics Curriculum?', *Australasian Journal of Economics Education Volume*, vol. 11, no. 1 (2014), pp. 1–20.

Introduction

In recent decades, the discipline of economics has been increasingly criticised for its inability to illuminate the workings of the real world and to provide reliable policy guidance for the major economic and social challenges of our time. Indeed, economics has been criticised for too easily providing intellectual cover for economic and social arrangements that are unwise, unsustainable and unjust. Simply put, the profession, and the analysis it produces, is not held in sufficiently high regard.

A recent wave of criticism of economics came as a result of the global financial crisis, an event that orthodox economists failed to foresee, prevent or adequately explain. Even the Queen of England felt compelled to ask Britain's leading economists why they did not see a crisis coming. Some have argued that the profession bears some of the responsibility for the crisis by providing intellectual support for many of the policy and regulatory changes that allowed a crisis to develop.

Another recent wave of criticism has come from university students who find the economics education they are offered to be inadequate and too narrow. In 2014, sixty-five student groups from across thirty countries formed the International Student Initiative for Pluralism in Economics Education (ISIPE), which released an open letter calling for major reform of the curriculum. ISIPE's establishment follows in the footsteps of the Post-Autistic Economics Movement that was first established in France in 2000 and which had various knock-on effects across the world.

Dissenting academic economists have also been increasingly visible, vocal and well organised. In 1993, they formed the International Confederation for the Advancement of Pluralism in Economics: a federation of thirty groups working to maintain diversity and innovation in methods, approaches and analysis of policy. Other initiatives include the 2011 formation of the World Economics Association, the establishment of the Association for Heterodox Economists, the Society for Heterodox Economists as well the creation of publications such as the *Heterodox Economics Newsletter*, *Real-World Economics Review* and the *Directory of Heterodox Economics*. Clearly, there is a significant number of people calling for real change in economics.

In the face of this criticism and agitation, orthodox economists have not responded in an adequate and reasonable manner. Part of the explanation for this is that many economists have a deeply held view that the theory and methods that they rely on are rigorous and meritorious. For them, economics is, and remains, the queen of the social sciences and a model for other disciplines to emulate. They see the criticism the profession has received in recent years as being misguided, naive or politically motivated. However, critics argue that economic theory is anything but rigorous and meritorious. Particular problems include an over-reliance on highly unrealistic theoretical assumptions, an over-use of mathematical modelling, the exclusion of many important variables and relationships, and the failure adequately to incorporate crucial insights from other academic disciplines such as politics, philosophy, psychology, history and sociology. Another line of criticism is that particular theories are persisted with long after empirical evidence has suggested they be abandoned or significantly altered (Quiggin 2010).

One way of understanding all the problems just described is to link them to the issue of non-plurality or monism. By this it is meant that contemporary economics lacks pluralism in its methods, theories, epistemology and methodology. It is to say also that it is insufficiently interdisciplinary in the sense that it has become less and less able to engage in a co-informing dialogue with other academic disciplines. Social and economic reality is so complicated that no discipline should so heavily close-off, and narrow-down, the methods and accumulated insights and approaches by which we may better understand the world around us.

Economics has not always been so monist. The discipline was once broader and richer. Indeed, even today there still exist other approaches (for example, institutional economics, Post-Keynesian economics, Marxian economics, feminist economics, ecological economics, and Austrian economics) but they are all marginalised within the profession. Similarly, the sub-disciplines of history of economic thought, economic history and development economics are also marginalised. The neoclassical approach – a quite narrow approach to economic and social analysis – has become ever more dominant over these minority schools and sub-disciplines. Whilst the neoclassical approach is not without some value, provided that its strengths and weaknesses are understood, it is inadequate as the sole option for economic analysis. A more plural economics is required.

One can also argue that a more interdisciplinary economics is also required. That is to say that economics should be more open to the learning of other disciplines and more able to enter into a co-informing dialogue with them. However, the very essence of pluralism is to be intellectually open. Thus it is understood in this book that to call for economic pluralism is necessarily to call also for increased interdisciplinarity within economics.

To argue for a more plural and interdisciplinary approach within economics denotes one as a radical within the profession. However, it is actually more accurate to say that those calling for such changes represent a traditionalist orientation and are seeking to remedy an extreme state of affairs. Contemporary economics *is* perverse, no other social science is non-plural to anywhere the extent that economics is (King 2012) and in no other discipline do students so regularly rebel against the narrowness of their instruction (Kay 2014). There is nothing about the nature of economic phenomena that dictates this monist approach. In fact, the complex and shifting nature of economic reality actively requires pluralism and interdisciplinarity (King 2012). One can also add that pluralism is consistent with traditional intellectual values of liberalism, tolerance and scepticism (including self-scepticism).

What this book is about

It is argued that the lack of pluralism within economics is currently its central failing and is tightly linked to most of its problems and deficiencies. For this reason, one focus of this book is to explain why economics is so non-pluralistic and why it has proven so difficult to reform. There has been real disquiet about its shortcomings at least as far back as the 1960s, yet various waves of protest have washed through to little or no effect. It is a strange and unfortunate state of affairs and it is important to try to understand why this is so.

The main focus of the book, however, is exploring and evaluating particular strategies for reform. Various reform strategies are examined to remedy the marginalisation of what are known as the 'heterodox' traditions of economics (institutional economics, Post-Keynesian economics, Marxian economics, feminist economics, ecological economics, and Austrian economics) and also to restore the fortunes of history of economic thought, economic history and development economics. It is argued that these areas of knowledge are best understood to constitute collectively 'political economy.' Notwithstanding improvements in neoclassical economics and the orthodox research frontier, restoring the fortunes of political economy is viewed as the most central means to restore plurality in economics.

It is to be emphasised at this point that this book, consistent with its espousal of pluralism, is not *against* orthodox economics per se, instead it is *for* political economy. Orthodox economics is currently very dominant in economics teaching, research and policy. It currently requires no attention, analysis or support to continue its ongoing existence. By contrast, political economy is very much in need of attention, analysis and support.

The strategies for reform that are examined are largely centred on reforming the way economics is taught and the way economics research is evaluated within the university system. Other reform strategies outside of the university system such as reforming high-school economics education or adult education (perhaps by utilising advances in information technology) are not the focus here. They are worthy of attention, but pursuit of them here is beyond the scope of a single book. In any event, a dedicated focus on the university is a good place to start given that this is where the discipline reproduces itself. Achieving real change here should have desirable flow-on effects to high school education and adult education.

Three broad pathways for reform are considered. The first pathway is to work for reform from within traditional centres of economics teaching (which is usually a university's economics department). The second pathway, 'reform from without', is to work for reform from outside traditional centres (for example teaching a pluralist economics in another department). The third pathway is to pursue a hybrid approach where one is simultaneously pursuing reform from inside and outside of traditional centres (for example, establishing Politics, Philosophy and Economics degrees that structurally integrate the study of economics with other disciplines). Within these broad strategies there are of course more fine-grained strategic choices to be made and these are also analysed.

It is argued that the strategies of working outside traditional centres of economics teaching and pursuing hybrid strategies may often, though not always, offer the most promising pathways for substantial reform. Indeed, one of the options put forward in this book is that political economy should conceive of itself, and operate as, something akin to a separate discipline that operates outside the orbit and control of departments of economics. However, it is also shown that working from within traditional centres of economics teaching can be productive and will be the most appropriate option for some to pursue in some contexts. No particular strategy is presented as a panacea, and no strategy is condemned as being inherently hopeless. Indeed, a central argument of the book is that a pluralist economics will, perhaps not surprisingly, require a pluralism of strategies and a division of labour between universities and the individuals within them. The appropriate choice of reform strategy to be pursued within a particular university is dependent on the specific context of that university and the capacities and inclinations of those involved. However, one can better evaluate what to do in a specific context by learning what has occurred in similar contexts. Given this, a diverse range of case studies is offered up in the later chapters of the book to examine different reform strategies in action.

It is quite clear that to pursue pluralism within economics is not the simplest, quickest or easiest of tasks. However, it should be emphasised that there is no *good* reason why greater pluralism should not occur. In particular, it *is* possible and practical to teach economics in a plural manner. Evidence indicates that introducing students to a range of approaches need not create confusion; indeed, the evidence shows that, if handled skilfully, it can promote depth of intellectual understanding (Barone 1991; Dawson 2007). As John Stuart Mill long ago asserted, one cannot fully understand any argument until one also understands the relevant counterarguments. There is no good reason to shield students from controversy or debate, as William Becker argues we should 'quit lying and embracing the controversies' (Becker 2007, p. 3). Furthermore, there is also good research to show that exposure to a diversity of views, combined with an ever-present critical perspective, develops the general skills that are required of graduates by employers and by society itself (O'Donnell 2010).

Why reform is needed

Before summarising the content of the chapters to come, it is worth noting why the achievement of a plural economics is important and of considerable practical consequence.

Economists currently exert a particularly strong influence on policymaking. For example, treasury departments are usually the most influential departments in any country's public service. These departments are nearly always primarily managed and staffed by economists. As Pusey (1991) has shown, the economics education that public sector economists receive has a very direct effect on how they then think and analyse policy options. A narrow and uncritical education in neoclassical economics is a poor foundation for good policymaking.

The nature of an economics education also has direct effects on the thinking of many non-economists. Many millions of students across the world choose, or are required, to undertake at least one introductory economics subject while at university. What these students learn in these introductory classes affects how they make sense of the economy, society and themselves for the rest of their lives. Introductory economics exerts a strong influence over what a society views to be acceptable economic analysis and policy advice. It influences society's view about what is and is not possible and how certain objectives may be best achieved.

Another cause for concern is that the current curriculum appears to be detrimental to students' social and ethical development. For example, researchers who undertook a number of free rider/prisoner's dilemma games, found students with a training in economics to be more aggressive, less cooperative, more pessimistic about the prospects of cooperation, and more prone to cheating than students who had not undertaken any economics subjects (note that selection bias was controlled for in these experiments). The characteristics that developed as a result of taking these economics courses persisted long after their education had finished (Frank, Gilovich & Regan 1993, 1996).

Another identified problem lies in the content of the curriculum being neither properly understood nor retained by students (Clarke & Mearman 2001). Those who have undertaken an introductory economics subject at high-school or university retain little of their knowledge; indeed, within a few months of completing their studies, doing little better than those who had not studied any economics at all (Hansen, Salemi & Siegfried 2002). Furthermore, few undergraduates are able 'to express an opinion of any greater insight regarding economic affairs than a member of the general public' (Sheehan, Embery & Morgan 2015, p. 215). This poor level of insight and retention suggests that an enormous waste of society's resources is occurring.

A further problem is that the current curriculum, primarily due to its non-plural nature, is not only deficient as an input towards providing a liberal education and an informed society, it also fails adequately to supply the graduate knowledge, skills and attributes required by many employers (O'Donnell 2007). Again, this amounts to a missed opportunity and a large waste of resources.

In summary, it is hard not to agree with former Greek Minister of Finance, and Professor of Economics, Yanis Varoufakis (2009, p. 46) that the currently inadequate education of economists amounts to 'a powder keg buried deep in the foundations of complex liberal societies'. Certainly, a reformed plural economics is needed to assist in addressing the major challenges of our time, such as climate change and ecological constraint, increasing inequality and economic and social instability.

Structure of the book

It is useful at this point to provide a broad overview of the chapters to come and to emphasise the 'bare bones' of some of the major arguments made in the book. 'Bare bones' is probably an apt phrase to use as some of the arguments, in their skeletal form, and without supporting flesh and muscle, might initially be alarming to some.

Chapter 1 'The sociology of scientific knowledge', examines the central tenets of the sociology of scientific knowledge (SSK). It places SSK in the context of the breakdown of the received view of science and then follows its development from Thomas Kuhn through to 'Strong Programme' and the 'Social Constructivists'. The chapter includes a case study of Shapin and Schaffer's *The Leviathan and the Air-Pump* and provides some useful concepts and ideas for making sense of contemporary economics thus providing a foundation for later chapters. A key argument advanced is that solutions to the problem of knowledge are inseparable from solutions to the problem of social order.

Chapter 2, 'The changing face of economics', examines the extent to which economics might be reformed via developments within the research frontier of orthodox economics. Particular consideration is given to the argument that many critics of contemporary economics are neither recognising, nor capitalising on, the changing nature of economics, and are instead persisting with outdated and counterproductive habits of thought and action. The response in the chapter to these ideas and arguments is that whilst orthodox economics has become less monolithic, it is a mistake to expect too much of the orthodox research frontier in terms of its capacity to create a more plural and adequate economics.

Chapter 3, 'Economic pluralism and economics as a science', provides the intellectual case for a more plural economics curriculum. The ideas of theory as simplification, and of economic and social reality existing as an open system, are the central rationales put forward to support pluralism. The latter half of the chapter applies the concept of pluralism to differing conceptions of what is scientific, with particular emphasis on conceptions of science within orthodox economics.

Chapter 4, 'Orthodoxy, heterodoxy and political economy', is concerned with matters of definition and categorisation. A detailed intellectual and practical argument is put forward for conceiving of a distinct area of knowledge called 'political economy' which could be seen as either a separate discipline to economics, or as existing as one side of a dualism in economics with the other side of that dualism being 'orthodox economics'. Alternatively, political economy could be categorised in other ways including as a trans-disciplinary area of knowledge or even as a branch of politics. The argument is also put forward that the term 'heterodox economics' is problematic and warrants being used only in a quite narrow and specific manner.

Chapter 5, 'The global student movement for pluralism', provides an overview of student agitation for reform of economics. The chapter includes an examination of how the Post-Autistic Economics Movement emerged in France around 2000, as well as an analysis of the International Student Initiative for Pluralism in Economics (ISIPE) that emerged in 2014. The analysis includes a survey of the activities and views of twenty-four student groups associated with ISIPE. It is argued that the student movement is a significant development and has significant potential to drive reform. It is suggested that greater communication, coordination and cooperation between these student groups and academics would be desirable.

Chapter 6, 'Economics textbooks', analyses the contemporary economics textbook. The chapter includes a case study of Mankiw's *Principles of economics*, the world's leading introductory textbook, finding it to be deeply problematic. There is also an analysis of *Principles of economics in context* by Goodwin et al., a text designed to replace problematic textbooks such as Mankiw's. The chapter concludes with an examination of the Institute for New Economic Thinking's *Core Econ* an open-access online textbook, which is found to be an inadequate response to calls for curricular reform in economics.

Chapter 7, 'Economics departments', examines the institutional features of economics departments and gives particular focus to the problem of teaching work being undervalued relative to research work. The bias against political economy research is also examined. The chapter includes survey analysis of how the curriculum within economics departments has changed since 1980. The main argument put forward is that the current realities of economics departments suggest that political economists should seek to establish greater independence and differentiation from orthodox economics.

Chapter 8, 'Reform from within', contains two case studies of how economic pluralism has developed within the traditional base for economics in the university system – the economics department. The case studies are drawn from Kingston University in the United Kingdom and Western Sydney University in Australia. Both case studies illustrate that, despite some challenges, establishing a pluralist economics department is possible. How these pluralist departments were developed and managed is given particular attention.

Chapter 9, 'Reform from without', examines two case studies where universities have divided their economics departments into two, creating on one hand, a department primarily, or exclusively, focused on neoclassical economics, and on the other, a pluralist department that is partly, or largely, a political economy department. The case studies are of Notre Dame University (where separation was counterproductive) and the University of Sydney in Australia (where separation has brought success). It is argued that despite clear challenges and risks, the model of institutional separation does, in certain situations, offer a promising means to achieve a more plural and adequate economics.

Chapter 10, 'Hybrid strategies', considers a strategy for the reform of economics whereby its curriculum is structurally integrated with other disciplines. It contains a case study of La Trobe University's Politics, Philosophy and Economics (PPE) degree. This degree represents a 'hybrid strategy' for reform in that the degree acts as a means to drive reform of economics from *inside* the economics department, but it also drives reform of economics from *outside* the economics department by virtue of the fact that political scientists and philosophers end up becoming involved in economics teaching and economics research, as well as influencing the economics makeup of the economics component of the degree.

Chapter 11, 'The market for economic knowledge', is focused on what employers currently require from economics graduates. Employer needs are a potentially powerful driver of reform, as students and university administrators are increasingly keen for a university education to meet the needs of employers. A pluralistic economics curriculum does appear to have very strong capacities to develop the knowledge, skills and attributes that many employers require. However, the evidence in the chapter suggests there is work to be done in creating a greater awareness of the link between pluralism and the graduate attributes.

Chapter 12, 'The three purposes of economics', seeks to explain the nature of contemporary economics by relating it back to the functions it is asked to perform. The chapter is indebted to an unduly overlooked article by Warren Samuels who, building on the work of Robinson, Shackle and others, argues that there are three interrelated purposes for economics in society: scientific explanation, social control and psychological comfort. It is argued that these three purposes exert a powerful influence on the nature of economics and that a proper understanding of them, including an understanding of their circular and cumulative interrelationship, offers a useful way to summarise and connect the various forces that shape contemporary economics.

References

Barone, C. A. 1991, 'Contending Perspectives: Curricular Reform in Economics', *The Journal of Economic Education*, vol. 22, no. 1, pp. 15–26.

Becker, W. E. 2007, 'Quit Lying and Address the Controversies: There Are No Dogmata, Laws, Rules or Standards in the Science of Economics', *American Economist*, vol. 51, no. 1, pp. 3–12.

Clarke, P. & Mearman, A. 2001, 'Heterodoxy, Educational Aims and the Design of Economics Programmes', *Economic and Social Policy*, vol. 5, no. 2, pp. 1–14.

Dawson, R. 2007, 'Judging Economics Teaching and Textbooks', *Journal of Australian Political Economy*, vol. 60, December, pp. 73–97.

Frank, R. H., Gilovich, T. & Regan, D. T. 1993, 'Does Studying Economics Inhibit Cooperation?', *Journal of Economic Perspectives*, vol. 7, no. 2, pp. 159–71.

Frank, R. H., Gilovich, T. & Regan, D. T. 1996, 'Do Economists Make Bad Citizens', *Journal of Economic Perspectives*, vol. 10, no. 1, pp. 187–92.

Hansen, W. L., Salemi, M. K. & Siegfried, J. J. 2002, 'Use it or Lose it: Teaching Literacy in the Economics Principles Course', *American Economic Review*, vol. 92, no. 2, pp. 463–72.

Kay, J. 2014, 'Angry Economics Students Are Naive – and Mostly Right', *Financial Times*, London, p. 1.

King, J. E. 2012, *A Case for Pluralism in Economics* Academy of the Social Sciences in Australia, Melbourne.

O'Donnell, R. 2007, 'Teaching Economic Pluralism: Adding Value to Students, Economies and Societies', paper presented to Second International Conference for International Confederation of Associations for Pluralism in Economics, University of Utah, 1–3 June.

O'Donnell, R. 2010, 'Economic Pluralism and Skill Formation: Adding Value to Students, Economies, and Societies', in R Garnett, E K Olsen & M Starr (eds), *Economic Pluralism,* Routledge, New York, pp. 262–77.

Pusey, M. 1991, *Economic Rationalism in Canberra: A Nation Building State Changes Its Mind*, Cambridge University Press, Cambridge.

Quiggin, J. 2010, *Zombie Economics: How Dead Ideas Still Walk among Us*, Princeton University Press, Princeton.

Sheehan, B., Embery, J. & Morgan, J. 2015, 'Give Them Something to Think About, Don't Tell Them What to Think: A Constructive Heterodox Alternative to the Core Project', *Journal of Australian Political Economy*, vol. 75, Winter, pp. 211–31.

Varoufakis, Y. 2009, 'Where the Customers Are Always Wrong: Some Thoughts on the Societal Impact of a Non-Pluralist Economic Education', *International Journal of Pluralism and Economics Education*, vol. 1, no. 1/2, pp. 46–57.

1   The sociology of scientific knowledge

This book is essentially concerned with how ideas in economics persist, spread, contract or are just simply ignored. It is therefore appropriate to commence the analysis by examining the key ideas and concepts within the Sociology of Science Knowledge (SSK) which is a particular branch of the philosophy of science that seeks to explain the persistence, spread and contraction of intellectual ideas in general. The chapter provides a general exposition of SSK, resisting the temptation immediately to start applying the ideas to economics to any great degree. The application of the ideas will come in the chapters ahead.

SSK seems rather removed from a traditional conception of what the philosophy of science is. Hands (1998, p. 474) points out that the philosophy of science has generally been concerned with epistemic justification for rules that are said to dictate proper scientific method. By contrast, SSK examines a scientific community, first and foremost, as a social group whose behaviour is significantly determined by the same sorts of factors that determine how individuals act within other social groups. This view of science is different from simply assuming that science is a straightforward mechanical process whereby hypotheses or theories are developed, tested against evidence and then discarded or provisionally accepted and where social forces do not impinge.

SSK arose because of the failure of earlier philosophies of science, such as logical positivism and Popperian falsificationism, to provide a rule-based approach for classifying theory as being either scientific or unscientific (see Chapter 3). SSK, along with rhetorical and postmodern approaches, can be seen as constituting a 'naturalistic turn' whereby we examine what scientists actually do, rather than prescribe what they should do (Hands 2001b). SSK views the old rule-based approach of the received view as being untenable, arguing that observation cannot be 'objective' and needs to be seen as being both theory-laden and social-context laden (Hands 2001a). SSK asserts that socialisation and institutions are crucial to how scientific endeavour plays out. Socialisation and the signals and incentives of particular social structures often lead scientists unquestioningly to believe certain things and look at things in a specific way. Science, for all its claims to be an objective pursuit of the truth, cannot totally transcend the social, even if scientists themselves, or the society they serve, would like to, or feel they need to, imagine otherwise.

SSK originates with the publication of *The Structure of Scientific Revolutions* by Thomas Kuhn (1962). Kuhn's book was a landmark and has had a significant impact on both the philosophy of science and economic methodology. The literature on Kuhn's work is vast, but the essential ideas can be outlined reasonably succinctly. It is argued that most of the time science practice is in a state of 'normal science', where there is a single ruling paradigm. A paradigm is an overall framework or research programme that defines the thinking and behaviour of a particular community of researchers. Kuhn later refined his idea of paradigm by arguing that it is composed of a disciplinary matrix (Dow 2002). This disciplinary matrix stipulates the models and methods to be used, but also provides a general world-view that includes things such as the values by which theories are to be judged (Dow 2002). Exemplars also form part of the disciplinary matrix, demonstrating an (apparently) impressive solution to a particular problem (Pheby 1987). Within economics, textbooks immediately come to mind as important components of the disciplinary matrix.

Kuhn argued that paradigms are incommensurate with one another. Such an assertion conflicts with the traditional conception that science builds on the knowledge contained in older theories and that later theories will be getting closer and closer to the truth (Boumans et al. 2010). Incommensurability provides some of the explanation of why scientists from different paradigms have enormous problems trying to communicate with each other and to respect each other's positions. It was Kuhn's reading of Aristotle's *Physica* that provided the genesis for his main ideas. Kuhn noted that Aristotle's observations of biology and political behaviour had impressively stood the test of time as searching and profound. However, his study of motion, to Kuhn, read as absurd. Stranger still, was the fact that these absurd ideas of Aristotle were taken so seriously for a very long period of time (Kuhn 1977 p. xi). Kuhn eventually resolved his puzzlement by concluding that Aristotle's analysis of motion was written within an older paradigm. Aristotle's writing only seemed preposterous to Kuhn because he was viewing it through the lens of a later paradigm.

Paradigms are resistant to change and have many processes that are conservative in nature. However, they are not permanent and can be overthrown from time to time; notably, this is said to occur via a *revolutionary* rather than an incremental process (Kuhn 1962; Pheby 1987). The starting point for a revolution is the building up of anomalies and problems that are so serious that they can neither be ignored nor accommodated via minor adjustments to the currently dominant paradigm. This situation is seen as a state of 'crisis', which is resolved by scientists abandoning the established paradigm and taking refuge in a new paradigm (Pheby 1987).

Kuhn developed his ideas by looking at the history of the natural sciences rather than the social sciences. It is generally accepted that Kuhn's ideas do not transfer quite as well to the social sciences as the natural sciences. Backhouse (1998) has outlined some problems in regard to how Kuhn's ideas apply to the history of economics. First, it is difficult to clearly establish the start and end of particular paradigms: has there been a single paradigm since Adam Smith? Or are there various paradigms, such as the classical, neoclassical and Keynesian? The second problem is that it is difficult to argue that particular paradigms have enjoyed near-monopoly status, as asserted by Kuhn. While there is a dominant orthodox economics, there are also dissident schools that coexist with this dominant paradigm. In the social sciences, paradigms seem to accumulate, rather than replace each other (Hettne 1995).

While Kuhn's thinking does not map seamlessly on to the history of economics, his concept of a paradigm has broad applicability to economics; in particular that 'prior acceptance of a paradigm defines what one will look for and what he/she will see' and that 'adherents to different paradigms literally live in different worlds and find it virtually impossible to communicate with one another across that perceptual barrier' (Bartlett 1995 p. 1259). The concept of a paradigm is also particularly valuable in prompting questions and lines of inquiry in seeking to understand contemporary economics. The problem of *sharply* defining where a paradigm starts and ends is usually difficult, but this does not negate its usefulness.

Developments in SSK since Kuhn

Since the publication of *The Structure of Scientific Revolutions*, SSK has been extended in various directions. One of the most important of these extensions has been the 'strong programme' of the Edinburgh School, which strongly asserts that all scientific knowledge, including SSK itself, should be seen as a social construction (Bloor 1991; Dow 2002). Boumans et al. (2010) argue that the four cornerstones of the strong programme are as follows:

> Causality: identify the causal conditions that bring about the beliefs of scientists;
>
> Impartiality: be impartial between true and false, or rational and irrational, beliefs;
>
> Symmetry: the same type of cause should be used to explain both true and false beliefs;
>
> Reflexivity: the explanations offered should also be applicable to the sociology of science.

The strong programme's position on the issues of symmetry, causality and reflexivity has had some influence in the case studies undertaken in later chapters, though the analysis is obviously written by somebody who has a commitment to economic pluralism. However, some effort has been made to try to understand how different protagonists appear to understand their situations.

Another key branch of SSK is the anthropological approach of the social constructivists (this variant is sometimes referred to as the 'Bath School' – reflecting its origins at the University of Bath). The emphasis of the social constructivists is on micro-studies of what actually occurs in particular settings where science is undertaken, such as a laboratory (for an example of this work see Knorr-Cetina

1981). Indeed, this branch of SSK is sometimes known as the 'laboratory studies approach' (Boumans et al. 2010). The social constructivist approach is anthropological, as it requires 'the social scientist to spend a substantial amount of time doing fieldwork at the site of the scientific activity and to understand the particular details of the knowledge production process . . . to follow scientists around' (Hands 1998 p. 476). This book can be seen as having some affinity with the social constructivist approach, through the participant-observation approach that is adopted in Chapter 10, which draws on eleven years of working in economics departments and twenty years working within universities.

This examination of SSK will now be concluded by examining two ideas that are particularly important for the purposes of this study. The first idea is the proposition that new ideas get accepted on the basis of how desirable they are in terms of the current preferences, predilections and interests of particular groups of scientists. The second idea is the proposition that larger social debates and struggles, particularly those concerned with social and political order, are decisive in shaping what is accepted as science.

SSK argues that scientists, particularly social scientists, have no recourse to some privileged and objective process whereby they can uncover the unambiguous truth. They are prone to persist with ideas and concepts that they are attached to and feel fond of and which are advantageous to them: 'the acceptance of a scientific theory is dependent upon its compatibility with the social interests of the scientific community rather than its success in terms of explaining the state of the world' (Boumans et al. 2010, p. 122). There are certainly clear sunk costs of investing in a particular paradigm: abandoning it may lead to the loss of status and income and may also require people to acquire radically different knowledge and techniques. This could plausibly result in significant psychological stress, as scientists might well have to come to terms with having committed much of their professional lives to a failed project. This might create a strong conscious, or at least unconscious, incentive to remain committed to the status quo. Certainly, a number of dissenting economists have looked to arguments of sunk costs (Freedman 2000) and emotional and psychological distress to help explain the resistance to pluralism (Nelson 2001).

While a focus on how academics think and respond to their self-interest is important, it is also necessary to acknowledge the role that larger political and social forces play in the spread of scientific ideas. To link larger political and social forces to the spread of economics ideas is familiar territory for radical political economists and other heterodox economists (see for example Lee 2009), but it is also a cornerstone of SSK. A classic case study in the SSK tradition that illustrates this is Shapin and Schaffer's *Leviathan and the Air-Pump* (1985).

Shapin and Schaffer, working within the tradition of the strong programme, undertook an innovative analysis of a well-known scientific dispute that occurred between Thomas Hobbes and Robert Boyle in the 1660s and early 1670s. At the surface level, the dispute was about the scientific legitimacy of Boyle's air-pump experiments. These experiments involved a suction pump being attached to a glass bulb. The pump would evacuate the air, and thus create what in today's terms would be called a vacuum. However, back then, what exactly was created by the evacuation of the air was a matter of intense disagreement between Hobbes and Boyle, with Hobbes strongly attacking the significance and legitimacy of Boyle's work.

Initially, Shapin and Schaffer make a familiar point from SSK, namely that *internal* social pressures from within a scientific community are important:

> [T]he member who poses awkward questions about 'what everybody knows' in the shared culture runs a real risk of being dealt with as a troublemaker or an idiot. Indeed, there are few more reliable ways of being expelled from a culture than continuing seriously to question its taken-for-granted intellectual framework.
>
> (Shapin & Schaffer 1985, p. 6)

Many dissenting economists would agree with such an assertion, but their analysis quickly goes beyond this basic point to stress how political philosophy and a given social order can exert a substantial influence over the spread of ideas.

The dispute between Hobbes and Boyle was centred on matters of method and methodology. Hobbes argued that the path to absolute certainty was via a deductive epistemology that utilised logic and geometry and recognised no boundaries between the natural, human and the social. It was an approach that left no scope for dissent. Shapin and Schaffer argue that Hobbes's adoption of such a methodological position cannot be separated from his controversial views on social order, specifically his arguments concerning the desirability and legitimacy of a strong state (i.e. a Leviathan) to determine what is true and correct and what must be obeyed. Hobbes's particular method of knowledge production, and the supposed degree of certainty it could deliver, was seen as having profound implications for societal order. Shapin and Schaffer argue that for Hobbes, it was a case of 'show men what knowledge is and you will show them the grounds of assent and social order' (Shapin & Schaffer 1985, p. 100). It was on this basis that Hobbes viewed Boyle's air-pump experiments, not as interesting and promising scientific experiments that impressively utilised empirical, inductive and probabilistic methods, but as misguided attempts at knowledge creation that provided a basis for civil war:

> The vacuism Hobbes attacked was not merely absurd and wrong, as it was in his physical texts; it was dangerous. Speech of a vacuum was associated with cultural resources that had been illegitimately used to subvert proper authority in the state.
>
> (Shapin & Schaffer 1985, p. 91)

Shapin and Shafer point out that 'for Hobbes, the rejection of vacuum was the elimination of a space within which dissension could take place' (Shapin & Schaffer 1985, p. 109)1.

Boyle was also aware of the larger significance of his debate with Hobbes over experimental methods. Boyle realised that defending the air-pump experiments was about defending the legitimacy of an inductive and experimental approach to knowledge that relied on probabilistic reasoning. If this approach to knowledge creation could be defended, a political philosophy that recognised a pluralism of views could also be defended; for if our knowledge is only partial, a pluralism of views is valid. In other words, his 'adversary's civic philosophy and theology could be invalidated if it were shown that his physics was unsound' (Shapin & Schaffer 1985, p. 207). Hobbes's claim that there could be a leader who could determine what is correct and what must be obeyed would thus be robbed of its supposed intellectual basis and would become a failed project:

> The quest for necessary and universal assent to physical propositions was seen as inappropriate and illegitimate. It belonged to a 'dogmatic' enterprise, and dogmatism was seen not only as a failure, but as dangerous to genuine knowledge.
> (Shapin & Schaffer 1985, p. 24)

Shapin and Schaffer argue that the dispute between Boyle and Hobbes was afflicted with Kuhnian incommensurability: there was no common ground on which to settle the dispute (Jennings 1988). Shapin and Schaffer also argue that Boyle's views prevailed because they were in keeping with the political tides of the time. For Shapin and Schaffer this scientific debate was a case of 'he who has the most, and the most powerful, allies wins' (Shapin & Schaffer 1985, p. 342). In other words, there can be no intellectual success without success in gaining a minimum level of social and institutional support (King 2002, p. 241).

Ultimately, what Shapin and Schaffer conclude from their analysis of the dispute is that solutions to the problem of knowledge are totally enmeshed with finding solutions to the problem of social order so that 'the form of life in which we make our scientific knowledge will stand or fall with the way we order our affairs of the state' (Shapin & Schaffer 1985, p. 344) and that 'the problem of generating and protecting knowledge is a problem in politics, and, conversely, that the problem of political order always involves solutions to the problem of knowledge' (Shapin & Schaffer 1985, p. 21).

This chapter has provided an exposition of the key ideas of SSK. It was emphasised that science cannot be understood as a straightforward or mechanical process whereby hypotheses or theories are developed, tested against evidence and then discarded or provisionally accepted. Whilst hypothesising, theorising and testing are important to science in all its forms, science is also a social activity and social institutions constrain and facilitate the preservation and replacement of scientific ideas. Institutions and larger political and social and historical forces exert their influence on scientific practice, however much any group of people, including economists, might wish to convince themselves otherwise.

Note

1 In arguing all this, Hobbes could not be more diametrically opposed to a viewpoint put forward, much later, by the philosopher and mathematician A N Whitehead who argued,

'Never swallow anything whole. We live perforce by half-truths and get along fairly well as long as we do not mistake them for whole-truths, when we do so mistake them, they raise the devil with us' (Whitehead in Price 2001, p. 298).

References

Backhouse, R. E. 1998, 'Paradigm/Normal Science', in J. B. Davis, D. W. Hands & U. Mäki (eds), *The Handbook of Economic Methodology*, Edward Elgar, Lyme, pp. 352–54.

Bartlett, R. 1995, 'The Role of Economic Theory', *Journal of Economic Issues*, vol. 29, no. 4, pp. 1257–59.

Bloor, D. 1991, *Knowledge and Social Imagery*, University of Chicago Press, Chicago.

Boumans, M., Davis, J. B., Blaug, M., Maas, H. & Svorencik, A. 2010, *Economic Methodology: Understanding Economics as a Science*, Palgrave Macmillan, Basingstoke.

Dow, S. C. 2002, *Economic Methodology: An Inquiry*, Oxford University Press, Oxford.

Freedman, C. 2000, 'Economic Convictions and Prior Beliefs: Akerlof Wrestles with the Ghost of John Maynard Keynes', *Journal of Economic and Social Policy*, vol. 4, no. 2, pp. 71–87.

Hands, D. W. 1998, 'Sociology of Scientific Knowledge', in J. B. Davis, D. W. Hands & U. Mäki (eds), *The Handbook of Economic Methodology*, Edward Elgar, Lyme, pp. 474–77.

Hands, D. W. 2001a, 'Economic Methodology Is Dead – Long Live Economic Methodology: Thirteen Theses on the New Economic Methodology', *Journal of Economic Methodology*, vol. 8, no. 1, pp. 49–63.

Hands, D. W. 2001b, *Reflection without Rules: Economic Methodology and Contemporary Science Theory*, Cambridge University Press, Cambridge.

Hettne, B. 1995, *Development Theory and the Three Worlds: Towards an International Political Economy of Development*, Longman, Harlow.

Jennings, R. C. 1988, 'Review Article: Leviathan and the Air-Pump', *The British Journal for the Philosophy of Science*, vol. 39, no. 3, pp. 403–10.

King, J. E. 2002, *A History of Post-Keynesian Economics since 1936*, Edward Elgar, Cheltenham.

Knorr-Cetina, K. 1981, *The Manufacture of Knowledge: An Essay on the Constructivist and Contextual Nature of Science*, Pergamon, Oxford.

Kuhn, T. S. 1962, *The Structure of Scientific Revolutions*, University of Chicago Press, Chicago.

Kuhn, T. S. 1977, *The Essential Tension: Selected Studies in Scientific Tradition and Change*, University of Chicago Press, Chicago.

Lee, F. S. 2009, *A History of Heterodox Economics: Challenging the Mainstream in the Twentieth Century*, Routledge, London.

Nelson, J. A. 2001, 'Why the P.A.E. Movement Needs Feminism', *Post-Autistic Economics Review*, no. 9, September.

Pheby, J. 1987, *Methodology and Economics: A Critical Introduction*, Macmillan, Basingstoke.

Price, L. (ed.) 2001, *Dialogues of Alfred North Whitehead*, David R. Godine, Boston.

Shapin, S. & Schaffer, S. 1985, *Leviathan and the Air-Pump: Hobbes, Boyle, and the Experimental Life: Including a Translation of Thomas Hobbes, Dialogus Physicus De Natura Aeris by Simon Schaffer*, Princeton University Press, Princeton.

2 The changing face of economics

This chapter provides an exposition of a set of arguments that constitute a distinctive view about the direction of contemporary economics, including what forces drive change, what change strategies work and what desirable change in economics looks like. The arguments are a useful prelude to much of the analysis contained in subsequent chapters as they introduce some of the key debates and literatures around the issue of pluralism. The chapter gives particular focus to what can be termed 'conservative reformism', though perhaps the term 'mild reformism' might be just a good a descriptor to use. In any case, the position in question argues that contemporary economics, whilst currently less than perfect, is currently transitioning to something better. The key driver of change is developments within the orthodox research frontier. Indeed, some have argued that substantial and desirable change in economics has *already* occurred and they chastise critics inside and outside the profession for not properly recognising this.

Traditionalists, dissenters and conservative reformers

It is useful, for the purposes of this chapter, to set up a simple three-way taxonomy of traditionalists, dissenters, and conservative reformists to classify contemporary economics. It is conceded at the outset that such a taxonomy is a rather rugged simplification. It is also conceded that there are also other similar, competing taxonomies that exist, such as 'orthodoxy versus heterodoxy'. Nonetheless, the proposed three-way category is the appropriate structure to use at this point. Issues of categorisation will be more fully explored in Chapter 4, 'Orthodoxy, heterodoxy and political economy'.

Traditionalists

Traditionalists constitute the majority of economists in academia, the public service and the private sector. These are economists who are committed to, and demonstrably satisfied with, standard neoclassical economics for the purposes of research, teaching and policy. Traditionalists have no real appetite for change, demand no change, and do not appear to see any real change coming. The degree of self-confidence possessed by traditionalists can be striking. For example, a graduate student in economics, when asked whether economists have a relevant role to play in society, replied, 'yes, they are the only careful, structured, empirical thinkers on most economic, political, and social issues' (cited in Colander 2005a, p. 193). Many similar examples of this sense of superiority and strong self-confidence abound (see for example Lazear 2000; Levitt & Dubner 2009; Mankiw, Gans & King 2009). Traditionalists are, in Kuhnian terms, the practitioners of normal science. In a Lakatosian sense, they are the protectors of the hard core. Traditionalists are highly prominent in the literature on economics education, where they focus almost entirely on innovative pedagogical practices to teach a curriculum that is taken as given and largely immutable (for a good example see Mixon & Cebula 2009).

Dissenters

The next category for examination is that of the dissenters. This group of people, with whom I would myself identify, usually describe themselves as heterodox economists or political economists. Dissenters are critical of much orthodox economics and economics teaching. It is not that they usually reject orthodox economics per se (though there are exceptions), but they are critical of its dominance, the uncritical way it is taught, and the way other approaches to economics are marginalised by it. Dissenters also have little confidence that positive change will be automatic, inexorable or imminent. The following excerpts, both made by prominent dissenting economists, capture much of the dissenting economist's mind-set:

> [N]eoclassicism's stranglehold over the economics mainstream is as strong as it has ever been. Indeed, the more it seems to 'loosen up', the greater its power over the hearts and minds of economists, politicians and business. This claim is based on the observation that, at close inspection, the centrifugal forces occasioned by dissatisfaction with the original formalist neoclassical position, after initially pushing the mainstream away from the neoclassical nucleus, eventually subside, turning centripetal. At that point, they return the analysis either to the original neoclassical position or, even worse, to a position at a higher plane of neoclassical abstraction on which the original problem not only remains unsolved but is, indeed, amplified and potentially more misleading.
>
> (Varoufakis & Arnsperger 2009, p. 6)

> Suggestions that mainstream economics has been a failure and that the discipline is in a state of crisis have been repeatedly made over the past 40 years … Critics of the mainstream are much better organized in institutional terms (with societies, websites and their own journals, and much easier communication via email) than they were four decades ago, but there is little sign that they are having any significant impact on the economics establishment. If anything, mainstream economics is in a stronger position to

resist internal pressures for change than it ever was, and it can use the growing information asymmetry between itself and the wider public about what it does to put 'spin' on its contributions and deny it is failing.

(Earl 2010, p. 222)

Dissenters do not assume that some bright new dawn is imminent or that cold logic or hard evidence will necessarily be sufficient to achieve reform. Furthermore, the idea of the orthodox research frontier riding to the rescue as some sort of 'white knight' to remedy economics is seen as implausible.

Given the difficulties and dynamics they describe, dissenters have proposed various strategies to bring about the required reform. The strategies are quite diverse, spanning reasoned pleas (Sent 2003), collective struggle and protest (Butler, Jones & Stilwell 2009) and operation by stealth (Earl & Peng 2012). However, there is a common thread: they assume that change will not come automatically and that it will have to be induced by one strategy or another.

Conservative reformers

The two positions just described are reasonably straightforward: traditionalists are happy with the status quo, dissenters seek substantial change, via deliberate action of some sort. The third category is that of conservative reformism. This obviously oxymoronic phrase captures the fact that, on one hand, some reform is seen as desirable, but on the other hand the level of change is quite qualified and sits alongside a strong desire for some considerable continuities with the status quo. The means by which reform is sought are also quite conservative. The emphasis is on a mild and diplomatic dialogue within orthodoxy to help ease through the inexorable changes being driven by advances at the orthodox research frontier.

A good example of a conservative reformer is Diane Coyle, whose book *The Soulful Science: What Economists Really Do and Why It Matters* (Coyle 2007) argues that economics is now in a new and exciting phase. She sees the early to mid-1980s as the high watermark for neoclassical economics. According to Coyle it was at this point that the neoclassical research programme came to be recognised as having become excessive, indulgent and faintly ridiculous. Since this time it is seen as having been in a process of steady retreat from absurdity. She accuses critics of economics of not having recognised these changes in the discipline.

A later work edited by Coyle, *What's the use of Economics? Teaching the Dismal Science after the crisis* (Coyle 2012), despite its rather bold-sounding title, is also consistent with the conservative reformist position. As Andrew Mearman (a dissenting economist) notes, the book seemingly calls for substantial change, but it actually undercuts this by setting sharp limits on the boundaries of what that change must be. The core of the discipline is seen to be sound and it still in needs to be taught. Indeed, Mearman suggests that one reading of the book is that it represents a defensive move to prop up an orthodoxy that is currently under sustained criticism:

[T]hroughout the book, very bold opening gambits are weakened by defensive moves denying the necessity of radical reform. More economic history is necessary; greater interdisciplinarity is desirable; more awareness of complexity is sorely needed; insights from other disciplines can be valuable; insights from behavioural economics should be (and are) included in Economics curricula. Beyond that, though, the core of the subject remains sound. It is stated that, for a variety of reasons, teaching must communicate that core. Quite short shrift is given to those who now, or have in the past raised fundamental criticisms of mainstream economics. It is perhaps significant that the book also does at times evaluate barriers to fundamental change. One reading of the book is indeed that the book itself demonstrates the potential for inertia.

(Mearman 2014, pp. 155–6)

A prominent conservative reformist is David Colander (see Colander 2000a, 2000c, 2003a, 2003b, 2005a, 2005b, 2008, 2009b). Colander has made diverse, interesting and valuable contributions to the history of economic thought and economic methodology (among several other areas of economics). Colander has also sought to play a positive and engaged role of messenger and mediator between orthodoxy and heterodoxy that is commendable. Consistent with his general eclecticism, Colander also puts forward the conservative reformist position in its strongest form. Analysing Colander's conservative reformist position offers a useful test case for the conservative reformist position in general.

Colander, like Coyle and other conservative reformers, argues that economics has changed significantly since the 1980s. Earlier concerns that he himself had about the profession and in particular, how economists are educated are now much attenuated and modified:

I am known as a critic of graduate education in economics, but my critique in this study is quite different from my critique of 20 years ago. Then, my critique was not only of graduate education in economics, but also of economics itself – its rigidity of assumptions, its lack of empirical grounding and its failure to bring the models to the data in a serious way. However, I believe that economics has changed, and it is now attempting to bring the models to the data in a much more meaningful way than it used to. Theory for the sake of theory has been reduced.

(Colander 2005a, p. 197)

... economics has changed significantly since the 1980s, and graduate students today are happier with their training than they were. One reason why these changes have occurred is that the way economics is done has changed, as have economists' view of themselves.

(Colander 2009a, p. 192)

In regard to undergraduate education, he has, on occasion, made some particularly sunny comments. It is not viewed as mendaciously narrow and in urgent need of extensive reform, but instead as representing the 'just right' liberal arts major that serves as an instructive example for other social sciences to follow:

> As an economist I like to think that economics has become so popular because of its intellectual rigor, broad appeal, and importance to understanding the world. ... Modern economics is an exciting and dynamic field of study that has changed considerably in recent years; specifically, it has become more quantitative and scientific. Today's economists bring technical expertise to interesting and novel questions.
>
> (Colander 2009c, p. 72)

The key to understanding the conservative reformist position of Colander is to understand his belief that neoclassical economics is dying or is in some senses already dead (Colander 2000c), as well as his belief that economics is, and should be, primarily a modelling science that develops mathematical models and then empirically tests these models to see if they fit with the data. It is this model-building focus that separates it from more scientifically 'ambiguous' disciplines such as political economy (Colander 2008) – note here how political economy is seen as another discipline (though what its boundaries and form are understood to be in this instance is not clear).

Colander believes that neoclassical economics is being replaced by the orthodox research frontier (this is understood to include areas such as behavioural economics, experimental economics, evolutionary game theory and complexity economics), which is said to said to be bringing about a desirable revolution in economics (Colander 2000a, 2000c, 2003a, 2005a, 2005b; Colander & Klamer 2007; Colander, Rosser & Holt 2004). It is a revolution that will touch on economic policy (Salzano & Colander 2007); economic teaching (Colander 2000a, 2003a); and even the history of economic thought (Colander 2000b):

> Economists today are not neoclassical according to any reasonable definition of the term. They are far more eclectic, and concerned with different issues than were the economists of the early 1900s, whom the term was originally designed to describe.
>
> (Colander 2000c, p. 130)

> There is a revolution going on in the trenches of computational economics, complex systems theory, behavioural economics, experimental economics, evolutionary game theory, and 'general to specific' econometrics.
>
> (Colander 2005b, pp. 341–2)

> ... economics is currently at a turning point: it is moving away from a strict adherence to the holy trinity – rationality, greed, and equilibrium – to a

more eclectic trinity of purposeful behavior, enlightened-self interest and sustainability.

(Colander, Rosser & Holt 2004, p. 1)

This revolutionary force will be necessarily attenuated by institutional inertia, but it will only delay, rather than stop, the rising tide of change. In particular, it is assumed that what starts at the research frontier will inevitably reach both the postgraduate and undergraduate curriculum.

What then are the causal relationships that will effect these profound changes? The central trigger is the changing research interests of postgraduate students and younger staff members at elite universities in the United States:

> Most of the change in economics has come about from the inside, from young professors at top schools who start doing economics in a different way than was previously done … the key to understanding change is the choices new graduate students are making about dissertation topics.
>
> (Colander 2003a, p. 1)

In Colander's view, graduate students will choose research topics that are part of the orthodox research frontier, and some of these students will then go on to become academics. It is then assumed that such academics will incorporate cutting-edge developments into the curriculum. The students who are the recipients of this renovated curriculum will then go further in expanding the research frontier when they choose their dissertation topics. Some of this second generation of students will then become academics and renovate the curriculum still further. The pattern continues to replicate itself, driving desirable change to an ever-greater degree. Over time there is an exit of the old guard and a repopulating of the profession by the new. Colander is adamant that it is these replicator effects that are key; other factors are, at best, of minor significance:

> The economics profession changes as cohorts with older-style training are replaced with cohorts with newer style training. In many ways, the replicator dynamics of graduate school play a larger role in determining economists' methodology and approach than all the myriad papers written about methodology.
>
> (Colander 2005a, p. 175)

Colander provides two explanations for why graduate students and younger staff members will strike out into cutting-edge research. The first explanation is that the neoclassical research paradigm is becoming 'exhausted' (Colander 2003a, p. 1). This exhaustion appears to have less to do with running out of interesting puzzles to solve than it does with orthodox economists themselves wanting to transcend the accumulated problems of the neoclassical programme (Colander 2000a):

[M]ainstream economists know the standard problems with economics, and they are working to change them. Who does not want economics to be empirically grounded? Who does not want economics to be relevant? Who does not recognize that formalism sometimes runs amok? The debate is how to change economics, not whether it has problems. Economists working in the eclectic mainstream tradition are working to solve those problems, especially in cutting edge research.

(Colander 2005b, p. 338)

A key assertion to note (aside from the contestable rhetorical questions) is the belief that orthodox economists recognise real problems in their approach and are working to remedy these problems.

The second reason given for younger staff members and graduate students to embrace the orthodox research frontier is the arrival of low-cost and high-power computing. This allows economics to continue to be a model-building and model-testing discipline. For Colander, this is what makes economics scientific and thus superior to political economy. What exactly are these new methods that have been opened up by advances in computing? The key method is numerical simulation. Previously, in the absence of modern computing, numerical simulation was largely impractical. Model building had to be constructed out of algebraic solutions. However, most dynamic equations cannot be solved analytically (algebraically); thus the scope for formal model building was quite limited.

The increase in mathematical methods at our disposal is seen as offering a type of salvation, or redemption, for heterodox economists. Colander argues that heterodox economists increasingly can, and should, discard their former predilections for analysis via informal methods, and utilise advances in computing to pursue their analysis via formal (mathematical) methods. Even prestigious non-technical orthodox economists must do this or their work will lose its currency and influence. This will make then for a more scientific economics:

I believe that the non-technical work of North, Williamson, or Coase is not the future of economics. Instead the future of economics is increasingly technical work that is founded on the vision that the economy is a complex system.

(Colander 2003a, p. 6)

Note here the assertion that acceptance of economy and society as a complex system (something many dissenting economist would agree with) then leads to an assertion that many dissenting economists would reject: that a complex system should always be analysed via increasingly 'technical', computer-driven methods.

Colander places considerable hope and importance on a particular variant of the orthodox research frontier: complexity economics. This is clearly seen as a game-changer for the discipline and the social sciences in general:

Dateline 2050. Researchers today announced the development of a unified theory of the social sciences... . The theory, which is also called a unified social systems theory, ties together the various social sciences that in the nineteenth and twentieth centuries diverged into anthropology, sociology, history, geography, economics, political science, and psychology ...

(Hunt & Colander 2011, p. 5)

Complexity economics is a branch of the science of complexity. Complexity science itself is somewhat of an umbrella term and its exact boundaries are not clear as it incorporates other areas of science such as chaos theory and network theory. At the core of complexity is a conception of a system that is characterised by evolutionary processes of change and that is (to some extent) adaptive and self-organising. Such systems are characterised by emergence, increasing returns and path-dependence. They exist in historical time. They are also characterised by non-linearities and are very dependent on initial conditions (Beinhocker 2006; Kauffman 1995).

Much of the early work in complexity economics originated at the Santa Fe Institute, where financial backing from Citibank has been rather central. However, it is very important to realise that explicit evolutionary theorising within economics goes back as far as Veblen. Institutional and evolutionary economics, which embraces much of what is understood as complexity, has arisen earlier and independently of the Santa Fe Institute and other bases of contemporary complexity science.

Because complexity economics usually rejects many of the tenets of neoclassical economics (such as equilibrium and perfect rationality) and because it also embraces non-neoclassical concepts (such as emergence and evolution) then one might assume that complexity economics is something that is (or should be) best understood as in keeping with heterodox traditions in economics. This is not how Colander views complexity, arguing that the commitment to formal methods aligns complexity with orthodox economics:

[T]he complexity vision raises deep questions about some of the fundamental assumptions of economics, and thus it has been associated with heterodox economists who have emphasized those questions in many of their critiques. I, for one, do not see that association fitting the reality. As I stated above, all good economists have raised these questions; standard economists have simply felt that the alternative approaches used by heterodox economists, which have usually involved heuristic analysis rather than formal analysis, were unacceptable. Complexity economics differs from heterodox economics in that it is highly formal; it is a science that involves simplification and the search for efficient means of data compression. Thus, complexity economics will be more acceptable to standard economists because it shares the same focus on maintaining a formal scientific framework, and less acceptable to many heterodox economists who otherwise share its general vision.

(Colander 2000a, p. 5)

Note again the assertion that 'good' orthodox economists have always raised the same questions and identified the same issues that heterodox economists have. This is not an unreasonable point in itself, but it does beg the question 'what proportion of orthodox economists are, in Colanders terms, 'good' economists?' There is an obvious danger that he could be mistaking a small fringe of innovators or mild dissenters to be more significant, and influential, than they actually are.

Colander argues that there is a strong desire within orthodoxy for stronger empirical grounding, more real-world relevance, more careful deployment of formal methods, and for improvement in general (Colander 2009b). He argues that heterodoxy has been unwilling or unable to follow suit. In general, he sees them being an irrelevance and as having had little role in changing economics (Colander 2005b, 2009b). Radical critics pursuing radical change via direct and collective means is clearly seen as irrelevant, or even counter-productive (Colander 2005b, 2009b):

> Heterodox economists, often implicitly, see that process of change as occurring through an outside revolution, as mainstream economists see their mistaken ways and change their views to a new reality. In this view change comes from the outside – ideally from heterodox economists' views being accepted. I don't see it that way. Most of the change in economics has come about from the inside.
>
> (Colander 2003a, p. 1)

What explains the marginalisation of heterodoxy? Colander's emphasis is *not* on problems of discrimination, intolerance and suppression that are perpetrated by orthodoxy against heterodoxy – an explanation favoured by many heterodox economists (Jones & Stilwell 1986; Lee 2009, 2012; Stilwell 2006, 2011). Rather, his emphasis is on the purported poor conduct, misconceptions and bad attitudes of heterodox economists.

For Colander, the key failure of many heterodox economists is their inability to recognise, or capitalise on, the fact that orthodox economics is changing; indeed heterodox economists are seen as attacking a straw man (Colander 2005b). Another failing is a lack of diplomatic skills and judgement with which to advance their interests. They adopt the wrong 'attitude' and 'tone' towards their orthodox colleagues, alienating potential allies and collaborators within eclectic orthodoxy:

> [I]t is not beliefs that separate mainstream from heterodoxy; it is attitude and a willingness to compete within a given set of rules and institutional structures. Mainstream economists are willing to compete within those rules; heterodox economists aren't.
>
> (Colander 2009b, p. 37)

In our view … inside-the-mainstream critics, want to separate themselves from that heterodox tone and attitude, not necessarily from heterodox ideas. It is because of the tone and attitude between the lines in heterodox writing that Rodrick, and other inside-the-mainstream critics, go to great lengths to disassociate themselves from heterodoxy.

(Colander, Rosser & Holt 2010, p. 404)

Heterodox economists, with their out-dated ideas and their bad attitude and tone, are self-marginalising. What advice is offered to heterodox economists to allow them to redeem themselves? First, they should stop describing themselves to others as heterodox. Second, they need to work on the assumption that orthodox economists are actively working to change and improve economics (Colander 2005b) – this is described as 'giving the mainstream its due'. Third, and most significantly, they have to fundamentally change how they go about their *own* work as economists. This involves worrying less about methodology than about forming alliances with orthodox economists who can help repackage heterodox ideas into a more formal (thus more respectable and scientific) guise.

Assessing conservative reformism

Whilst a full assessment of the conservative reformist position relies on the evidence and reasoning put forward in later chapters it is still possible to offer some initial response to various aspects of the position now.

In regard to the assertion that orthodox economics is changing, one can readily agree that, whilst neoclassical economics is definitely not 'dead', it is less monolithic than it was two or three decades ago. In making this argument conservative reformists are actually in concert with the prominent heterodox economist John B Davis who has also recognised a fracturing in orthodoxy economics (see in particular Davis 2006; Davis 2007, 2008a; Davis 2008b). Davis argues that it is untenable to take the position that orthodoxy (what he terms the 'mainstream') is 'still at bottom or in essence identical with neoclassical economics' (Davis 2008a, p. 55). However, and in contrast with the conservative reformist position, Davis also makes the valid point that this new diversity within the orthodoxy occurs within quite *narrow* parameters, remaining strongly wedded to a closed-system ontology and deductivist formal methods. Davis conceives of a rationality–individualism–equilibrium nexus that is very different from the heterodoxy's institutions–history–social structure nexus (Davis 2008a). In particular the theory of the individual is generally very different between orthodoxy and heterodoxy (Davis 2008a). One of the scenarios for the future that Davis ponders is that of there being 'increasing tolerance for new approaches within the mainstream, combined with a continuing, shared intolerance toward heterodox economics' (Davis 2008a, p. 61). To summarise, the dominant orthodox branch of the profession, whilst having become less monolithic, is still narrow and insufficiently pluralist.

The assertion that advances in computing will allow for a new, and desirable, wave of formalist modelling in economics is overstated and appears to rest on some misconceptions about what we can and cannot expect from formalist methods. It is true that advances in computing do allow a wider range of mathematical methods to be deployed in economics and that economic modelling using dynamic numerical simulations and agent-based modelling can be useful and interesting (see for example Epstein & Axtell 1996). It is also true that mathematics plays a legitimate role in economics and that it is useful in clarifying and communicating ideas, including various ideas associated with heterodox traditions (Chick 2000; Keen 2009). However, none of this dictates that complex mathematically modelling represents the dominant or even singular future of the profession.

Mathematical modelling, like any particular method of analysis, has limitations as well as strengths. For all that formalism offers, and whatever our advances in computing, there still exists the substantive problem that as mathematical models become more like reality, the modelling process itself becomes more difficult. Consider the following rumination on the general limitations of modelling:

> [W]hen one makes one's model more realistic by introducing more complex premises, one also thereby increases – sometimes dramatically – the problems involved in applying it. The more degrees of freedom in a model, the more parameters that have to be estimated, giving more potential sources of error. Moreover, the number of possible interrelationships that must be precisely specified grows geometrically with the number of parameters involved. The conclusions reached as the model is made more complex become less robust – more sensitive to small variations in the initial parameters – and greater and greater precision in the data inputs is needed to avoid reaching indeterminate conclusions. The result is often an elegant and complex but relatively useless model that cannot produce determinate results unless one has recourse to an often unavailable comprehensive and precise data set. This problem of unwieldiness is particularly likely to occur when the refinements introduced into a model require the measurement of subjective factors – such as changes in attitudes or limitations on cognitive capabilities that are inherently difficult to measure and quantify, and to relate to other, more tangible factors in mathematically precise ways.
>
> (Crespi 1997 p. 154)

These types of issues will continue to bedevil economic modelling and help to explain Goodwin's (2008) argument that fifty years of experimenting with more sophisticated mathematical techniques have failed thus far to confirm the hypothesis that more complex tools could unlock greater understanding of the richness and complexity of reality. Whilst it is not being argued here that formal methods are of no value, Goodwin's questioning of what sophisticated mathematical techniques have delivered thus far, and what they may offer in the future, is legitimate and relevant to consider.

Complexity does increase the challenges of modelling social reality dramatically because complexity is all about the recognition of non-linearities, path-dependencies, processes of emergence and shifting networks. Powerful and cheap computing may be of some help, and any assistance it can offer would be welcome, yet it will only be able to go so far. Accurately specifying the characteristics of agents and the environment they operate is generally an enormously challenging thing to do, with the margin for error being very small because complex systems are generally highly dependent on initial conditions. Small measurement errors, or the omission of very minor variables, can make an enormous difference in results. Given this, particular caution and modesty would be required about any implications such modelling offers for public policy. None of this is to say that such work in modelling and simulation might not yield something useful and that some further research in these areas is not a valid and desirable thing for particular communities of researchers to undertake. However, what is being argued here is that it would be undesirable for agent-based and complexity modelling to ever displace other forms of analysis. Indeed, the sensible thing for policymakers, and everyone else, is to evaluate the results of complexity analysis against the results of other forms of analysis. In other words, pluralism of theory and of method becomes more, rather than less, important.

Another claim worth examining at this point is the advice given by conservative reformists for political economists to repackage heterodox ideas in mathematical form. In some respects, such a view is not without merit. If heterodox ideas can be translated into mathematical form without any loss of insight or power then this will promote a co-informing dialogue across the intellectual divide, allowing further development of the ideas themselves. However, the advice given by conservative reformists fails adequately to acknowledge that many political economy concepts and theories do not fit, and may never fit, into mathematical form, at least not without some serious loss of potency or insight. Consider the concept of circular and cumulative causation. In 1944, when Myrdal was developing Veblen's original concept, he initially thought he should be able to put it into an interconnected series of quantitative equations for a truly 'scientific' solution (Argyrous 2011). Note here Myrdal's initial belief in the association between mathematics and truly scientific analysis. However, by 1978 Myrdal came to the conclusion that this earlier ambition to realise his analysis in completely mathematical form was not possible, concluding that there was a requirement for 'detailed historical analysis of the particularity and peculiarities of individual industries and countries' (Argyrous 2011, p. 150). While Myrdal thought that certain aspects of circular and cumulative causation might be suitable to mathematical measurement and modelling, this could only provide part of the explanation; fieldwork, historical case studies and the methods and ideas of the other social sciences were also required (Argyrous 2011). In other words, pluralism and interdisciplinarity were required. This is an intellectually solid and warranted position. Advances within mathematics or computing are unlikely to ever make it otherwise.

Complexity is interesting. As one student from Monash University who undertook a subject focused on agent-based models and complex adaptive systems, stated: 'This was the most amazing unit I have ever done. It blew my mind (numerous times), changed my world, infiltrated (and dominated) every part of my life, and left me hopelessly craving more. Absolutely loved it!!' (cited in Angus, Parris & Hassani 2011, p. 18). It is heartening to see such high levels of excitement and engagement. However, the capacity for complexity to induce such giddy levels of excitement carries the dangers that people will suspend their critical faculties as to the limitations of the approach. As King notes, the history of science is littered with 'prophets spurned, old truths forgotten or neglected, even older heresies enthusiastically embraced, and egregious errors pursued at great speed to the end of the appropriate cul-de-sac' (King 2002, pp. 241–2). There is an obvious danger that complexity could be incorporated into economics in a manner that exhibits all these problems.

Complexity can only be genuinely useful to economics if it is incorporated into economics in a way that is methodologically sensible. We can't assume this will happen of its own accord given that economics has regularly been able to steal obscurantism out of the jaws of insight. For example, Blaug (1997) points out that when game theory first started gaining a profile in economics it was hoped that it would subvert established economic orthodoxy and lead to richer models of rational agency (Hargreaves-Heap & Varoufakis 2004). This has not occurred. As Randall Wray has pointed out, one economist's 'cutting edge research frontier' can all too easily be someone else's frontier of nonsense (Randall-Wray cited in Cohen 2009, p. 1)

To assume that economic and social systems are complex systems does not then dictate that economics should become even more mathematically focused than it currently is. Human social systems, whilst complex, have important differences from the computer-created complex systems that are prone to generate excitement amongst budding complexity enthusiasts. Human systems are inhabited by agents that undergo complex and culturally specific socialisation from birth. They have behavioural dispositions that are biological in nature, but their behaviour and thinking is shaped by habits and social institutions. Whilst people often do respond to simple material incentives, their behaviour is also governed by ideas, norms, values and habits. The sources of stability in human social systems are habits, routines and institutions that co-determine one another in a manner that would be hard to represent within numerical simulations and complexity models. Advances will occur, and understanding a complex system with these characteristics may well be aided by numerical simulations and agent-based modelling. However, it is very hard to see how they will also not continue to require the heavy deployment of methods, concepts and theorising that have been central to the social sciences. Philosophers, anthropologists, sociologists, historians, political scientists, political economists, along with psychologists and others, will need to continue to do the work that they do, using the type of methods and theories that they have found most useful for their work and complementing this with new methods and theories where appropriate and helpful. It seems implausible and in any case undesirable for it to be otherwise, unless the purpose is for *scientistic* rather than scientific social science analysis. A greater appreciation of all this may be at least as helpful to the economics profession as anything that is currently flowing back to us from the orthodox research frontier within economics.

A complexity approach will struggle (just like any other approach) with the same problems that have always beset social and economic analysis. Conceiving of the economy as a complex adaptive system is of little more practical use than is conceiving of the economy as an open system: *it is just an ontological starting point*. If one wants to make operational theory, one is faced with the very familiar challenges of where to make the provisional closures and abstractions. It is at this point that all the very familiar methodological schisms open up: *plus ça change, plus c'est la même chose*. Given the greater methodological literacy of political economists, and also their familiarity with concepts such as path-dependence and evolution, complexity economists might therefore profitably seek the assistance of political economists, rather than the vice-versa arrangement that Colander advises.

We might also question assumptions about how strong the demand is within orthodoxy for a complexity revolution. The idiographic, unpredictable and difficult-to-model nature of complex systems may turn out to be too unpalatable for the profession. Complexity economics does not give rise to clear and unambiguous answers, does not offer elegant theoretical proofs and does not generate analysis that can reliably serve the given social and economic order. To understand the economy as a complex adaptive system is, above all else, an invitation to modesty rather than hubris. Will any of this capture the imagination of most orthodox economists? A marketing perspective is useful in respect of this point:

> In many ways then the success of a theoretical approach should be understood just as a marketing manager would attempt to understand the success of a consumer or industrial product. If it is launched at an inopportune moment, is poorly packaged, is too complex for the consumer to grasp, and fails to appeal to traditional values, then it will not find a market.
>
> (Dow & Earl 1982, pp. 177–8)

The demand for a complexity revolution does not appear to be all that strong. The profession has been accused of either ignoring or misunderstanding complexity. Leombruni and Richiardi conducted survey research on papers on agent-based modelling (ABM), which is a cornerstone of the complexity approach, and found almost nothing in the top orthodox journals: eight articles out of a total of 26,698 articles published in the top journals since Arthur's classic edited work on complexity and economics in 1988 (Leombruni & Richiardi 2005). Lehtinen and Kuorikoski, argue that the numerical simulations said by Colander to be at the centre of the revolution continue to be shunned by economists because they conflict with economists' underlying commitment to the established orthodox economic axioms (Lehtinen & Kuorikoski 2007).

The survey articles just cited are a few years old. It may eventually be the case that complexity economics (in *some* form) gains some *substantial* traction within economic orthodoxy. However, even if this did occur, there is significant potential for complexity to be misunderstood. The history of economics often shows that when new insights are discovered, they are either ignored, or absorbed into orthodoxy on orthodoxy's own terms. The tendency is to preserve as many core orthodox tenets as possible, with the more revolutionary insights often being adopted (or remaining) within heterodoxy/political economy. This syndrome leads to the production of various schisms: neoclassical Keynesian versus post-Keynesian economics, old and new institutional economics, old and new behavioural economics. This pattern may be repeating itself yet again with respect to complexity. For example, Steve Keen, a prominent Post Keynesian, has raised concerns that some current work in complexity economics is incorporating IS-LM models and rational expectations, and in general lacks awareness of the history and debates with economic thought and methodology (Gallegati et al. 2006; Keen 2003). Colander's own work in trying to push the complexity revolution along has been seen by some as 'a disservice to those of us who would like to promote a complexity vision for, and of, economic theory, applied economics and the history of economic thought' (Velupillai 2003, p. 4). Such critiques indicate that we could end up with, or that we already have, a 'new' and 'old' complexity economics.

As this book is concerned with the reform of economics, with a particular emphasis on making it more plural and interdisciplinary, this chapter has appropriately directed its main focus to evaluating the 'conservative reformist' position that asserts that there is an inexorable process of reform under way and that it is primarily driven by developments that have occurred within the orthodox research frontier over the last three decades. Whilst it is conceded that developments at the orthodox research frontier have made orthodox economics less monolithic, the orthodoxy is still insufficiently pluralist and interdisciplinary. Might developments within the orthodox frontier eventually result in sufficient levels of pluralism and interdisciplinarity? The possibility cannot be completely discounted, but the reasoning and evidence put forward in this chapter, as well as in chapters to come, suggest this is very unlikely in the short-term, and is only an outside chance in the mid- and long-term. It is not a possibility that anybody should be counting on. There are good reasons for those interested in a plural and interdisciplinary economics to look to a different vision of economics than that advocated by conservative reformists, and also to explore means to realise that vision that go beyond simply waiting on what the orthodox research frontier may or may not deliver.

References

Angus, S. D., Parris, B. & Hassani, M. 2011, 'Embracing Complexity in Economics Education: Experiences from a New Unit in Complex Adaptive Systems and Agent-Based Modelling', paper presented to Australian Conference of Economists, Australian National University, 13 July.

Argyrous, G. 2011, 'Cumulative Causation', in G. Argyrous & F. J. B. Stilwell (eds), *Readings in Political Economy: Economics as a Social Science*, Tilde University Press, Prahan, pp. 144–51.

Beinhocker, E. D. 2006, *The Origin of Wealth: Evolution, Complexity, and the Radical Remaking of Economics*, Harvard Business School Press, Boston.

Blaug, M. 1997, 'Ugly Currents in Modern Economics', *Policy Options*, September, pp. 3–8.

Butler, G., Jones, E. & Stilwell, F. J. B. 2009, *Political Economy Now! The Struggle for Alternative Economics at the University of Sydney*, Darlington Press, Sydney.

Chick, V. 2000, 'On Knowing One's Place: The Role of Formalism in Economics', *Economic Journal*, vol. 108, no. 451, pp. 1859–69.

Cohen, P. 2009, 'Ivory Tower Unswayed by Crashing Economy', *New York Times*, p. 10.

Colander, D. C. 2000a, *The Complexity Vision and the Teaching of Economics*, Edward Elgar, Cheltenham.

Colander, D. C. 2000b, 'The Death of Neoclassical Economics', *Journal of the History of Economic Thought*, vol. 22, no. 2, pp. 127–43.

Colander, D. C. (ed.) 2000c, *Complexity and the History of Economic Thought: Perspectives on the History of Economic Thought*, Routledge, London.

Colander, D. C. 2003a, 'Caveat Lector: Living with the 15 Per Cent Rule', Discussion Paper No. 03–26, Department of Economics, Middlebury College, Vermont.

Colander, D. C. 2003b, 'The Complexity Revolution and the Future of Economics', Discussion Paper 3–19, Department of Economics, Middlebury College, Vermont.

Colander, D. C. 2005a, 'The Crisis in Economics: The Post-Autistic Economics Movement: The First 600 Days – Review Article', *Journal of Economic Methodology*, vol. 12, no. 2, pp. 336–42.

Colander, D. C. 2005b, 'The Making of an Economist Redux', *Journal of Economic Perspectives*, vol. 19, no. 1, pp. 175–98.

Colander, D. C. 2008, 'Foreword', in C Arnsperger (ed.), *Critical Political Economy Complexity, Rationality, and the Logic of Post-Orthodox Pluralism*, Routledge, New York, pp. xviii–xxiii.

Colander, D. C. 2009a, 'Economics Is the "Just Right" Liberal-Arts Major', *The Chronicle of Higher Education*, vol. 55, no. 26, p. 72.

Colander, D. C. 2009b, *The Making of a European Economist*, Edward Elgar, Cheltenham.

Colander, D. C. 2009c, 'Moving Beyond the Rhetoric of Pluralism: Suggestions for an 'inside-the-Mainstream' Heterodoxy', in R F Garnett, E Olsen & M Starr (eds), *Economic Pluralism*, Taylor & Francis, Hoboken, pp. 36–47.

Colander, D. C. & Klamer, A. 2007, *The Making of an Economist, Redux*, Princeton University Press, Princeton.

Colander, D. C., Rosser, B. J. & Holt, R. P. F. 2004, *The Changing Face of Economics: Conversations with Cutting Edge Economists* University of Michigan Press, Ann Arbor.

Colander, D. C., Rosser, B. J. & Holt, R. P. F. 2010, 'How to Win Friends and (Possibly) Influence Mainstream Economists', *Journal of Post Keynesian Economics*, vol. 32, no. 3, pp. 397–408.

Coyle, D. 2007, *The Soulful Science: What Economists Really Do and Why It Matters*, Princeton University Press, Princeton.

Coyle, D. (ed.) 2012, *What's the Use of Economics? Teaching the Dismal Science after the Crisis*, London Publishing Partnership, London.

Crespi, G. S. 1997, 'Review: Does the Chicago School Need to Expand Its Curriculum?', *Law & Social Inquiry*, vol. 22, no. 1, pp. 149–69.

Davis, J. B. 2006, 'The Turn in Economics: Neoclassical Dominance to Mainstream Pluralism?', *Journal of Institutional Economics*, vol. 2, no. 1, pp. 1–20.

Davis, J. B. 2007, 'The Turn in Economics and the Turn in Economic Methodology', *Journal of Economic Methodology*, vol. 14, no. 3, pp. 275–90.

Davis, J. B. 2008a, 'Heterodox Economics, the Fragmentation of the Mainstream, and Embedded Individual Analysis', in J. T. Harvey & R. F. Garnett Jr (eds), *Future Directions in Heterodox Economics*, University of Michigan Press, Michigan, pp. 53–72.

Davis, J. B. 2008b, 'The Turn in Recent Economics and Return of Orthodoxy', *Cambridge Journal of Economics*, vol. 32, no. 3, pp. 349–66.

Dow, S. C. & Earl, P. E. 1982, *Money Matters: A Keynesian Approach to Monetary Economics*, Robertson, Oxford.

Earl, P. E. 2010, 'Economics Fit for the Queen: A Pessimistic Assessment of Its Prospects', *Prometheus*, vol. 28, no. 3, pp. 209–25.

Earl, P. E. & Peng, T. C. 2012, 'Brands of Economics and the Trojan Horse of Pluralism', *Review of Political Economy*, vol. 24, no. 3, pp. 451–67.

Epstein, J. M. & Axtell, R. L. 1996, *Growing Artificial Societies: Social Science from the Bottom Up*, Brookings Institution Press, Washington.

Gallegati, M., Keen, S., Lux, T. & Ormerod, P. 2006, 'Worrying Trends in Econophysics', *Physica A: Statistical Mechanics and its Applications*, vol. 370, no. 1, pp. 1–6.

Goodwin, N. R. 2008, 'From Outer Circle to Centre Stage: The Maturation of Heterodox Economics', in J. T. Harvey & R. F. Garnett Jr (eds), *Future Directions in Heterodox Economics*, University of Michigan Press, Michigan, pp. 27–52.

Hargreaves-Heap, S. P. & Varoufakis, Y. 2004, *Game Theory: A Critical Introduction*, Routledge, London.

Hunt, E. F. & Colander, D. C. 2011, *Social Science: An Introduction to the Study of Society*, Pearson Education, Boston.

Jones, E. & Stilwell, F. J. B. 1986, 'Political Economy at the University of Sydney', in B. Martin, C. M. A. Baker, M. Clyde & C. Pugh (eds), *Intellectual Suppression: Australian Case Histories, Analysis and Responses*, Angus & Robertson, Sydney, pp. 24–38.

Kauffman, S. 1995, *At Home in the Universe: The Search for Laws of Self-Organization and Complexity*, Oxford University Press, New York.

Keen, S. 2003, 'Standing on the Toes of Pygmies: Why Econophysics Must Be Careful of the Economic Foundations on Which It Builds', *Physica A: Statistical Mechanics and its Applications*, vol. 324, nos. 1–2, pp. 108–16.

Keen, S. 2009, 'Mathematics for Pluralist Economists', in J Reardon (ed.), *The Handbook of Pluralist Economics Education*, Routledge, London, pp. 150–68.

King, J. E. 2002, *A History of Post-Keynesian Economics since 1936*, Edward Elgar, Cheltenham.

Lazear, E. P. 2000, 'Economic Imperialism', *Quarterly Journal of Economics*, vol. 115, no. 1, pp. 99–146.

Lee, F. S. 2009, *A History of Heterodox Economics: Challenging the Mainstream in the Twentieth Century*, Routledge, London.

Lee, F. S. 2012, 'Heterodox Economics and Its Critics', *Review of Political Economy*, vol. 24, no. 2, pp. 337–51.

Lehtinen, A. & Kuorikoski, J. 2007, 'Computing the Perfect Model: Why Do Economists Shun Simulation?', *Philosophy of Science*, vol. 74, no. 3, pp. 304–29.

Leombruni, R. & Richiardi, M. 2005, 'Why Are Economists Sceptical About Agent-Based Simulations?', *Physica A*, vol. 355, pp. 103–9.

Levitt, S. D. & Dubner, S. J. 2009, *Freakonomics: A Rogue Economist Explores the Hidden Side of Everything*, Harper Perennial, New York.

Mankiw, N. G., Gans, J. & King, S. 2009, *Principles of Microeconomics*, Cengage Learning Australia, South Melbourne.

Mearman, A. 2014, 'Review a of "What's the Use of Economics? Teaching the Dismal Science after the Crisis"', *Economic Issues*, vol. 19, no. 1, pp. 155–6.

Mixon, F. G. & Cebula, R. J. 2009, *Expanding Teaching and Learning Horizons in Economic Education*, Nova Science Publishers, New York.

Salzano, M. & Colander, D. C. 2007, *Complexity Hints for Economic Policy*, Springer, New York.

Sent, E.-M. 2003, 'Pleas for Pluralism', *Post-Autistic Economics Review*, vol. 18, February.

Stilwell, F. J. B. 2006, 'The Struggle for Political Economy at the University of Sydney', *Review of Radical Political Economics*, vol. 38, no. 4, pp. 539–50.

Stilwell, F. J. B. 2011, *Political Economy: The Contest of Economic Ideas*, Oxford University Press, South Melbourne.

Varoufakis, Y. & Arnsperger, C. 2009, 'A Most Peculiar Failure: On the Dynamic Mechanism by Which the Inescapable Theoretical Failures of Neoclassical Economics Reinforce Its Dominance', Working Paper, Department of Economics, University of Athens, Athens.

Velupillai, K. 2003, Economics and the Complexity Vision: Chimerical Partners or Elysian Adventurers?, Working Paper 7, Università degli Studi di Trento.

3 Economic pluralism and economics as a science

This book is concerned with achieving greater pluralism in economics, but there is obviously a requirement to explain why greater pluralism would be desirable. There is also a need to examine the question of what limits, if any, should be placed upon pluralism. Is pluralism a case of anything goes? If not, what criteria can be deployed to determine what is and is not acceptable? This chapter examines such issues and questions. It also examines how pluralism articulates with conventional notions about what constitutes scientific practice, particularly inside the discipline of economics.

What is economic pluralism?

Economic pluralism asserts that multiple approaches to economics are valid and useful in building up our understanding of economic and social reality. No single approach is seen as having a monopoly of the truth (Dow 2007). Provided analysis meets standards of logic and reasoning regarded as acceptable by a particular scientific community, multiple approaches should not be seen as anomalous or embarrassing. Pluralism contrasts with monism, which asserts that a single and complete understanding exists and is obtainable. Pluralism is a concept that started to gain traction in economics in the 1990s. For example, in May 1992, forty-four leading economists, mainly heterodox, but also some orthodox economists (Samuelson, Modigliani and Tinbergen), published a one-page statement in the *American Economic Review* that called for greater pluralism. The statement criticised the dominance of particular methods and core simplifying assumptions, calling for greater pluralism in scientific debate, in the range of contributions that were published in the leading journals and also in the training and hiring of economists. This, they argued, would promote, not erode, the rigour of scientific argument within economics (Hodgson, Maki & McCloskey 1992).

Not everyone views pluralism as desirable. The concept is foreign to most orthodox economists, who, if they ever considered it at all, might well assume that the concept sounds dubious and antithetical to the idea of economics as a rigorous science. Even amongst heterodox economists the concept is controversial, with some arguing that it is neither intellectually warranted, nor of practical use to the heterodox agenda (Davidson 2004).

The rationale for pluralism

The simplest way to explain why pluralism is both necessary and desirable is to see it as an inescapable by-product of theory construction. Such an argument is an adaptation and extension of a line of argument from Stilwell (2011), who in turn draws on Boulding (1970) and Duesenbury (1958). Theory construction, at least within the social sciences, involves, in some respects, the *loss* of knowledge. This loss of knowledge may take the form of using simplifying assumptions, classing some variables as exogenous, adopting unidirectional sequences of causation, ignoring the potential for emergence, etc. Whilst theory can be complicated, the world that it seeks to explain is usually more so. Given this, theorists are usually forced to make difficult and uncertain decisions about how to simplify the world around them. This resulting simplification can give rise to a tunnel vision (of one sort or another), which Leff argues is the price we must pay for avoiding total blindness (Leff 1974).

Not only are our theories of the economic and social world simplistic, but the decisions to omit or simplify certain variables are often contested. Previously it was thought that approaches such as logical positivism or Popperian falsificationism could provide some reliable and mechanical adjudication on whether one attempt at simplification was superior to another, but this hope is now seen as misguided (Hands 2001; Pheby 1987). In summary, the very process of theory construction, with its necessary simplifications and abstractions, provides a strong *prima facie* case for pluralism.

As theory construction is, in part, a process of deliberate simplification, architects of a new theory will likely have been aware that they have engaged in what amounts to something approaching a sleight of hand. However, it is less probable that those who subsequently simply apply the theory will be as aware of the sleight of hand involved and will be more prone to see it as truth from above or some type of magical looking-glass. A good example of this is how the architects of modern general equilibrium theory such as Arrow and Debreu have always stressed how little their work has to say about the real word, yet this has not stopped their theoretical contributions being adapted into becoming a cornerstone of policy advice (Ackerman 1999). This tendency to claim a level of theoretical relevance that is at odds with the real world has been a general problem in orthodox economics: as Blaug notes, analytical and expository convenience can be a very good excuse for various lines of theoretical simplification but 'the temptation to read more significance into the analysis than is inherent in the procedure is irresistible and most neoclassical writers have succumbed to it' (Blaug 1997, p. 692).

Another rationale for pluralism is that theories or approaches differ in what they seek to explain and predict; in other words, theories differ as a result of having a differing explanatory focus. For example, orthodox economists, following the Austrian-influenced Robbins (1932), usually consider economics as studying the allocation of scarce means towards given ends. By contrast, institutionalists consider that the origin and evolution of the ends themselves is the central problem that cries out for explanation.

Pluralism is also a corollary of the issue of historical specificity. Theories tend to be developed in, and for, particular historical terrains. As the world and the economy changes, so might we have to change our theories (Dasgupta 1986). The economy is a human construction and not an entity that predates us like the natural world, which is subject to physical laws like gravity or thermodynamics. The issue of historical specificity is underpinned by the concepts of the idiographic and the nomothetic. If economic and social reality is inherently idiographic in its nature then economics needs to be inherently pluralist. By contrast, if economic and social reality is nomothetic in nature then the concept of economic pluralism is far more difficult to justify. Indeed, Lawrence Summers' claim that 'the laws of economics are like the laws of engineering: one set of laws works everywhere' (cited in Klein 2007, p. 218) would be a lot more plausible than it actually is.

Yet another rationale for pluralism is the need for comparison. Even if a single theory can be seen as satisfactorily explaining a particular phenomenon better than any other theory, there is a practical requirement to establish that this is the case by comparison with competing theories. As Hodgson explains:

> [E]ven correct theories have to be visibly tested by counter-arguments and alternatives. Even the medieval Catholic Church recognized this, with its institution of the 'Devil's Advocate'. A priest was employed to make the strongest possible arguments against Catholic doctrine, in order to test and demonstrate its strength. Even today, if a single theory were correct, it would become stronger through its demonstration of superiority against its rivals. If it contained flaws or blemishes, such dialogue could assist in its clarification and refinement.
>
> (Hodgson 2004, p. 21)

This 'devil's advocate' rationale is consistent with John Stuart Mill's already mentioned argument that one does not fully understand one's own argument unless one understands the arguments of those who criticise it.

Different levels of pluralism

Pluralism exists at a number of levels: method, theory, methodology, epistemology and ontology. Pluralism of method occurs when there are multiple ways of doing economics. Questions of method are about *how* economists provide explanations and descriptions (Boumans et al. 2010), that is, they pertain to the choice of techniques. Such techniques include differential calculus, interviews, econometrics, case studies, etc.

Theoretical pluralism exists when multiple theories exist to explain particular phenomena. The implication of this is that there is a plurality of description, explanation, prediction and prescription available to economists on the phenomena in question (Dow 2007). Multiple theories can exist within an overall school or approach; one example of this is how, within orthodox economics, real business cycle theory and the neoclassical synthesis provide rival explanations and prescriptions for macroeconomic instability.

Epistemological pluralism argues that there are multiple types of knowledge. Such a plurality exists most obviously in the long-standing debates concerning rationalism versus empiricism as a source of knowledge. Within economics the most famous manifestation of this dispute was in the *Methodenstreit* of the late nineteenth century that was initiated by Menger and Schmoller.

The most challenging level of pluralism is that of methodological pluralism, for it asserts that there is no single criterion, or set of criteria, by which economists can rule on which is the best theory (Dow 2007). The concept of methodological pluralism can be seen as a corollary of the breakdown of the 'received view' in the philosophy of science and economic methodology. The 'naturalistic turn', and the rise of rhetorical and sociological approaches, has led to the abandonment of a strict rule-based approach to methodology (Boumans et al. 2010; Hands 2001).

Is the acceptance of methodological pluralism a bridge too far? Does it promote nihilism and a rejection of the idea of scientific progress? No, or at least, not quite. In practice, the proliferation of rival methodologies is ultimately limited by social forces, in that each methodology needs to be validated, accepted and practised by a particular scientific community to have any standing, influence or institutional support (Dow 2004). This does not mean the knotty issue of relativism is entirely resolved, but it does provide some counter to the claim that methodological pluralism can be directly equated with saying 'anything goes'.

The final level of pluralism is at the level of ontology. Ontology is concerned with fundamental questions about the nature of reality. Economic ontology is concerned with questions as to the essential nature of the economy and of society. One's ontological commitments, what Schumpeter would call the 'pre-analytic vision', are of great importance to any analysis one undertakes. Ontology is particularly important to the issue of pluralism, as one's ontological commitments can heavily influence one's stance towards pluralism at the levels of epistemology, methodology, theory and method; as Dow has argued, 'the crucial point is to recognise the origins of theoretical approaches in methodological approaches and ultimately in conceptions of reality' (Dow 2007, p. 33).

Open versus closed systems

The central ontological commitment is whether one presupposes that economic and social reality is an open or a closed system. An open system is one where:

> [N]ot all the relevant variables can be identified, and where the external boundaries of the system are therefore not knowable. The system is subject to outside influences which cannot be accounted for in advance (where 'account for' includes knowledge that an outside influence, or relationship, is random). Further, within the system, there is scope for change in the relationships between variables which cannot be identified in advance, and indeed for change in the nature of the constituent variables themselves. Since the system

in reality cannot be understood in terms of constituent parts of a fixed nature, it is pluralist.

(Dow 2007, p. 28)

By contrast, a closed system is one where:

> All the relevant variables can be identified, where the boundaries of the system are knowable, so that variables can be classified as endogenous or exogenous, and where the relationships between variables are knowable and unchanging (so that all change in the system can be accounted for). The constituent parts of the system are of a common, fixed nature, with an independent existence (as in atoms or rational individuals).

(Dow 2007, pp. 27–8)

In a closed system, the theorist can expect to find what Lawson (1997) would call 'event regularities' – if event 'A', then event 'B'. This creates the alluring prospect of finding the 'laws of economics' – a distinctly nomothetic ambition. A closed-system reality is certainly inconsistent with epistemological and methodological pluralism and is also very limiting, if not totally limiting, on questions of method.

Different ontological presuppositions provide an important part of the explanation as to why disagreement between economists can often be so intractable. It is less to do with them 'having no ears', as some have asserted (Keen 2001, p. 1), and more to do with the fact that they are often presupposing entirely different realities. On this basis, it would be futile to convince an economist of the merits of pluralism of method, theory, methodology and epistemology, if they are knowingly, or more likely, unknowingly, committed to a closed-system ontology. Mutual incomprehension is a likely outcome. A mutual understanding of differing ontological presuppositions is a necessary, though probably not sufficient, basis for productive communication.

To presuppose an open-system reality seems warranted, yet it also needs to be conceded that in practice all theory, particularly if it is be used for applied purposes, requires us to impose some closures, boundaries and fixities. The key distinction then becomes whether theorists accept that they are overlaying a closed framework over an open system reality, or whether they are overlaying closed theory on top of what they also assume is a closed-system reality. In the former case, an individual would probably understand that they are engaging in a temporary and provisional closure (Lawson 2003). The theorist should therefore be quite aware that something of some importance might be missed, distorted, over-emphasised or under-emphasised. This means that researchers should be naturally modest, tentative and open to persuasion about their conclusions as there is recognition by the theorist of the difference between the closed system ontology of the theory and the open system nature of reality. By contrast, if a theorist is overlaying a closed system theory on what they assumed is a closed-system reality, the theorist is in pursuit or possession of a singular and immutable truth; intellectual debate and discussion becomes very constrained.

Anything goes?

As mentioned previously, the most challenging level of pluralism is that of methodological pluralism. This level of pluralism can be understood as being a by-product of a breakdown of the received view of science and the absence of criteria that can convincingly function as judge, jury and executioner against a particular theory. In the absence of a simple rule-based methodology, a scientific community needs to exercise judgement. The term 'judgement' is understood to be the use of practical reason and ordinary logic practised under the weight of uncertainty and drawing on a range of methods to arrive at a conclusion which is necessarily uncertain (Dow 2007). To exercise judgement sounds somewhat vague, yet it is something that can be approached in a structured way and there are concrete things that can be done to develop it.

What exactly can be done to improve one's judgement? One can be informed about the range of theories and concepts that are available. This not only involves understanding the strengths and weakness of the contending theories and methods (be they quantitative or qualitative), but also involves developing one's knowledge of economic methodology, economic history, history of economic thought and political philosophy. A knowledge of other social sciences and also biophysical sciences, particularly psychology, is also beneficial. Of course, this is a daunting brief. It recalls Keynes's daunting list of attributes required of the master economist:

> [T]he master-economist must possess a rare combination of gifts. He must be mathematician, historian, statesman, philosopher – in some degree. He must understand symbols and speak in words. He must contemplate the particular in terms of the general, and touch abstract and concrete in the same flight of thought. He must study the present in the light of the past for the purposes of the future. No part of man's nature or his institutions must lie entirely outside his regard. He must be purposeful and disinterested in a simultaneous mood; as aloof and incorruptible as an artist, yet sometimes as near the earth as a politician.
>
> (Keynes 1933 [1963], p. 56)

This is too ambitious for most of us to achieve, myself included, but intimidating as it is, it is nonetheless valuable for clarifying the sort of destination towards which we might to try to advance ourselves. One can also reflect on the extent to which economists are currently trained in any manner consistent with this conception of a master economist.

We can also try to make our judgements in a structured way, by which it is meant that there are lines of questioning which, while falling short of a rule based methodology, are still demanding and worth pursuing. Table 3.1 below (adapted from Coates 2005) provides us with a good example of the structured lines of questioning and evaluation that are open to us:

The first grouping, 'explanatory coherence', demands that a theory be internally consistent at the level of logic. It can argued, rather strongly, that a theory has no

Table 3.1 Criteria for the evaluation of theory

Explanatory coherence
The number and quality of linkages in the explanatory chain
The number of unlinked elements in the explanation
The degree to which linkages stretch back to an organising concept
The elegance and clarity of the explanation

Explanatory power
Capacity to handle evidence
Degree of vulnerability to facts
Clarity on counterfactual tests
Number of special exceptions being canvassed

Explanatory reach
Range of issues covered
Scale and importance of matters ignored/unexplained
Degree of depth – status of unexplained independent variable
Degree to which as range expands, coherence diminishes

Explanatory openness
Capacity to absorb new circumstances/new lines of research
Openness to articulation with additional lines of explanation
Degree to which that openness is compatible with original coherence
Openness to criticism and to self-reflection

Explanatory impact
The social consequences of applying its prescriptions
The pattern of winners and losers associated with its prescriptions
The interests privileged
The values structuring the approach

Source: Coates 2005, p. 267

claim of offering knowledge about the world when it does not even make sense as a set of ideas. Some specific failures of explanatory coherence in economics include problems of circularity (assuming what one seeks to explain) and logical inconsistency. A noted example of such a problem is the neoclassical conception of capital and the consequent problems it creates within the aggregate production function (Harcourt 1972). It is not uncommon that a requirement for explanatory coherence is seen as a minimum requirement for theory to be seen as legitimate, even amongst those who accept the concept of pluralism (Chick & Dow 2001; Hodgson 2001; King 2011). The general position on pluralism amongst such economists is that we should expect and accept contradictory ideas existing within the community of economists, but we should not accept contradictory ideas within particular theories or concepts (Hodgson 2001).

The next grouping, 'explanatory power', pertains to how a theory fits with evidence. A theory may be internally (logically) elegant, but externally irrelevant in that it cannot explain or predict real-world phenomena. Despite facts being theory-laden and the difficulties of empirically testing theory (Boumans et al. 2010; Dow 2007), it is beneficial to our interests to care about empirical evidence that might be of assistance in corroborating or contradicting our theoretical assertions (Blaug 2010; Lavoie 2009). Theories that shy away from empirical evidence like Dracula from a stake should generally invoke circumspection.

The third grouping, 'explanatory reach', examines the scope or boundaries of explanation. A key consideration here is what is left as exogenous and unexplained. One might initially think that the more a theory explains the better, but greater explanatory scope is not always a good thing. There are some good examples that demonstrate this. The economics imperialism of Becker is one example of the dangers of over-reach (Harcourt 1979; Harcourt & Kerr 1982). Becker extends the rational choice framework to matters of marriage, crime, sleep and other social phenomena. Yet the flawed and sometimes ludicrous nature of some of this work reveals that it has little claim to offer a general theory of human behaviour. Furthermore, Hodgson (2001) argues that the pursuit of excessive generality can result in the elimination of important features that are common to a particular subset of economic and social reality; in other words, the price of generality can be vacuousness (Bowles 2005). Different theories, resting on different foundations, are often required to understand different phenomena.

The grouping of 'explanatory openness' examines how brittle and inflexible a particular approach is. Can an approach interact meaningfully with other approaches or is it a self-enclosed package deal that cannot articulate with other approaches? Again, economics imperialism provides a relevant illustration of this problem of insularity: assumptions of full rationality and exogenous preferences badly limit orthodoxy's ability to interact and benefit from other approaches in the social sciences. That practitioners of this approach often see themselves as offering scientific salvation for their fellow social scientists compounds the problem further (for an unwitting example of this problem see Lazear 2000).

The grouping 'explanatory impact' prompts us to consider how analysis can be closely intertwined with the interests of particular groups in society. Certain groups will benefit or suffer on the basis of how we choose to understand the working of the economy. Indeed, beliefs about the economy are themselves working parts of the economy (Stretton 1999). Economics is, among other things, a conduit for the expression of social, economic and political interests (Halevi 2002). The popular currency of an idea or approach may have less to do with its explanatory merit than with its ability to serve the interests of particular groups. This line of argument has long been used by Marxian and radical political economists to explain the continuing persistence of neoclassical economics. We can also connect it back to Shapin and Schaffer's point about solutions to the problem of knowledge and the problem of social order being inseparable.

Economics as a science

This chapter has put forward a case for pluralism in economics on intellectual grounds. One could describe this as having mounted a *scientific* case for pluralism. However, it is useful to reflect a little further on what science and scientific explanation are. First, because it is so tied into the intellectual case for pluralism.

Second, because different groups of people have quite different understandings of what it is to be a science, and their acceptance or rejection of pluralism is heavily contingent on *their* conception of science. Understanding what these differing conceptions of science are is helpful in mapping out strategies to promote greater pluralism in economics.

One way to answer the question 'what is science?' is simply to look to the experts: professional philosophers of science. This is a good place to start, but such specialists cannot really give us a simple or clear answer to the question, at least not one upon which they would all agree (Boumans et al. 2010; Dow 2002). The history and philosophy of science shows marked shifts on what is, and what is not, considered scientific, and things have become less, rather than more, straightforward over recent times.

As has already been discussed earlier in this chapter, it was once hoped that we could develop a rules-based approach that could distinguish the scientific from the non-scientific. For example, Whewell in the nineteenth century argued that 'the philosophy of science ... would imply nothing less than a complete insight into the essence and conditions of all real knowledge, and an exposition of the best methods for the discovery of new truths' (Whewell 1840, p. 3). This is a very attractive vision of science: a looking glass with which we shall be able to see the singular truth. This vision of science is well summarised by Hands:

> [T]he Enlightenment view of scientific knowledge that has been handed down from Bacon, Descartes, and other philosophers. The view that knowledge of the causal structure of the world could be obtained with certainty if the proper method were followed, and even though philosophers have differed radically about what the proper method actually is, the idea that it – the scientific method – is the secret of epistemic success is common to all the various philosophical approaches.
>
> (Hands 2001, p. 4)

The logical positivists of the Vienna Circle, Popper's falsificationism and Friedman's instrumentalism are all good examples of this rule-based approach to scientific analysis – otherwise known as the received view of science (Hands 1998). This received view of science fits awkwardly (if it all) with the concept of pluralism: if there is a reliable rule-based methodology then we should able to find the best theory.

While the received view of science still has some currency, the philosophy of science has moved on somewhat. It is argued that the received view has now broken down and that the issues of under-determination, theory-ladenness, the social nature of science, relativism, anti-foundationalism and naturalism expose the old rules-based approach as untenable (Boumans et al. 2010; Hands 2001). Furthermore, examining the history of science as practised (rather than as professed) shows that our understanding of scientific advance is closely connected with institutional success and social acceptance (King 2002). This post-received view of science meshes well with the concept of pluralism: in the absence of a decisive rule-based methodology to decide between theories we should be open to consideration of multiple theories and to a degree of eclecticism and synthesis.

Looking at the views of professional philosophers of science and economic methodologists is richly illuminating, but as was earlier stated, there is not a single and agreed-upon answer as to what is proper science and scientific analysis. In reality, an examination of the specialists' views of the question is more an opening up of further debate about the question rather than a provision of a final answer that closes off all debate (Dow 2002). That this is so is partly a reflection of the fact that the philosophy of science draws on basic epistemological and ontological debates that go back to the birth of philosophy. What then is to be done? It would not be hard to fill the rest of this chapter (and book) with a discussion of how philosophers of science and economic methodologists understand the idea of science, and how this then relates to pluralism. However, this task is best left to professional economic methodologists. What is worth doing at this point is to focus more on the non-specialist understanding of the nature of science and scientific explanation because it is, regardless of its intellectual justification, a powerful variable in the spread of intellectual ideas.

Economics as a science within orthodox economics

Within economics there is something of a schism. Heterodox economists are usually quite aware, and often much concerned with, debates in economic methodology and philosophy of science; indeed, some heterodox economists argue, sometimes too much so. In any case, within heterodoxy there is a general intellectual context to which the issue of economics pluralism can be related. By contrast, orthodox economists rarely have an active interest in, or any real awareness of, debates in economic methodology and the philosophy of science (Fullbrook 2009; Lawson 1997, 2001). For example, Samuelson famously asserted that 'those who can, do science; those who can't prattle about its methodology' (Samuelson 1992, p. 240). This general aversion to methodological discussion and reflection within orthodoxy makes it a much harder forum in which to sell pluralism as an idea.

Of course, having no interest in methodology does not mean an absence of methodological position: it just means that one does not care to articulate, examine, defend or compare the position one holds. Orthodox economists usually hold to some version of the received view of the philosophy of science and economic methodology. Some (probably incoherent and superficial) blend of Popperian falsificationism and Friedmanesque instrumentalism would be the most common methodological stance, regardless of whether these economists actually practise the rules they espouse (Canterbury & Burkhardt 1983; Hutchison 1960). Orthodox economists are usually proud and confident in their methodological stance. It is not hard to see why: it is most helpful for getting articles published in highly ranked journals, finding employment and in helping to impress audiences of other economists and policymakers. Ignoring the critique of economic methodologists and philosophers of science is a relatively easy thing to do. It may continue to be so for some time to come.

The dominance of the received view helps to explain some of the intolerance and persecution to which heterodox economists have often been subjected. If orthodox economists are confident and committed to a relatively simple rule-based methodology to determine what is and is not science, and orthodox economists believe that they follow such rules, and believe that heterodox economists do not, then it easy to see why orthodoxy is so often hostile to heterodoxy. Indeed, a heterodox economist could easily be seen as being akin to a creation scientist who has somehow found employment in a department of biology: they are a threat to the reputation of that department, someone who will confuse and mislead in their teaching. Such a person is also a threat to everyone's hard work and hopes for the future.

There is much to indicate that pluralism in economics is currently unduly constrained by the received view of science (Negru 2009) and a consequent inability to understand that real science is pluralist (Fullbrook 2001). In fact, economists are often very keen to indicate a level of consensus about their discipline. For example, Samuelson argued in his highly influential textbook that a scientific consensus exists about what constitutes good economics – i.e. that there is a set of foundational concepts, methods and propositions that is 'accepted by all but a few extreme left-wing and right-wing writers' (Samuelson 1970, pp. 197–8). Davis (2008) argues that the entire history of economic thought has been heavily shaped by a fear that pluralism endangers a scientific economics. He views the history of economics as an ongoing alternation between periods of pluralism and the dominance of a single approach. Orthodoxy is understood to emerge out of heterodoxy in a core–periphery relationship that regularly reconstitutes itself. An economist may have licence to be plural and eclectic in approach during a phase of high pluralism, but will come to grief as the tide of pluralism then recedes to leave a rigid orthodoxy dominating the landscape. Davis extends his analysis to offer a number of scenarios, the most interesting one of which forecasts that if the orthodox research frontier is to progress, some part of it will have actively to destroy the standing of neoclassicism (Davis 2008, p. 350); thus the orthodox research frontier, or perhaps established heterodoxy, may coalesce into something approaching a unified whole so that it can seize the crown of dominance. These are very interesting claims, yet they appear to discount the possibility that the current orthodoxy might just continue to dominate. There is much evidence in subsequent chapters indicating that whilst research at leading universities may continue to move in any number of directions, teaching and policy work, and the profession as a whole, may continue to be largely unchanged for quite some time. Given this, and given the fact that some new monism (whatever that may be) is not desirable, it seems prudent to consider strategies by which genuine pluralism might be engineered.

This chapter outlined an intellectual basis for greater pluralism in economics. Two arguments were most central. The first was that theory arises out of simplification and abstraction, and that there is no simple or assured way to simplify and abstract. Complete and definitive theory therefore becomes elusive. The second argument supporting pluralism was ontological: economic and social reality exists as an open (rather than closed) system and this is a fundamental basis for pluralism. It was then asked whether pluralism means 'anything goes'. It was argued that it does not. In large part this is because there are structured ways in which we can form judgements about our analysis and the frameworks we choose to undertake that analysis. The final part of the chapter examined how pluralism sits with conventional conceptions of science, particularly within orthodox economics. It was argued that a lack of methodological awareness constrains orthodoxy's capacity to embrace pluralism.

References

Ackerman, F. 1999, Still Dead after All These Years: Interpreting the Failure of General Equilibrium Theory, Working Paper 00-01, Tufts University, Global Development and Environment Institute.

Blaug, M. 1997, *Economic Theory in Retrospect*, Cambridge University Press, Cambridge.

Blaug, M. 2010, 'Popper's Logic of Discovery', in M. Boumans & J. B. Davis (eds), *Economic Methodology: Understanding Economics as a Science*, Palgrave Macmillan, Basingstoke, pp. 84–91.

Boulding, K. E. 1970, *Economics as a Science*, McGraw-Hill, New York.

Boumans, M., Davis, J. B., Blaug, M., Maas, H. & Svorencik, A. 2010, *Economic Methodology: Understanding Economics as a Science*, Palgrave Macmillan, Basingstoke.

Bowles, S. 2005, *Microeconomics: Behavior, Institutions, and Evolution*, Princeton University Press, Princeton.

Canterbury, E. R. & Burkhardt, R. J. 1983, 'What Do We Mean by Asking 'Is Economics a Science?'', in A. S. Eichner (ed.), *Why Economics Is Not yet a Science*, Macmillan, London, pp. 15–40.

Chick, V. & Dow, S. C. 2001, 'Formalism, Logic and Reality: A Keynesian Analysis', *Cambridge Journal of Economics*, vol. 25, no. 6, pp. 705–21.

Coates, D. 2005, *Varieties of Capitalism, Varieties of Approaches*, Palgrave Macmillan, Basingstoke.

Dasgupta, A. K. 1986, *Epochs of Economic Theory*, Oxford University Press, Delhi.

Davidson, P. 2004, 'A Response to King's Arguments for Pluralism', *Post-Autistic Economics Review*, issue 24, March, pp. 1–5.

Davis, J. B. 2008, 'The Turn in Recent Economics and Return of Orthodoxy', *Cambridge Journal of Economics*, vol. 32, no. 3, pp. 349–66.

Dow, S. C. 2002, *Economic Methodology: An Inquiry*, Oxford University Press, Oxford.

Dow, S. C. 2004, 'Structured Pluralism', *Journal of Economic Methodology*, vol. 11, no. 3, pp. 275–90.

Dow, S. C. 2007, 'Pluralism in Economics', in J Groenewegen (ed.), *Teaching Pluralism in Economics*, Edward Elgar, Cheltenham, pp. 22–39.

Duesenbury J. 1958, *Business Cycles and Economic Growth*, McGraw-Hill, New York.

Fullbrook, E 2001, 'Real Science in Pluralist', *Post-Autistic Economics Review*, issue 5, March, pp. 30–4.

Fullbrook, E (ed.) 2009, *Ontology and Economics: Tony Lawson and His Critics*, Routledge, London.

Halevi, J 2002, 'High Priests and Run-of-the-Mill Practitioners', *Post-Autistic Economics Review*, issue 14, June, pp. 20–4.

Hands, D W 1998, 'Sociology of Scientific Knowledge', in J B Davis, D W Hands & U Mäki (eds), *The Handbook of Economic Methodology*, Edward Elgar, Lyme, pp. 474–77.

Hands, D W 2001, *Reflection without Rules: Economic Methodology and Contemporary Science Theory*, Cambridge University Press, Cambridge.

Harcourt, G C 1972, *Some Cambridge Controversies in the Theory of Capital*, Cambridge University Press, London.

Harcourt, G C 1979, 'The Social Science Imperialists', *Politics*, vol. 14, no. 2, pp. 243–51.

Harcourt, G. C. & Kerr, P. 1982, *The Social Science Imperialists: Selected Essays of G.C. Harcourt*, Routledge, London.

Hodgson, G. M. 2001, *How Economics Forgot History: The Problem of Historical Specificity in Social Science*, Routledge, New York.

Hodgson, G. M. 2004, 'Is It All in Keynes's General Theory?', *Post-Autistic Economics Review*, issue 25, May, pp. 21–4.

Hodgson, G. M., Maki, U. & McCloskey, D. 1992, 'A Plea for a Rigorous and Pluralistic Economics', *American Economic Review*, vol. 82, no. 2, p. xxv (back matter).

Hutchison, T. W. 1960, *The Significance and Basic Postulates of Economic Theory*, A. M. Kelley, New York.

Keen, S. 2001, 'Economists Have No Ears', *Post-Autistic Economics Review*, issue 7, July, pp. 7–9.

Keynes, J. M. 1933 [1963], *Essays in Biography* Norton, New York.

King, J. E. 2002, *A History of Post-Keynesian Economics since 1936*, Edward Elgar, Cheltenham.

King, J. E. 2011, 'Arguments for Pluralism in Economics', in F J B Stilwell & G Argyrous (eds), *Readings in Political Economy: Economics as a Social Science*, Tilde University Press, Melbourne, pp. 54–6.

Klein, N. 2007, *The Shock Doctrine: The Rise of Disaster Capitalism*, Allen Lane, Camberwell.

Lavoie, M. 2009, 'After the Crisis: Perspectives for Post Keynesian Economics', paper presented to Encontro Internacional de Associação Keynesiana Brasileiro, Porto Alegre, 5 September.

Lawson, T. 1997, *Economics and Reality*, Routledge, London.

Lawson, T. 2001, 'Back to Reality', *Post-Autistic Economics Review*, issue 6, May, pp. 12–18.

Lawson, T. 2003, *Reorienting Economics*, Routledge, London.

Lazear, E. P. 2000, 'Economic Imperialism ', *Quarterly Journal of Economics*, vol. 115, no. 1, pp. 99–146.

Leff, A. 1974, 'Economic Analysis of Law: Some Realism About Nominalism', No. 2820, Yale University Faculty Scholarship Series, Yale University.

Negru, I. 2009, 'Reflections on Pluralism in Economics', *International Journal of Pluralism and Economics*, vol. 1, nos. 1 and 2 pp. 7–21.

Pheby, J. 1987, *Methodology and Economics: A Critical Introduction*, Macmillan, Basingstoke.

Robbins, L. 1932, *An Essay on the Nature and Significance of Economic Science*, Macmillan, London.

Samuelson, P. A. 1970, *Economics*, McGraw-Hill, New York.

Samuelson, P. A. 1992, 'My Life Philosophy: Policy Credos and Working Ways', in M. Szenberg (ed.), *Eminent Economists: Their Life Philosophies*, Cambridge University Press, New York, pp. 236–47.

Stilwell, F. J. B. 2011, *Political Economy: The Contest of Economic Ideas*, Oxford University Press, South Melbourne.

Stretton, H. 1999, *Economics: A New Introduction*, UNSW Press, Sydney.

Whewell, W. 1840, *The Philosophy of the Inductive Science*, John W Parker, Cambridge.

4   Orthodoxy, heterodoxy and political economy

For a book such as this, concerned as it is with explaining the current state of economics and assessing strategies for its improvement, careful consideration of how best to comprehend and categorise the various strands of economics is an elemental concern. Categorisations structure and frame the way we make sense of economics. They also have significant strategic implications, impacting on where the teaching of economics might occur within universities and how, and by whom, different strands of economics research are assessed. Categories such as 'heterodoxy', 'orthodoxy' and 'political economy' create an 'us' and 'them' or 'insiders' and 'outsiders'. It is worth considering who falls into which camp or whether particular individuals or schools could span both camps. Do established categories reflect substantial *intellectual* difference or are they instead really just social and ideological constructs? Is there sufficient intellectual difference within economics to justify not only teaching parts of it in separate university departments but even to separate one part of it as an independent academic discipline?

This chapter is focused on categorisation and nomenclature economics, giving particular focus to dualisms such as orthodox economics versus heterodox economics and political economy versus economics. After some discussion, it is argued that dualisms of this type, while inherently reductionist, can sometimes still be intellectually defensible and practically useful. However, it is also emphasised that economics, like many other disciplines, is not a simple object and that it cannot be captured entirely cleanly by any simple dualism. Notwithstanding these limitations, a particular dualism is put forward that is primarily intellectual, rather than social in nature. It rests on an argument that there is an ontological schism in economics based on whether one presupposes a 'complicated' or 'complex' economic system. It is argued that orthodox economics is largely compatible with a complicated system ontology, and a pluralist social science orientated economics is compatible with the ontology of a complex system. It is then argued that this dualism is capable of being extended to the point where it is possible to justify the existence of two separate disciplines where there is normally assumed to be just one. One of these disciplines would be 'economics', which would be comprised of neoclassical economics and much of the orthodox research frontier. The other discipline would be 'political economy', which would be comprised of heterodox economics, economic history, history of economic thought and development economics. Whilst arguing for two disciplines as just described is reasonable, it also recognised that it is not always necessary or desirable to push the level of differentiation quite this far. For example, one could use the same reasoning to argue that there is a political economy that constitutes a particular 'wing' or 'branch' of economics rather than it being an entirely separate discipline. One could also argue for the existence of a political economy that is a sub-discipline of political science, or a cross disciplinary or trans-disciplinary, area of knowledge. In any case, the key point that is stressed is that *some form* of collective differentiation as 'political economy' for the areas of heterodox economics, economic history, history of economic thought and development economics, would be desirable. The specific form of differentiation would be dependent on the particular context that exists within particular countries and in particular universities.

This chapter also makes the argument that it would be desirable for the term 'heterodox economics' to be used somewhat more narrowly and carefully. It appears best limited to *internal* use within the discipline of political economy – a term to be used 'within the trade' so to speak. Whilst it is currently a serviceable term to describe the schools of institutionalism, Post-Keynesianism, Marxism, Austrian economics, ecological economics and feminist economics, it is nonetheless a confusing term to outsiders. It also has a number of other characteristics that make it less than ideal. As a consequence of this, it is suggested that those working in the intellectual traditions just listed may wish to consider referring to themselves, in the first instance, as practitioners of a particular school (for example, as an institutionalist), and in the second instance, referring to themselves as 'political economists'.

Orthodoxy and heterodoxy in economics

It is appropriate to start an examination of categorisation in economics by looking at 'orthodox economics' versus 'heterodox economics', which is a dualistic categorisation of economics that enjoys some currency at the moment, at least amongst self-identified heterodox economists. First consider established general understandings of the words 'orthodox' and 'heterodox'. The *Oxford Dictionary* describes orthodoxy as follows:

1   Holding correct, or currently accepted opinions, especially on matters of religious belief; not independent-minded, conventional.
2   Of opinion, doctrine, etc.: right, correct, in accordance with what is accepted or authoritatively established.
3   In accordance with what is regarded as proper or usual; conventional, approved.
4   Psychology. Of sleep: characterised by the absence of, rapid eye movement and (probably) dreams, and by a lower level of physiological activity than paradoxical sleep.

(Brown 1993, p. 2025)

By contrast, heterodox[1] is described as follows:

> A. An unorthodox opinion. B. Of an opinion or a person: unorthodox.
> (Brown 1993, p. 1226)

Clearly, this is a dualistic relationship, and a very tidy one at that: heterodoxy is simply what orthodoxy is not. There is a strong suggestion that this is an exhaustive classification: all possible cases divide into being either orthodox or heterodox.

Little appears to change when we move from simply examining orthodox versus heterodox as general terms to examining 'orthodox economics' versus 'heterodox economics'. In particular, there is usually an implicit or explicit suggestion of exhaustiveness (Mearman 2010). Later sections of this chapter assess whether or not this assertion of exhaustiveness is justifiable.

When one looks at how different groups of economists view their discipline, and themselves in relation to it, there is much evidence of non-orthodox economists identifying themselves as heterodox. This is apparent in publications such as *Heterodox Economics Newsletter* and in organisations such as the *Association of Heterodox Economists*. Within such circles, the general understanding is that orthodoxy is neoclassical economics and heterodoxy is an umbrella grouping that includes Austrian economists, feminist economists, institutional economists, Marxian-radical economists, Post-Keynesian and ecological economists[2] (Fullbrook 2003, 2004).

At first blush such a taxonomy seems reasonable: most economists working under these approaches would see themselves as being in a minority approach that is different from a dominant orthodox approach and many would not chafe against being labelled as heterodox economists. Most orthodox economists would also view these economists as being non-orthodox, though some may not use the term 'heterodox economics' to describe them; this may be because they have never even heard of the term 'heterodox economics'.

A common rationale for identifying oneself as heterodox is that one is opposed to key parts of orthodox theory. For example, in macroeconomics one may reject the quantity theory of money, rational expectations theory, IS-LM, Say's law or the efficient markets hypothesis. Another common rationale is methodological: perhaps some ontological or epistemological commitment that is at clear variance from the orthodox view. A third rationale is ideological, perhaps an opposition to 'neoliberalism' or 'globalisation', though it would be rare for most economists to base their opposition solely on ideological grounds.

Is heterodoxy united in anything other than opposition to orthodoxy? There is a social point of commonality in that heterodox schools are all minority approaches, but whether there is intellectual commonality is a matter on which opinions vary. Some argue that heterodox schools have substantive theoretical and methodological differences from each other, perhaps to the point that some schools can barely comprehend one another (Hopkins 2013). However, some, particularly Lee, have argued that there is a broad and emerging intellectual unity (Lee 2009, 2012). Whether there is an emerging unity or ongoing diversity is perhaps now less of an

Table 4.1 The conventional view of the orthodox heterodox divide

Category	Orthodox	Heterodox Economics
Schools	Neoclassical economics	Austrian economics Feminist economics Institutional economics Evolutionary economics Marxian-radical economics Post-Keynesian Social economists Ecological economists
Key feature	Common methodological core: equilibrium, self-interest, rationality	Diverse, only unified in opposition to neoclassical economics
Status	Dominant	Marginalised

issue than it once was, given the increasing currency of pluralism among many, though not all, heterodox economists.

How is orthodoxy usually understood? The standard way to define orthodoxy is as neoclassical economics, particularly the textbook neoclassical economics of Samuelson, or its progeny such as Varian and Mankiw. This is an economics that, at its core, assumes fully informed, rational, utility-maximising individuals engaged in constrained optimisation, with methodological individualism and a closed system ontology facilitating the heavy, and often uncritical, use of mathematics. Fundamental uncertainty, in a Keynesian or Knightian sense, is usually reduced to quantifiable risk and the full implications of a monetary economy are usually not acknowledged. The focus is not on production, but on allocation under scarcity.[3] Such a definition of neoclassical economics can include much of game theory and, to a large extent, the new institutional economics of Williamson. It can also incorporate neoclassical-synthesis Keynesianism. The standard conceptions of orthodoxy and heterodoxy as just discussed are illustrated in Table 4.1.

What is wrong with the conventional categorisation?

The conventional view of the orthodox–heterodox divide has a number of problems. First, it does not really tell us where other currently marginalised areas of economics sit in relation to it. What about economic history, history of economic thought and development economics? Not acknowledging these sub-disciplines with the scheme of categorisation is both a strategic and intellectual error. In regard to the strategic error, these sub-disciplines, like the heterodox schools, are also currently marginalised by the orthodoxy and there is an obvious logic for all four parties to conceive of themselves, and to operate, in a more collective manner. In regard to the intellectual error, it will shortly be argued that there is also a significant degree of intellectual affinity between these areas of knowledge and the heterodox schools.

The content of Chapter 2 alerts us to another problem with the conventional orthodox–heterodox divide: arguing that orthodoxy is synonymous with neoclassical economics is not really possible because of the development of the orthodox research frontier. For this reason any definition of economic orthodoxy has to include both neoclassical economics and the orthodox research frontier. Indeed from this point forward in this book the term 'orthodox economics' and 'orthodoxy' will refer to neoclassical economics plus the mainstream research frontier.

Whilst the existence of the orthodox research frontier cannot be denied, it is still worth emphasising further that the significance, implications and meaning ascribed to it is a matter of debate. Consider the case of behavioural economics. Some argue that it has degenerated into a defensive move to prop up the degenerating research programme of neoclassical economics (Earl 2010). There is now a 'new' behavioural economics that is acceptable to orthodoxy (and which many orthodox economists view as an extension of orthodox economics) and that is in many ways a betrayal of the initial vision of those who developed the 'old' behavioural economics found in the 1950s and 1960s by Herbert Simon and others (Earl 2010; Sent 2004):

> For heterodox economists who have long been employing and advocating the approach of the old behavioural economists, watching the rise of new behavioural economics is an experience akin to that suffered by a European art-house movie director whose film is re-made Hollywood-style and in the process is 'dumbed down' and has its ending changed.
>
> (Earl 2010, p. 218)

The conservative nature of much of the 'new' behavioural economics is evident enough in the assertions of its key contributors and textbooks. It is seen as an approach that 'extends rational choice and equilibrium models; it does not advocate abandoning these models entirely' (Ho, Lim and Camerer, cited in Wilkinson 2008, p. 4). The prominent new behavioural economist Matthew Rabin states that, 'in terms of many critiques of the mainstream, I actually feel like a conservative' (Rabin 2007, p. 151).

The existence of a 'new' and 'old' behavioural economics extends a pattern that has provided us with a 'new' and 'old' institutionalism and a Keynesian and Post-Keynesian economics. The pattern is in part the result of paradigmatic strictures within orthodoxy preventing a proper engagement with, and understanding of, the original ideas (Earl 2013). If new ideas (from heterodoxy or from outside economics) are to be absorbed into orthodoxy, it tends to occur on the orthodoxy's own terms. The problem with this is that the more genuinely original and challenging aspects of an idea tend to be ignored or debased.

Turning to other problems in the conventional understanding of the orthodox–heterodox divide, one can often see the issue of the explicit or implicit assumption of exhaustiveness; in other words, there is an inability to acknowledge fully that there is a level of common ground between what is conventionally seen as either heterodox or orthodox. Consider Lee (2009), who asserts that heterodoxy is a complete and 'blasphemous' rejection of orthodoxy. In fact, the situation is not quite so simple. This is clearly demonstrated by King (2012), who provides various examples whereby rejecting the validity of core neoclassical concepts such as the law of demand, externalities and elasticity would be damaging to one's personal credibility and could also lead to detrimental public policy. It is also relevant to note that Earl and Peng found that their attempts to categorise research programmes had overlaps between programmes and that from their perspective 'no single existing brand of economics has a fully heterodox profile' (Earl & Peng 2012, p. 461).

One solution to this problem of commonalities is to treat the less problematic components of neoclassical economics as useful contributions to the economic toolbox, with the ever-present caveat that any tradesman would endorse: each tool needs to be fully understood, carefully used with regard to its limitations, applied to a task to which it is suited, and employed in conjunction with other tools if it is appropriate and helpful to do so. Such an approach is consistent with what many heterodox economists actually do in practice (Mearman 2010, 2011). The other way of understanding the situation is to say that concepts such as elasticities and externalities are not necessarily just the intellectual property of neoclassical economics. This, however, only reinforces the point that there are clearly some concepts and theories in common between orthodox and heterodox economists.

Illustrations of commonality between orthodoxy and heterodoxy are easily made. Kirzner (1987) points out that the neoclassical and Austrian economics share a commitment to methodological individualism, methodological subjectivism, marginalism and opportunity cost. One may counter that we should therefore classify Austrian economics as orthodox. This is not an option, since later developments in Austrian economics, such as viewing markets and competition as a process of learning and discovery, choice under uncertainty, and a rejection of mathematical methods, all make Austrian economics incompatible with neoclassical economics. Furthermore, if one looks at the later work of Hayek, it is evolutionary, rather than static, in nature.

Commonalities can also be seen in the 'special case' game that sometimes gets played between different schools of economics. For example, the prominent Post-Keynesian Paul Davidson argues that Post-Keynesian economics absorbs neoclassical economics as a special case (Davidson 2004). Similarly, the leading 'old institutionalist' economist Geoffrey Hodgson argues that institutionalism absorbs neoclassical economics as a special case (Hodgson 2004). Admittedly, both authors stress just what a special case the incorporation of neoclassical economics is. However, the fact that this game of incorporation can be played at all is a further illustration of commonality.

A clear and simple categorisation of the orthodox–heterodox divide seems elusive. There seems little ground for thinking this will change. Mearman (2010) examines over twenty attempts to define heterodoxy versus orthodoxy and finds them all wanting in one way or another. To help us understand why each of these dualisms runs into problems he makes some important points about the nature of categorisation itself. These points allow us to see that the orthodox–heterodox dualism (or any similar type of dualism such as 'political economy' versus 'economics') needs to be a 'modern' rather than 'classical' form of categorisation.

A classical approach to categorisation is characterised by fixed, mutually exclusive categories that should have no effect on the objects we classify. The presumption that a classical approach can be deployed to categorise economics is quite common amongst many versions of the orthodox–heterodox divide (see Mearman 2010). However, economics appears to be a complex object and classical categorisation of a complex object is usually intellectually problematic (Mearman 2010). In particular, classical categorisation cannot cope with the type of commonalities between orthodoxy and heterodoxy that have just been identified. Classical categorisation requires mutually exclusive and exhaustive categories that cannot be generated in this case.

The alternative to classical categorisation is to opt for a 'modern' approach where categories can be fuzzy, non-exhaustive, evolving, constructed for purposes beyond classification and are also able to exert an influence over the target object itself (Mearman 2010). While this is not as tidy and precise as classical categorisation, it is much more flexible and useful. For example, by utilising a 'fuzzy' set, an entity can simultaneously hold *fractional* membership of both sides of a dualism. The (very) corny song from the 1970s by Donny and Marie Osmond about each them being 'a little bit country, *and* a little bit rock and roll' seems illustrative here. Given that many self-identified heterodox economists say that they are not fully heterodox and hold views that they see as being orthodox (Mearman 2010, 2011), i.e. that they accumulate dual membership scores across orthodox and heterodox categories, it would seem that modern, non-classical categorisation is the only plausible approach to adopt.

An ontological dualism between economics and political economy

While adopting a classical approach to categorisation seems untenable for economics, a broad dualism can still be identified (albeit one of a modern, fuzzy kind) between political economy on the one hand and orthodox economics on the other. The basis for this broad dualism is ontological. As explained in Chapter 3, ontological differences are differences of view about the underlying nature of reality. Within economics, this comes down to questions such as: what does theory X presuppose about the nature of reality? In other words, what is the larger (and usually less obvious) package deal one is signing up for when one accepts the validity of a particular theory? Ontology is of decisive importance in understanding differences in economic analysis (Dow 2007; Lawson 1997, 2003). Schumpeter has explained the importance of ontology as well as anyone ever has (albeit by using the terminology of 'pre-analytic vision' rather than ontology):

> Analytic effort is of necessity preceded by a preanalytic cognitive act that supplies the raw material for the analytic efforts … This preanalytic cognitive act will be called Vision. It is interesting to note that vision of this kind not only must precede historically the emergence of analytic effort in any field

but also must re-enter the history of every established science each time somebody teaches us to see things in a light of which the source is not to be found in the facts, methods, and results of the pre-existing state of the science.

(Schumpeter 1954, p. 41)

What is the nature of this ontological divide within economics? It is not the presupposition of an open system in heterodoxy and a closed system within orthodoxy. This in an inadequate basis for any division: as was mentioned in Chapter 2, all theory requires at least some provisional closure. The valid and useful ontological dualism hinges on whether one presupposes a complex system versus whether one presupposes a complicated system (Potts 2000).

The ontological difference exists in the geometry of economic space (Potts 2000). In orthodox economics, the economic system is complicated (not complex). The system exists as an integral field (the concept of a field is taken from graph theory). The components of the system are all fully connected to each other, meaning that responses to change are fully determined and predictable. In such a system it is the agents themselves (rather than the connections between them) that hold centre stage. Such a system can be quite *complicated* (the many pages of equations that comprise general equilibrium theory are a good example of this). However, beyond this *seeming* complexity the consistent nature of the connections between agents means that, in essence, the system is *simple*; indeed some have even described such systems as *simple*, rather than complicated (see for example Foster 2005). Certainly, for all its superficial complication, it is a fully determined system and exhibits the type of event regularities that make it well suited for the deployment of formal methods to gain knowledge of its workings and to generate precise predictions. Furthermore, economic change is also rather simple: it is about substitution that is driven by changes in relative prices, with such prices being driven by changes in supply and demand (Earl 2006).

The alternative ontology is to conceive of economic reality nested inside a *complex* (rather than complicated) system. In a complex system, all agents are not all fully connected to each other. This puts the focus on connections and it is changes in the connective structure of the system that create the system dynamics. For example, technology is understood as being a set of connections between materials and institutions. Organisations are understood as connections between people. Furthermore, learning and knowledge are understood as emergent properties of new connections (Schmid 2003). An important characteristic of a complex system is that not all agents are connected with each other (as is the case in a complicated system). Full connectivity is prevented by fundamental uncertainty and bounded rationality, but also by organisational, spatial, temporal, market and social structures (Schmid 2003). The connections that do exist are the product of path-dependent historical time. The system is not entirely deterministic, agents are rule followers but have a degree of latitude in their responses. Structure and agency co-evolve and there is both change within the system and change in the nature of the overall system. While formalism and computer simulations may indeed be useful to analyse such a system, they are not necessarily the only

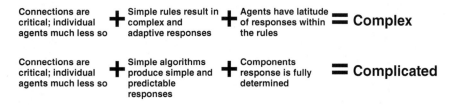

Figure 4.1 Complex versus complicated systems

method, or even the dominant method to be deployed. The differences between a complicated and complex system are summarised in Figure 4.1 which is reproduced from Potts (2007).

The ontology described by Potts is generally compatible with established heterodox approaches such as the Austrian, Post-Keynesian, institutionalist and Marxian schools. It does provide an underlying conception of economy and society that is compatible with so many important heterodox ideas. For example, that the economy is an evolving and historical entity, that we do not have full information about our choices before we choose, that we seldom accurately process the information we do have, and that we are followers (and creators) of habits, routines and institutions rather than being pure and perfect rational calculators. In this view of reality, the human agent is not the mindless and isolated prisoner of an exogenously given preference function: human beings are social beings who carry knowledge and create new knowledge via their interaction with others (Potts & Nightingale 2001).

It is immediately conceded that what is generally understood as heterodox economics does not always and everywhere sit perfectly inside a complex ontology. For example, some of the work of the Sraffian School would appear to have more affiliation with a complicated ontology. However, it is to be remembered that it is a 'modern' not 'classical' categorisation that is being put forward here. As such, categorisations are fuzzy, non-exhaustive, evolving, constructed for purposes beyond classification, and are also able to exert an influence over the target object itself (Mearman 2010).

As well as locating the heterodox traditions within a complex ontology we can also base the sub-disciplines of economic history, history of economic thought and development economics there as well. It is conceded that each of these four sub-categories of economics as a social science still have some distinct strands that still share the more complicated ontology of orthodox economics (history of economic thought being the most obvious). It must also be conceded that these sub-disciplines can be studied in a neoclassical way (development economics – which can just become applied orthodox microeconomics – being the most obvious example). However, these sub-disciplines, like most of the social sciences, share, at their most basic level, a general orientation towards a complex systems ontology.

The complex versus complicated system ontology also helps to make better sense of the orthodox research frontier. As has already been discussed, the orthodox research frontier is acceptable to orthodox economists (this is apparent enough in its name really), yet it is different from the neoclassical economics that is usually understood as defining the orthodoxy. An important clue to understanding this puzzle is provided by reflecting upon the previous discussion of the new versus the old behavioural economics. The 'old' or 'original' behavioural economics, with its focus on satisficing (rather than optimising) and on rule following, was much closer to heterodox economics and its complex ontology. By contrast, the 'new' behavioural economics is much closer to orthodoxy and its complicated ontology. Similarly, neoclassical synthesis Keynesian economics aligns closely with a complicated ontology, whereas Post Keynesian economics significantly aligns with a complex ontology. The same pattern is evident with the new institutional economics (essentially orthodox and with a complicated ontology) versus the old institutional economics (heterodox in nature and with a complex ontology). In other words, there is an ontological divide between neoclassical economics and much of the orthodox research frontier on one hand, and heterodox economics on the other.

The categorisation of orthodoxy is also necessarily non-exhaustive and fuzzy. The most obvious case of fuzziness would be in regard to complexity economics within the orthodox research frontier. However, it must be said that even the boundary might turn out to be less fuzzy than one might assume. To be more specific, it is entirely plausible, that a division within complexity economics could emerge. On the one hand there could be an 'old' or original complexity economics which is genuinely complex and has strong affinities with economic heterodoxy. On the other hand, there could be a 'new' complexity economics that betrays or distorts key aspects of complexity science and whose ontological foundations might even tend towards being complicated rather than complex. If so, it would only be slightly more incredible than the previously established cases of the 'new' and 'old' behavioural economics, the 'new' and 'old' institutionalism and 'Keynesian' and 'Post Keynesian' economics.

On the basis of the reasoning presented above we can divide economics on ontological lines as presented in Table 4.2.

Table 4.2 Economics and political economy as separate areas of knowledge

Area of knowledge	Incorporates
Orthodox Economics	1 Neoclassical economics 2 The orthodox research frontier
Political Economy	1 Heterodox economics (Institutionalism, Marxian economics, post Keynesian economics, Austrian economics, feminist economics, ecological economics) 2 Economic history 3 History of economic thought 4 Development economics

Political economy and economics

Having established the broad but somewhat fuzzy entities of political economy and orthodox economics as areas of knowledge, how exactly should they be categorised in a taxonomic sense? Specifically, are the areas of knowledge in the left column of Table 4.2 separate disciplines or branches of the same discipline? Could political economy be a cross-disciplinary or trans-disciplinary subject spanning economics and politics, or perhaps spanning economics, politics and philosophy? Could political economy be regarded as a branch of politics?

Before answering any of the questions just posed, it is worth reiterating that disciplinary differentiation in the social sciences is characterised by fuzzy boundaries and overlaps (COSS 2003; Garforth & Kerr 2011). The established boundaries are consistent with 'modern' rather than 'classical' categorisation; that is, they are fuzzy, non-exhaustive, evolving, constructed for purposes beyond classification and are also able to exert an influence over the target object itself. The creation of disciplines is shaped by both intellectual and non-intellectual considerations; the latter includes tradition, size, power and influence, tradition and convention. One could also stress issues of path-dependence in the way disciplinary categories have evolved. For all these reasons, we should not be too fearful or constrained about proposing changes to our understanding of how many disciplines exist and where the boundaries are between them. This is particularly so if it is thought that any proposed disciplinary categorisation is *at least* as intellectually valid as some of the more conventional categorisations, and if the categorisation is also likely to assist in the protection and development of the fields of knowledge that fall under any proposed categorisation. In other words, if a categorisation appears to be more useful, and is of comparable intellectual validity, then it is worthy of open and active consideration.

Now, to return to the question of how *exactly* to categorise political economy, it can be argued that differentiation could, and perhaps should, take a number of forms, with the choice of the precise form being shaped by context. Some options for the precise categorisation of political economy include categorising it as a separate discipline, a distinct 'social science' branch of economics, a trans- or cross-disciplinary area of knowledge, or as a branch of politics. The first two of these options will now be discussed with options three and four examined in Chapter 10 in the context of a discussion about the nature of politics, philosophy and economics degrees.

Political economy as an independent academic discipline

To assert separate disciplinary status is a novel and rather bold step. To the best of my knowledge not even the political economists who established Sydney University's Department of Political Economy (examined in Chapter 9) have ever argued that they represented an entirely separate academic discipline. However, in some respects political economy does function there (and elsewhere) as something close to an academic discipline, and occasionally one sees reference to the idea of political economy being a separate discipline (see for example the reference to the 'scientifically ambiguous' discipline of political economy in Colander 2008). Given all this, it is surely worth reflecting on the idea, at least as a thought experiment.

The first thing to be said is that the shift to full disciplinary separation is in some ways rather seamless and subtle. Table 4.2 would remain exactly the same, except that the upper leftmost cell would change from 'Area of Knowledge' to 'Academic Discipline', and the cell below it would change from 'Orthodox Economics' to simply becoming 'Economics', thus economics and political economy exist as related but separate academic disciplines.

There is also much precedent for a disciplinary differentiation such as this. The creation of disciplines – and even more so, academic departments – is significantly shaped by non-intellectual considerations such as administrative convenience, tradition, path-dependence and the distribution of institutional power within universities. The degree of intellectual difference that exists between economics and political economy is comparable to the difference that exists between other disciplines such anthropology and sociology or economics and finance. Indeed, none of these disciplines could point to any intellectual difference that delineates itself and its most closely related disciplines to anything like the same degree as the ontological difference between economics and political economy.

It is true that political economists would have to cede the term 'economics', but they have ready recourse to the arguably superior term of 'political economy' – the original name for economics up until the marginal revolution of the 1870s, and a name that better reflects the activities of the various research traditions that would fall under this proposed discipline. Meanwhile, orthodox economists, a group of people who in the main have proven to be so incapable of comprehending the value of pluralism, have a discipline to themselves – an outcome they themselves would most probably find satisfactory.

All the intellectual traditions in the proposed category of political economy not only have intellectual affinities via their common ontological foundations, and their general orientation around a institutions–history–social structure nexus, they also have common interests and face common problems of marginalisation by a dominant and intolerant economic orthodoxy. Becoming a single discipline would probably promote both the level of intellectual interaction and the more effective collective pursuit of common ends.

A crucial issue for all the intellectual traditions under the proposed discipline of political economy is the problem they face in getting their research assessed in a fair manner, owing to the dominance of orthodox economists on research assessment panels and in the drafting and design of the research assessment exercises. As a consequence, even more moderate orthodox economists can become terrified that the presence of non-orthodox staff in their department will drag their department's research ranking down. However, under full differentiation this problem could evaporate as political economy research could be assessed as a separate discipline by other political economists. Any ranking received by a department for the discipline of political economy would be separate from its ranking in the discipline of economics. Such a move could foster more effective cohabitation – for example a department of economics and political economy (like a department of economics and finance, which is a common form of disciplinary cohabitation within universities) might have better prospects of success if economists and political economists did not have to worry constantly about how their own research output might suffer for being assessed and aggregated alongside the other's research output.

Political economy as the 'social science wing of economics'

A more modest approach that is more in keeping with the conventional wisdom is to argue that political economy should conceive of itself as a distinct branch of economics. What this means is that Table 4.2 stays essentially unchanged but for the fact that political economy and orthodox economics are understood to be two branches of the single discipline of economics (rather than just two distinct areas of knowledge). Given political economy's ontological foundations, and its focus on the institutions–history–social nexus, one could perhaps subtitle political economy as the 'social science' wing of economics, thus denoting and further facilitating its connection with other social sciences.

Uniting the marginalised areas of heterodox economics, economic history, history of economic thought, and development economics under a category of political economy would promote intellectual collaboration and understanding. Just as crucially, it would unite these intellectual traditions under a common banner to lobby for reform within the discipline of economics. Currently, these marginalised areas of knowledge do not sufficiently conceive of themselves as a distinct entity, nor do they sufficiently try to advance their interests within the discipline as a distinct entity. They would probably get further if they did so.

It may seem unsettling to the reader that neither political economy nor economics is pinned down to a specific level or type of categorisation. It is true that if everybody does not file in behind one particular taxonomy then this could make the situation messy. However, most categorisation in the social sciences is necessarily messy because the social sciences are a complex object. In seeking to categorise such objects we can't use precise and tidy 'classical' categorisation and instead have to utilise 'modern' categorisation that is *always* intrinsically messy or 'fuzzy'. The salient point to consider is whether a different way of categorising the non-orthodox areas of economics might make things *better* and make more things *possible*. Is this not the key consideration? Perhaps over time things might generally (but never completely) coalesce around a particular understanding of what political economy is because that understanding has gained a level of success, support and understanding. In the meantime, the logic and merits of each option will depend on what individuals and groups judge to be viable and desirable for them in their country and their particular university. The main point to be stressed here (and it is a point that receives much support in subsequent chapters) is that *some* greater degree of differentiation and independence is highly desirable. The precise way political economy is to be understood can be shaped by the possibilities within particular contexts. In other words, the question is 'what works best in this place and at this time?' Pragmatism trumps purity in this instance because there are no pure or clean disciplinary categories.

Consider how the context might shape the choice of categorisation. In some countries an independent discipline of political economy may be the only vehicle that can really provide solutions to the profound problems of biased research assessment and intellectual suppression in the curriculum. In other countries, a distinct and well-organised branch of 'political economy' that exists within a discipline of 'economics' might be the most viable and desirable means for reform. In other situations the *only* plausible path forward is for political economists is to base themselves in departments of politics. In such cases conceiving of political economy as a branch of politics has a very strong logic and appeal. In yet other situations it may make sense to conceive of political economy as a cross-disciplinary or trans-disciplinary project. Such an approach may work best if one is in a school of social sciences and involved in cross-disciplinary degrees such as politics, philosophy and economics degrees.

Ruminating on how arbitrary and fuzzy disciplinary boundaries are carries the considerable virtue of liberating one's thinking and of opening the mind to the identification of possibilities, partnerships and solutions that might not otherwise be identified. This is true whether one considers political economy as a separate discipline, a separate branch of economics, a trans-disciplinary area of knowledge, or a branch of politics.[4] In summary, propagating a richer and more flexible understanding of what political economy is as an area of knowledge is something that it is intellectually warranted and strategically desirable.

The term 'heterodox economics'

Let us now turn to examining the term 'heterodox economics' more carefully. As per Table 4.2, it is usually understood to describe institutionalism, Marxian economics, Post-Keynesian economics, Austrian economics, feminist economics and ecological economics. With a reluctance that is borne of the knowledge that I will be upsetting many of my esteemed colleagues, it is argued that 'heterodox economics' is an awkward term. Indeed, one could argue that the term should be completely dispensed with, if not for the fact that the schools usually associated with it do, on occasion, need some collective descriptor, and heterodox economics at least has an established currency in this respect. However, there is a strong case for reserving it for internal use only, a 'within the trade' name to describe the various dissenting non-neoclassical schools. In most cases, and particularly when communicating with the outside world, it may work better for economists in these traditions to simply refer to themselves, in the first instance, as representing their particular school (for example institutionalism) and in the second instance as a political economist.

Why is it an awkward term? First, it is inherently negative in that it defines itself, in the first instance, by what it is not (i.e., it is *not* orthodox economics). Second, it is built for failure in that 'heterodox economics' is a brand name that 'would cease to make sense if it succeeded in usurping the current mainstream' (Earl & Peng 2012, p. 466). Third, there is no currently existing department that is titled 'Department of Heterodox Economics', and given the already mentioned problems with the term, such a department seems unlikely ever to emerge. By contrast, departments of political economy do exist (see Chapter 9). In general, the term 'heterodox economics' is poorly suited to facilitating success, growth, alliances and partnerships. As Stilwell notes, it is a term of questionable strategic savvy (Stilwell 2015).

The term 'heterodox economics' is also currently unintelligible to most people. Table 4.3 presents the results of a small survey on how the terms 'heterodox economics' and 'political economy' are understood amongst students and also amongst members of the general public. Political economy, whilst eliciting a range of responses, is still the more easily understood of the two terms. By contrast, nine out of ten people simply did not know what heterodox economics was. On this basis political economy offers a better foundation on which to build a discipline (or even something even approaching a discipline). The survey conducted had a small sample size, but it is consistent with what some self-proclaimed heterodox economists already know. As Stilwell (2015, p. 8) notes, 'the typical layperson's usual response to hearing the term "heterodox economics" – "what's that?" or just "huh?"'

Table 4.3 Understanding of the terms 'heterodox economics' and 'political economy'

Heterodox economics is:	Total	Percentage
Anti-economics	0	0
A particular subsection of economics	1	2
A particular subsection of politics	0	0
An independent academic discipline	1	2
Non-orthodox economics	3	6
Don't know	45	90
Other	0	0
Political economy is:		
Anti-economics	0	0
A particular subsection of economics	15	30
A particular subsection of politics	15	30
An independent academic discipline	1	2
Non-orthodox economics	0	0
Don't know	14	28
Other	5	10
Category of respondent		
Business student	13	26
Humanities student	16	32
Other Student	10	20
Non Student	11	22

Source: Thornton (2011)

The broader category of political economy is also the better term to use if one is considering basing the teaching of economics in faculties of social science, rather than in faculties of business where economics departments are often based. Political economy, with its lead term 'political', is suggestive of a subject that is relevant to other social scientists and their students. The term political economy suggests, and thus promotes, interdisciplinarity with the other social sciences.

There are some objections to using the term 'political economy'. It has been argued that it is either too closely associated with the left (particularly Marxian economics or radical political economy) or too closely associated with right (particularly public choice theory). Neither of these (contradictory) arguments is persuasive. Groenewegen (1987), in his examination of the history of the terms 'political economy' and 'economics', clearly demonstrates that both the terms 'economics' and 'political economy' have a rich, intermingled history. It is also clear that both terms have experienced changes in meaning over time, being colonised or abandoned depending on how well they served particular agendas at particular times. Both terms appear to have a 'use it or lose it' quality, in that the more a group of academics uses the title of political economy to describe its activities, the more the title of political economy is associated with those academics. The term has never fallen out of use amongst the non-neoclassical economics community; their frequent embrace of the term is evident in the books they write, the study groups they form, the conferences they run, the subjects and subject majors they create. It may actually be predominant over the term heterodox economics, though it would be hard to be sure without survey evidence. In any case, what is clear is that political economy is big enough, and worthwhile enough, to be far more comprehensively embraced by those seeking renewal and reform, and as a consequence of this, more clearly owned by them.

'Political economy' is also a superior term because it better allows reformers to frame their work and ideas within a long and rich tradition (Stilwell 2015). Reformers can then be seen (and can see themselves) less as dissenters, and more as representing the 'mainline tradition' within economics (Tabb 1999). Describing oneself, and understanding oneself, as a keeper of the true flame (rather than as a fringe heretic) seems more strategically savvy given the often cautious and conservative nature of universities. As Stilwell notes, an advantage of the term 'political economy' is:

> [I]ts long and respectable lineage. Political economy has a claim to actually *be* the mainstream, running from the eighteenth through to the twenty-first century and including seminal contributions from Smith, Ricardo, Marx, Keynes, Kalecki, Robinson, Myrdal, Galbraith, Heilbroner and numerous modern contributors to that broad tradition of economic and social inquiry. From this perspective, neoclassical economics can be seen as an initially interesting side-track that became a dead-end or cul-de-sac (albeit one with a massive volume of traffic going nowhere).
>
> (Stilwell 2015, p. 8)

In the light of all this, unless one needs to specifically organise or identify activities purely limited to institutional economists, Post-Keynesian economists, Marxian economists, ecological economists, feminist economists and Austrian economists, then simply opting for the broader term of political economy as the collective descriptor seems more prudent. Under such an arrangement one is first a practitioner of a particular school (for example, a Post-Keynesian) then one is a political economist.

Economics, political economy and heterodox economics defined for the chapters ahead

Earlier chapters of this book freely used the categories of heterodox economics, orthodox economics and political economy in keeping with their popular, and often loosely defined, meanings. However, given all the arguments made in this chapter, it is now possible to be more precise. How then should matters of categorisation be conducted from this point onwards in the book? One could speak only in terms of the discipline of political economy versus the discipline of economics. However, it is conceded that this is a novel categorisation and it might serve to distract and irritate some readers. More importantly, opting for the unrelenting use of a single (and quite novel) categorisation imposes a quite specific understanding of the terms political economy and economics which goes against the earlier argument that categorisation needs to be flexible, pragmatic and suited to context. Given the points just made it seems best from this point onwards to usually talk in terms of 'political economy' versus 'orthodox economics' existing within the single discipline of economics, thus Political economy and orthodox economics are defined as per Table 4.4 which the reader may want to refer back to when required.

This middle ground position (which casts orthodox economics and political economy as two branches of the discipline of economics) is not enormously different from the conventional wisdom within the discipline. However, it is somewhat different from the norm in that it is a dualism that acknowledges the existence of economic history, history of economic thought and development

Table 4.4 Orthodox economics and political economy as branches of the discipline of economics

Branch of economics	Incorporates
Orthodox economics	• Neoclassical economics • The orthodox research frontier
Political economy	• Heterodox economics (Institutionalism, Marxian economics, post Keynesian economics, Austrian economics, feminist economics, ecological economics) • Economic history • History of economic thought • Development economics

economics. Furthermore, the definition of orthodox economics[5] that is adopted includes both neoclassical economics *and* the orthodox research frontier, thereby avoiding the criticism of conservative reformists who complain that those attacking orthodox economics do not acknowledge that orthodox economics has changed and no longer simply consists of neoclassical economics.

Notes

1   Interestingly, the dictionary explains that the root for the closely related word 'heterodoxy' comes from the Greek word *heterodoxia*, which the Oxford Dictionary, at least at one point, relates it to 'error of opinion' (Brown 1993, p. 1226).
2   The list could be extended somewhat to include social economists, Georgian economists, Sraffian economists and others, but for the purposes of not having an unwieldy or overly contentious list I have listed only the most recognised heterodox traditions. I apologise for any offence, or error, caused in my personal determinations of what constitutes a major heterodox tradition.
3   The assumption of scarcity is selective in that rationality and institutions are usually assumed to be both abundant and costless (Pagano 2000, Hodgson 2004).
4   As already mentioned, see Chapter 10 for some further discussion on political economy as branch of politics or as trans-disciplinary area of knowledge.
5   I have avoided using the term 'mainstream economics' in this book as there is nothing – when measured by the standard of other social sciences – that is particularly mainstream about orthodox economics; indeed, it exhibits a lack of plurality and interdisciplinarity that is anything but mainstream.

References

Brown, L. 1993, *The New Shorter Oxford English Dictionary* Clarendon Press, Oxford.
Colander, D. C. 2008, 'Foreword', in C. Arnsperger (ed.), *Critical Political Economy Complexity, Rationality, and the Logic of Post-Orthodox Pluralism*, Routledge, New York, pp. xviii–xxiii.
COSS 2003, *Great Expectations: The Social Sciences in Britain*, Commission on the Social Sciences Academy of Learned Societies for the Social Sciences, London.
Davidson, P. 2004, 'A Response to King's Arguments for Pluralism', *Post-Autistic Economics Review*, issue 24, March, pp. 1–5.
Dow, S. C. 2007, 'Pluralism in Economics', in J. Groenewegen (ed.), *Teaching Pluralism in Economics*, Edward Elgar, Cheltenham, pp. 22–39.
Earl, P. E. 2006, Capability Prerequisites and the Competitive Process, Working Paper, Department of Economics, University of Queensland, St Lucia.
Earl, P. E. 2010, 'Economics Fit for the Queen: A Pessimistic Assessment of Its Prospects', *Prometheus*, vol. 28, no. 3, pp. 209–25.
Earl, P. E. 2013, *Comment on 'New' Versus 'Old' in the History of Economics*, Personal Communication, 18 January.
Earl, P. E. & Peng, T. C. 2012, 'Brands of Economics and the Trojan Horse of Pluralism', *Review of Political Economy*, vol. 24, no. 3, pp. 451–67.
Foster, J. 2005, 'From Simplistic to Complex Systems in Economics', *Cambridge Journal of Economics*, vol. 29, no. 6, pp. 873–92.
Fullbrook, E. 2003, *The Crisis in Economics: The Post-Autistic Economics Movement: The First 600 Days*, Routledge, London.
Fullbrook, E. 2004, *A Guide to What's Wrong with Economics*, Anthem, London.

Garforth, L. & Kerr, A. 2011, 'Interdisciplinarity and the Social Sciences: Capital, Institutions and Autonomy', *The British Journal of Sociology*, vol. 62, no. 4, pp. 657–76.

Groenewegen, P. D. 1987, '"Political Economy" and "Economics"', in J. Eatwell, M. Milgate & P. Newman (eds), *The New Palgrave: A Dictionary of Economics*, vol. 3, pp. 905–6.

Hodgson, G. M. 2004, *The Evolution of Institutional Economics: Agency, Structure, and Darwinism in American Institutionalism*, Routledge, New York.

Hopkins, B. 2013, 'Building Heterodox Community: Pluralism in Fragmented Epistemological Communities', in F. S. Lee & M. Lavoie (eds), *In Defense of Post-Keynesian and Heterodox Economics: Response to the Critics*, Routledge, London, pp. 133–57.

King, J. E. 2012, 'Post Keynesians and Others', *Review of Political Economy*, vol. 24, no. 2, pp. 305–19.

Kirzner, I. M.–1987, 'The Austrian School of Economics', in J. Eatwell, M. Milgate & P. Newman (eds), *The New Palgrave: A Dictionary of Economics*, Macmillan, London, pp. 145–51.

Lawson, T. 1997, *Economics and Reality*, Routledge, London.

Lawson, T. 2003, *Reorienting Economics*, Routledge, London

Lee, F. S. 2009, *A History of Heterodox Economics: Challenging the Mainstream in the Twentieth Century*, Routledge, London.

Lee, F. S. 2012, 'Heterodox Economics and Its Critics', *Review of Political Economy*, vol. 24, no. 2, pp. 337–51

Mearman, A. 2010, 'What Is This Thing Called 'Heterodox Economics'?, Working Paper No. 1006, Department of Economics, University of West England, Bristol.

Mearman, A. 2011, 'Who Do Heterodox Economists Think They Are?', *American Journal of Economics and Sociology*, vol. 70, no. 2, pp. 480–510.

Pagano, U. 2000, 'Bounded Rationality, Institutionalism and the Diversity of Economic Institutions', in F. Louçã & M. Perlman (eds), *Is Economics an Evolutionary Science? The Legacy of Thorstein Veblen*, Edward Elgar, Cheltenham, pp. 95–113.

Potts, J. 2000, *The New Evolutionary Microeconomics: Complexity, Competence, and Adaptive Behaviour*, Edward Elgar, Cheltenham.

Potts, J. 2007, Complexity and Creative Industries, Presentation paper, Centre for creative industries, Queensland University of Technology Brisbane.

Potts, J. & Nightingale, J. 2001, 'An Alternative Framework for Economics', *Post-Autistic Economics Review*, issue 10, December, pp. 12–15.

Rabin, M. 2007, 'Matthew Rabin', in D. Colander, R. Holt & B. Rosser (eds), *The Changing Face of Economics: Conversations with Cutting-Edge Economists*, University of Michigan Press, Ann Arbor, pp. 137–56.

Schmid, A. A. 2003, 'Review of the New Evolutionary Microeconomics by Jason Potts', *Economic Record*, vol. 79, no. 244, pp. 140–2.

Schumpeter, J. A. 1954, *History of Economic Analysis*, Allen & Unwin, London.

Sent, E.-M. 2004, 'Behavioral Economics: How Psychology Made Its (Limited) Way Back into Economics', *History of Political Economy*, vol. 36, no. 4, pp. 735–60.

Stilwell, F. J. B. 2015, 'Editorial', *Journal of Australian Political Economy*, no. 75, Winter, pp. 5–10.

Tabb, W. K. 1999, *Reconstructing Political Economy: The Great Divide in Economic Thought*, Routledge, London.

Thornton, T. B. 2011, *Survey on the Perception and Understanding of the Terms Heterodox Economics and Political Economy*, La Trobe University, Melbourne.

Wilkinson, N. 2008, *An Introduction to Behavioral Economics*, Palgrave Macmillan, Basingstoke.

5 The global student movement for pluralism

There is now an extensive worldwide network of student groups pushing for pluralism and their activities and views are the topic of this chapter. It is not a new phenomenon: as Kay (2014) points out, in no other discipline do students engage in such a level of organised protest against the content of their instruction. This chapter reveals that student groups are dynamic, interconnected and possessing a good grasp of the challenges they face within their own universities. Given all this, it is argued that it would be desirable for political economists and student groups to work together more closely. A foundation for greater partnership is mutual understanding; hence this chapter seeks to outline the history, activities and views of these groups.

Student protests in the twenty-first century

The epicentre of much of the current wave of student involvement has been in France. For example, the École Normale Supérieure (an elite school) has been protesting the lack of economic pluralism since 2000 (Lavoie 2015). It is from here that the 'Post-Autistic Economics Movement' was established. Elsewhere in France, student leaders also formed Pour un Enseignement Pluraliste de l'Economie dans le Supérieur (PEPS-Économie – for pluralist teaching in economics) and this organisation did most of the drafting of the May 2014 Open Letter published by the International Student Initiative for Pluralism in Economics (Lavoie 2015). This open letter follows other open letters such as the Kansas City Proposal of 2001 and Cambridge Proposal of 2001.

ISIPE

The International Student Initiative for Pluralism in Economics (ISIPE) is a network or consortium of more than sixty-five student organisations from across thirty countries that was established in 2014. Some of the member groups such as Network for Plural Economics (Germany) and Rethinking Economics (throughout the world and in the UK especially) are substantial network organisations in their own right. Many of the groups are also very active. For example, the Cambridge Society for Economic Pluralism, the Manchester Post Crash Society and the

Politics, Philosophy and Economics Society are highly engaged under their own auspices, producing email newsletters (which anyone can subscribe to) holding events and various other activities.

Table 5.1 lists ISIPE membership as of May 2014, when the open letter was originally released.

Table 5.1 ISIPE Membership as of May 2014

Country	Name of the group
Argentina	Sociedad de Economía Crítica Argentina
Australia	The PPE Society, La Trobe University
Austria	Society for Pluralist Economics Vienna
Brazil	Nova Ágora
Canada	Mouvement étudiant québécois pour un enseignement pluraliste de l'économie
Chile	Estudios.Nueva Economía
Chile	Grupo de estudiantes y egresados de la Facultad de Economía y Negocios de la Universidad de Chile
Denmark	Det Samfundsøkonomiske Selskab (DSS)
France	Pour un Enseignement Pluraliste de l'Economie dans le Supérieur (PEPS-Economie)
Germany	Arbeitskreis Plurale Ökonomik, Hamburg Arbeitskreis Plurale Ökonomik, Munich Ecoation, Augsburg Impuls. für eine neue Wirtschaft, Erfurt Kritische Ökonomen, Frankfurt Kritische WissenschaftlerInnen, Berlin LIE – Lost in Economics e.V., Regensburg Netzwerk Plurale Ökonomik (Network for Pluralist Economics) Oikos Köln Oikos Leipzig Real World Economics, Heidelberg Real World Economics, Mainz Student HUB Weltethos Institut Tübingen Was ist Ökonomie, Berlin
India	Javadhpur University Heterodox Economics Association
Israel	Economics Student Forum – Haifa (Rethinking Economics), Economics Student Forum – Tel Aviv
Italy	Rethinking Economics Italia
Mexico	Grupo de Estudiantes por la Enseñanza Plural de la Economía, UNAM
Russia	Oeconomicus Economic Club MGIMO
Slovenia	Movement for Pluralistic Economics
Spain	Asociación de Estudiantes de Económicas de la Universidad Autónoma de Madrid

Table 5.1 continued

Country	Name of the group
	Estudantes de Económicas e Empresariais, Universidade de Santiago de Compostela
	Post-Crash Barcelona
Sweden	Handels Students for Sustainability
	Lunds Kritiska Ekonomer
Switzerland	PEPS-Helvetia
UK	Alternative Thinking for Economics Society, Sheffield University
	Better Economics UCLU
	Cambridge Society for Economic Pluralism
	Glasgow University Real World Economics Society
	LSE Post-Crash Economics
	Post-Crash Economics Society, Essex
	Post-Crash Economics Society, Manchester
	Rethinking Economics
	SOAS Open Economics Forum

The Open letter itself is worth reading in full and is reproduced below:

An international student call for pluralism in economics

It is not only the world economy that is in crisis. The teaching of economics is in crisis too, and this crisis has consequences far beyond the university walls. What is taught shapes the minds of the next generation of policymakers, and therefore shapes the societies we live in. We, over 65 associations of economics students from over 30 different countries, believe it is time to reconsider the way economics is taught. We are dissatisfied with the dramatic narrowing of the curriculum that has taken place over the last couple of decades. This lack of intellectual diversity does not only restrain education and research. It limits our ability to contend with the multidimensional challenges of the 21st century – from financial stability, to food security and climate change. The real world should be brought back into the classroom, as well as debate and a pluralism of theories and methods. Such change will help renew the discipline and ultimately create a space in which solutions to society's problems can be generated.

United across borders, we call for a change of course. We do not claim to have the perfect answer, but we have no doubt that economics students will profit from exposure to different perspectives and ideas. Pluralism will not only help to enrich teaching and research and reinvigorate the discipline. More than this, pluralism carries the promise of bringing economics back into the service of society. Three forms of pluralism must be at the core of curricula: theoretical, methodological and interdisciplinary.

Theoretical pluralism emphasizes the need to broaden the range of schools of thought represented in the curricula. It is not the particulars of any economic tradition we object to. Pluralism is not about choosing sides, but about encouraging intellectually rich debate and learning to critically contrast ideas. Where other disciplines embrace diversity and teach competing theories even when they are mutually incompatible, economics is often presented as a unified body of knowledge. Admittedly, the dominant tradition has internal variations. Yet, it is only one way of doing economics and of looking at the real world. Such uniformity is unheard of in other fields; nobody would take seriously a degree program in psychology that focuses only on Freudianism, or a politics program that focuses only on state socialism. An inclusive and comprehensive economics education should promote balanced exposure to a variety of theoretical perspectives, from the commonly taught neoclassically-based approaches to the largely excluded classical, Post-Keynesian, institutional, ecological, feminist, Marxist and Austrian traditions – among others. Most economics students graduate without ever encountering such diverse perspectives in the classroom.

Furthermore, it is essential that core curricula include courses that provide context and foster reflexive thinking about economics and its methods per se, including philosophy of economics and the theory of knowledge. Also, because theories cannot be fully understood independently of the historical context in which they were formulated, students should be systematically exposed to the history of economic thought and to the classical literature on economics as well as to economic history. Currently, such courses are either non-existent or marginalized to the fringes of economics curricula.

Methodological pluralism stresses the need to broaden the range of tools economists employ to grapple with economic questions. It is clear that maths and statistics are crucial to our discipline. But all too often students learn to master quantitative methods without ever discussing if and why they should be used, the choice of assumptions and the applicability of results. Also, there are important aspects of economics which cannot be understood using exclusively quantitative methods: sound economic inquiry requires that quantitative methods are complemented by methods used by other social sciences. For instance, the understanding of institutions and culture could be greatly enhanced if qualitative analysis was given more attention in economics curricula. Nevertheless, most economics students never take a single class in qualitative methods.

Finally, economics education should include interdisciplinary approaches and allow students to engage with other social sciences and the humanities. Economics is a social science; complex economic phenomena can seldom be understood if presented in a vacuum, removed from their sociological, political, and historical contexts. To properly discuss economic policy, students should understand the broader social impacts and moral implications of economic decisions.

While approaches to implementing such forms of pluralism will vary from place to place, general ideas for implementation might include:

- Hiring instructors and researchers who can bring theoretical and methodological diversity to economics programs;
- Creating texts and other pedagogical tools needed to support pluralist course offerings;
- Formalizing collaborations between social sciences and humanities departments or establishing special departments that could oversee interdisciplinary programs blending economics and other fields.

Change will be difficult – it always is. But it is already happening. Indeed, students across the world have already started creating change step by step. We have filled lecture theatres in weekly lectures by invited speakers on topics not included in the curriculum; we have organised reading groups, workshops, conferences; we have analysed current syllabuses and drafted alternative programs; we have started teaching ourselves and others the new courses we would like to be taught. We have founded university groups and built networks both nationally and internationally.

Change must come from many places. So now we invite you – students, economists, and non-economists – to join us and create the critical mass needed for change. Click on 'Support us' to show your support and connect with our growing networks. Ultimately, pluralism in economics education is essential for healthy public debate. It is a matter of democracy.

Signed, the member organizations of the International Student Initiative for Pluralism in Economics.

This is an eloquent, well-argued letter that makes reasonable requests. It is not, and does not read as, a polemic. Despite this, relatively few economists have been prepared to add their names in support of the ISIPE petition. This demonstrates the capacity of the profession to close ranks when subjected to external scrutiny (Lavoie 2015). At the time of writing, none of the names that one would immediately associate with conservative reformists have signed. Neither have some prominent economists who are often seen as moderates (for example, Joseph Stiglitz, Paul Krugman and Robert Frank). One exception to this is Thomas Piketty. This lack of support for ISIPE underlies the point made in previous chapters that the appetite for reform in economics is really quite constrained. By contrast, many prominent political economists have supported the letter. It does seem that in this particular instance the divide between economists and political economists doesn't look very fuzzy at all.

Not every student who studies economics has felt strongly enough to actively join these groups, and so the question needs to be asked 'how broadly based and representative are these movements?' There is good evidence that dissatisfaction with the curriculum is broadly based, even if this does not cause open rebellion in every university. Guest and Duhs (2002) point out that economics is a subject that is rated very poorly by students in general. Similarly, Ward et al., drawing on survey evidence, argue that:

Economics is poorly perceived by potential students. It is viewed as: abstract and theoretical, difficult to study, rigorous and dull, thus reducing interest, unexciting, boring and lacking intrinsic interest, not relevant to 'real world' or 'real life' issues, lacking an ethical dimension, not being associated with a high profile profession or group of professions and reducing career prospects.

Ward, Crosling & Marangos 2000, p. 76)

Stilwell (2006) points to the dramatic attrition rate in economics as evidence of dissatisfaction. Many hundreds of students undertake first-year economics (usually on the basis that doing first-year economics is compulsory for business-based degrees), yet this huge catchment of students results in only a handful of students undertaking honours degrees in economics. Stilwell (2011) examines student survey responses undertaken within the Faculty of Economics and Business at the University of Sydney in 2003–7, finding that student evaluations for pluralist political economy courses produced the highest average scores for 'overall course satisfaction' in the faculty. By contrast, economics subjects produced the lowest average scores in the faculty. Subjects taught by other departments in the faculty such as accounting, finance, government, industrial relations, marketing and econometrics received scores between the two extremes of political economy and economics. The differences in ranking between economics and political economy were most extreme at the first-year level. That the polarisation of responses peaked at the first-year level probably indicates that subsequent self-selection occurs (the students with the most negative reaction to first-year economics subjects simply do not continue with the study of economics). The positive student feedback for political economy offers strong encouragement to the idea that any department offering such subjects has reasonable prospects of viable to strong enrolments.

Looking at national-level data, enrolments in economics have declined in many countries in recent decades, particularly if measured by percentage of market share. Each country has its own story, but in general, it is reasonable to say that the story varies from alarming rates of decline to, at best, relative underperformance. In some countries such as the United States and United Kingdom there has been a growth spurt in response to the global financial crisis (as students *presume* they will gain a satisfactory intellectual understanding of what occurred). Another explanatory factor might be sales of Dubner and Levitt's *Freakonomics* (Millmow & Tuck 2011). However, it is already clear that, in the United States at least, the short growth spurt has since 'stalled' (Siegfried 2014). Furthermore, in countries such as Australia and New Zealand, enrolments have not boomed as a result of the Global Financial Crisis (Agnew 2015; Millmow & Tuck 2011). In general, the study of economics has lost market share to other disciplines, particularly the business-based disciplines. For example in the United States, economics degrees account for only 1.6 per cent of all degrees awarded (Flynn & Quinn 2010). In general, the market signals suggest the need to renovate and renew what is offered. However, economics departments have generally been unwilling or unable to adapt sufficiently, which has at times has been described as committing 'academic suicide' (Round & Shanahan 2010, pp. 425–6) or opting for a 'quiet death' (Millmow 2002).

A survey of ISIPE member groups

It is illuminating to look at ISIPE's membership and to read its open letter. However, a more detailed analysis is warranted given the current and potential significance of ISIPE. Towards this end, an online survey was designed and run in October–November 2015. The results of this data will now be presented and discussed as required.

Data was gathered from thirty-six students collectively representing twenty-four of eighty-five ISIPE student groups. These twenty-four groups were distributed across seventeen of thirty countries where ISIPE groups exist. Seventy-eight per cent of respondents were male and 22 per cent were female. The average age of respondents was 24 years. Thirty-nine per cent were undergraduates, 11 per cent were honours students, 33 per cent were Masters students, and 17 per cent were PhD students.

Students were asked about their activities and beliefs as individuals. Students were also asked questions about their group. There were eight instances where more than one member of a particular group participated in the survey (which explains why there are thirty-six responses but only twenty-four groups). Multiple responses from within the same group were inevitable and unavoidable. In such instances the responses to most questions concerning group activity have been combined: this involved averaging numerical data, combining text responses and choosing the dominant multiple choice response.

The particular student groups that responded, and the estimates respondents gave about membership numbers in their group, are listed in Table 5.2 below.

Most of the groups are recently formed, one group formed in 2004, but the rest formed in 2010 or afterwards. The years 2013 and 2014 were the most productive years for group formation with eleven new groups forming in each of these years. The average membership size of the groups was forty. The groups are well connected with each other with twenty-two of the twenty-four groups (92 per cent) stating they have links of various types with the other ISIPE student groups, taking the form of joint public events (twelve groups – 50 per cent), joint social events for members (eight groups – 33 per cent), discussing and sharing strategies for change (nineteen groups – 79 per cent).

The groups themselves appear to be growing in membership size: four groups (17 per cent) said that membership had increased strongly, while twelve groups (50 per cent) said membership had increased slightly. Four groups (17 per cent) said membership was constant, two groups (8 per cent) said it had decreased, and two groups (8 per cent) did not respond to the question. On this basis, we can say that two-thirds of groups surveyed are growing.

The levels of activity within the groups has also increased with ten groups (42 per cent) stating it had increased slightly, eight groups (33 per cent) saying it had

Table 5.2 Survey responses by student group

Country	Name of the group	Formed	Membership
Australia	PPE Society, La Trobe University	2012	150
Austria	Gesellschaft für plurale Ökonomik Graz	2014	12
	Gesellschaft für plurale Ökonomik, Wien	2013	25
Belgium	Belgian Student Initiative for a Pluralist Economics Curriculum (BSIPEC)	2014	–
	Bureau des étudiants en ESPO (BDE ESPO)	–	
	Initiative louvaniste pour le pluralisme en économie	2014	10
Canada	Mouvement étudiant québécois pour un enseignement pluraliste de l'économie	2014	35
Chile	Estudios Nueva Economía (New Economy Studies), Universidad de Chile in Santiago	2011	20
Colombia	Consejo Estudiantil de Economía UPTC	2014	15
Denmark	Det Samfundsøkonomiske Selskab (DSS)	2013	10
France	Pour un Enseignement Pluraliste de l'Economie dans le Supérieur (PEPS-Economie)	2010	25
Germany	Humboldt University of Berlin, Network for Pluralist Economics	2012	15
	Student HUB Weltethos Institute Tübingen	2012	7
Pakistan	Quaid I Azam University Heterodox Economics Student Group	2013	15
Poland	SKN Ekonomii, Warsaw	2004	25
Slovenia	Gibanje za ekonomsko pluralnost, Ljubljana	2013	6
UK	Alternative Thinking for Economics Society, Sheffield University	2013	10
	Better Economics UCLU, London (with Rethinking Economics)	2015	7
	Edinburgh University Society for Economic Pluralism	2015	100
	Glasgow University Real World Economics Society (GURWES)	2013	90
	OPEN Economics, Leeds	2015	50
	Post-Crash Economics Society, Manchester	2012	11
	Rethinking Economics (Kingston University)	2014	
	Rethinking Economics (National)	2013	200

increased a lot, two groups (8 per cent) that it had stayed constant, three groups (13 per cent) that it had decreased slightly, and one group (4 per cent) stating they did not know. On this basis, we can say that 75 per cent of the respondent groups had increased their level of activity since their inception. Table 5.3 gives a summary of student responses about their group's activities.

What progress in promoting pluralism was reported? A total of ten of the twenty-four groups (42 per cent) indicated that they were aware of the creation of a new pluralist subject at their university. The particular subjects created were

Table 5.3 Activities undertaken by ISIPE student groups

Activity	Count/24	Per cent
Running pluralist subjects/courses/reading groups	15	63
Holding occasional seminars	21	88
Staging conferences	16	67
Holding regular group meetings	21	88
Organising social events	14	58
Maintaining a website or blog	19	79
Publishing a regular newsletter (email or print)	5	21
Producing group merchandise (badges/clothing etc.)	2	8
Other	14	58

varied; they included an honours subject in Post Keynesian Economics, subjects on methodology and the history of economic thought. Interdisciplinary subjects have also been established. One of these subjects focused on politics, philosophy and economics, while another subject on ecological economics was co-taught with staff from the law department and the biology department. In one instance there had not been progress in establishing a new subject but honours students were now able to undertake an elective subject from their university's economic history department – it is notable that such an option had not been available in the first place. Some pluralist economics subjects had been established in one university's business school, but not in that university's economics department. In another university a subject that offered differing perspectives on the financial crisis has been established, but it has been organised and run by the students themselves.

As well as the establishment of new subjects, nine groups (38 per cent) indicated that they knew of at least one case where an existing subject at their own university had been made more pluralist. In terms of how much individual subjects had been reformed, the general reaction was that improvements had been small, with words and phrases such as 'minor' and 'no significant change' predominating.

Students also had an awareness of what was going on in other universities within their country. For example, twelve (50 per cent) groups said they were aware of pluralist subjects being developed at other universities in their country. This was particularly the case in the UK where students could cite the existence of particular pluralist departments elsewhere in the country such as Kingston, Greenwich and SOAS.

Students were also asked to rank their personal perception of three different types of obstacles to pluralism. All thirty-six students responded and their rankings are listed in Table 5.4 below.

Fourteen of the thirty-six students (39 per cent) also took the opportunity to list other obstacles beyond the three obstacles listed above. The reasons vary, but most can be roughly nested inside the three broad categories listed in Table 5.4 above, though some cannot. The actual responses from the students are grouped and categorised below, albeit in a somewhat rough and ready way.

Table 5.4 Student perception of obstacles to economic pluralism

Answer options	not a factor	a minor factor	a major factor	the only factor	Response count
Lack of support from senior management in the university	6	9	21	0	36
Resistance by the department/ school that teaches economics	2	5	27	2	36
Lack of student support	5	23	8	0	36

Lack of student support:

> The main obstacle is students' high turnover that makes inertia a rewarding strategy for anyone in the department who opposes reforms.

> The fact that students are even unconscious of the lack of pluralism. And the fact that we are too few in the organisation, even if the students support us.

> It is important to emphasize a general lack of knowledge about heterodox economics both from students and mainstream professors.

Resistance by the department/Obstacles with the department:

> Lack of teachers who would be able to teach a pluralist course.

> Lack of heterodox economists available (possibly due to lack of publishing opportunities), and lack of ready teaching material.

> Deep-seated view of economics as a maths-based subject. Whilst changes to curriculum are possible and have occurred, heterodox models and teaching still seems to be peripheral.

> Lack of teachers with knowledge of non-mainstream schools of economics, with PhD degrees that could be available to teach new subjects.

> Ignorance of professors and university staff. They don't know and don't pay attention to critique, to history of economic thought and to various heterodox schools and economists.

> A lack of money to hire new heterodox professors (though this is often used as a convenient excuse).

Lack of support by senior management of larger institutional structures:

> Priority given to research by management; lack of resources; lack of reward for innovation and risk-taking in teaching.

The vast majority of faculty we talk to seem supportive of our cause but feel like they are powerless to do much about it.

The Research Excellence Framework, which ties the department's hands.

The Research Excellence Framework prevailing in UK universities.

Lack of support from the university.

There are institutional barriers that create disincentives for inter faculty cooperation on pluralist interdisciplinary subjects.

Factors outside the university:

Resistance from forces outside my university.

Negative influences by the business and the political community.

Restrictions on the economic course by national regulatory bodies.

Location of economic teaching

Students were asked to nominate where economics was taught in their own university. In eleven of the twenty-four groups (46 per cent) economics was taught in a college of arts/social science. In ten cases (42 per cent) it was taught in a college of business and in three cases (13 per cent) it was taught in neither of these particular types of colleges.

Understanding of the terms 'political economy' and 'heterodox economics'

One of the most interesting findings was student understanding of the term 'political economy'. Looking at the responses of each of the thirty-six individual students, two students (6 per cent) nominated the option that it 'describes all the non-neoclassical schools of economics', three students (8 per cent) nominated the term as having the same meaning as 'pluralist economics', one student (3 per cent) nominated the category 'don't know' and thirty students (83 per cent) nominated the category 'none of the above'. What exactly the thirty students who nominated 'none of the above' would understand to be the meaning of the term political economy is not clear at this point. Perhaps some linked it with Marxian radical political economy or with some of other ways the term can sometimes be used and understood? Obviously, it was an opportunity lost not to ask them to nominate their own understanding of the term. Whatever their precise definition of the term, they were open to using the term to describe a pluralist economics with twenty-six students (72 per cent) of students agreeing with the proposition that a pluralist economics could be taught in other social science departments (for example, in departments of politics) under the disciplinary title of 'political economy'. Five students disagreed (14 per cent) with the proposition and five students did not have an opinion either way (14 per cent).

Students were also surveyed on their understanding of the term 'heterodox economics' with thirty-two students (89 per cent) agreeing with the proposition that it described all the non-neoclassical schools of economics. Only one student (3 per cent) agreed that it had the same meaning as pluralist economics. There were three students (8 per cent) who stated that neither of these definitions described the term heterodox economics. The percentage of students who linked the term to the non-neoclassical schools of economics is high, though it should be remembered that these students are a pretty unique sub-section of society and that in Chapter 4 it was argued that in the wider world the term 'heterodox economics' mystifies most people.

Interactions with various levels of the university

Fifteen of the twenty-four groups (63 per cent) had undertaken discussions about promoting economic pluralism with senior managers in their university, seven groups stated they had not (29 per cent) and two groups stated that they did not know if their group had done so or not (8 per cent).

For the fifteen groups that had undertaken the discussions, four groups described the tone of these discussions to be 'respectful and open' (27 per cent), nine groups described the tone as 'polite but defensive' (60 per cent) and two groups as 'patronising and dismissive' (13 per cent). No students nominated the other available option of 'rude and disrespectful'.

The productivity of the discussions was rated as follows. There were three groups out of the fifteen groups (20 per cent) that rated the discussions 'moderately productive', two of the groups (13 per cent) did not know, two of the groups (13 per cent) rated the discussions unproductive, four groups elected the category 'other' (27 per cent) and three groups (20 per cent) did not respond. There was one group (7 per cent) that said the discussions were irrelevant because change was achieved via other means.

What can be concluded about student interaction with senior management from these results? It appears that speaking with senior management is not a magic wand, but the results suggest it is not a totally unpromising thing to do. Neither was it too dramatic or confrontational or difficult for the students with 87 per cent of respondents finding senior management either 'respectful and open' or 'polite but defensive'.

Students were also surveyed on whether they had approached the head of the department that teaches economics in their university. Sixteen of the twenty-four groups (67 per cent) had undertaken discussions. Of these sixteen groups, five groups (31 per cent) described the tone of these discussions to be 'respectful and open', five groups (31 per cent) 'polite but defensive', four groups (26 per cent) 'patronising and dismissive', and one group (7 per cent) 'rude and disrespectful'.

One group (7 per cent) selected the option 'other' and noted they have a heterodox and pluralist head of department. One student also reported that they tried on a number of occasions to meet with the Head of School. Three arranged meetings were cancelled. They ended up speaking to a Deputy instead; that person was sympathetic but unable to help.

The student groups rated the productivity of the discussions with the head of department as follows. None of the sixteen groups that responded described the discussion as 'very productive', eight groups (50 per cent) described these discussions as being 'moderately productive', five groups (31 per cent) as not productive, one group (6 per cent) as counterproductive, one group (6 per cent) did not know and one group (6 per cent) elected to pick the category 'other'.

What can we conclude about interactions with heads of departments? The record is mixed. The tone of the discussion was not as good as with senior management. However, that 50 per cent of groups found the discussions moderately productive is a significant finding, though in retrospect the survey missed the opportunity to better gauge what moderately productive meant in practice.

Students were then asked about their interactions with economics lecturers. Twenty-two out of twenty-four of the groups (92 per cent) indicated that members of their group had undertaken discussions about economic pluralism with individual staff members who teach economics at their university. For the twenty-two groups that had undertaken the discussions, twelve (54 per cent) described the tone of these discussions to be 'respectful and open', three groups (14 per cent) described the tone as 'polite but defensive', one group (5 per cent) 'patronising and dismissive', no students nominated the available category of 'rude and disrespectful'. There were six groups (27 per cent) who selected the category 'other' and then offered their own description of the tone:

varying, mostly polite but defensive, some respectful and open (enthusiastic even)

depends on who we talk to

some very open and some defensive

it depends. Two out of 15+ professors were supportive. The others ranked from 'neutral' or 'don't care' to 'I hate you ignorant students, I'm doing Science!'

some in favour of and other against

depends on the professors

it varies from highly enthusiastic to generally defensive, but all in all respectful some academics were helpful and understanding, others were respectful, and others dismissive.

In terms of the productivity of these discussions, only one of the twenty-two groups (5 per cent) described these discussions as being 'very productive', fourteen (64 per cent) moderately productive, four (18 per cent) as not productive, three groups (14 per cent) did not know. No students nominated the category 'counterproductive'. Two students added the additional comments, 'All professors agreed with the need for pluralism and more history. But not officially. They mentally support it but don't take an active role in promoting it' and 'it was moderately productive in the sense that even if we provoked outrage and panic (sometimes), they were obliged to react'. The interaction with individual staff members could be summarised as mixed, but the fact that 69 per cent of groups found the discussions productive is encouraging.

Twenty-one of the twenty-four groups (88 per cent) indicated that there was at least one heterodox economist/political economist working at their university. There were two of the twenty-four groups (8 per cent) that said there was not, and one group (4 per cent) did not know. When asked if heterodox economists worked in the same department as orthodox economists, two of these twenty-one groups said no (10 per cent), two groups (10 per cent) did not know and seventeen groups (81 per cent) said yes. Of the seventeen groups that said yes, five of these groups indicated that there are also heterodox/political economy staff working elsewhere within the university. The associated comments in this respect were:

some do, some don't

some do, some don't

some do, most don't

yes, but there are also political economists/Marxists in the political science department

one or two not-entirely-orthodox economists work in the mainstream department, but lots from the politics/geography/etc. departments do work that we would consider 'economics'.

Another student commented that whilst there was one remaining heterodox/political economist within the economics department, 'Some decades ago, several heterodox economists were working at the economic department. Now, there is just one, because the others complied (they had to sometimes), fired or left'. Another comment was that 'at my university most heterodox/political economy staff are old and that most of them will be retire in the next 10 years'. This comment captures a common reality that some heterodox economists/political economists do work in economics departments, having been employed when the situation was less difficult. These heterodox economists/political economists may not necessarily be harassed, but the salient issue is that they are not being replaced when they retire.

Of the twenty-one out of twenty-four groups (88 per cent) that had heterodox/political economists at their university sixteen of those twenty-one groups (76 per cent) indicated that these academics had provided their group with significant support. Four groups (19 per cent) said that such academics had not provided them with significant support and one group (5 per cent) did not know. Students were then asked if they would describe the interaction they have with their university's political economists/heterodox economists as being a close working partnership. Nine of the twenty-one groups (43 per cent) said yes, eight groups (38 per cent) said no and four groups (19 per cent) did not know. Additional comments were as follows:

> Some of them offer to give talks for free; they participate in their free time in our reading group.

> They like and support our campaign.

> Our university is crawling with heterodox staff, so it hasn't been the one-man stand typical in other departments.

Sixteen of the thirty-six students (44 per cent) subscribe to the Real-World Economics Review and fifteen students (42 per cent) subscribe to the Heterodox Economics Newsletter.

The final question was open-ended: 'Based on what you have learnt and experienced, do you have advice to offer other student groups that are seeking to promote economic pluralism?' In many ways, these responses are the most interesting and nearly all responses are reproduced below. In some instances they have been modified so that particular student groups, or particular individuals, cannot be identified.

> A greater future lies ahead.

> Just do it!

> Our aim must be the recruitment of new heterodox teachers (only after that can we have heterodox courses).

> Searching for support outside of the economic department is important. Creating a pressure in the media, for example. Having allies inside the economic department is also very important in order to transform the pressure into action.

Produce evidence-based reports to come up with figures and facts on the lack of pluralism when talking with staff and professors.

Try and appeal to a broad audience by making your events accessible if not you run the risk of simply being about ten economics students who run events for themselves and can easily be ignored.

Developing a well-thought agenda for change. Being specific about what should change and in what direction. Then finding staff members who would like to support you. Waiting for a good opportunity.

Be aware of the multiple layers of complexity that reinforce resistance to pluralism in economics in universities. Modern universities are not so much intellectual organisations, as they are bureaucratic organisations. Agents of change need to be cognisant of the mechanics of university bureaucracy. Students should not only make the intellectual case for pluralism, but should also make the 'business' case.

Get in touch with all professors and lecturers and find out what their interests are. Show them that students are interested as well in this field of economics and that a productive environment can be achieved via discussions and critical thinking. Slight confrontation might be helpful, but too much is normally counter-productive.

Just form a group, meet with the teachers, read a lot and discuss everything, don't be afraid to make mistakes.

To secure continuation, it is very important to focus on reaching out to the first-year students from the moment when they set foot on the campus, as they are quickly consumed by the race for prestige and good grades, rather than thinking critically in the manner that ISIPE promotes.

Engage with students so that economic staff can see a large and eager student body.

Establish structures that will last through time. Make sure new students will get involved in the movement. Significant changes in an economics department take years to achieve.

Get the students mobilised. Otherwise no proper pressure can be put on the departments.

Be constructive and do not dismiss mathematical tools or the value of neoclassical economics. Just focus on exploring alternative schools of thought, and don't be afraid to get in touch with any ISIPE members for support and ideas!

There is strength in numbers, both in terms of membership in local organizations and in the number of local organizations. Campaigning for pluralism takes a lot of time, and the more people you have who are energized and willing to work, the more we can do. Don't ignore simple things like making sure people feel included, are having fun, and are excited about the cause. In the UK we have built an incredible level of trust between the different local organizations by frequent UK-wide meetings. Once the people in the movement become your friends, you find yourself invested in a deeper and more profound way. There is no substitute for in-person meetings to keep people connected to each other and invested in the movement. Offering things such as free pizza can help build attendance and levels of engagement at face-to-face meetings. We all understand that this is going to be a long battle, and to give pluralism a fighting chance we're going to need as many energized active supporters as possible.

Yes. It can be very tough. We have been fighting for two years now against a curriculum which was, at the time we started, almost 95 per cent orthodox. We are also fighting against deeply convinced orthodox economists. Some of them openly hate heterodox economics, considering it as being nothing more than ideology and bullshit. As students, we faced many difficulties, including implicit threats (for grades and so on). It is important to acknowledge power relations in these cases. Alone, we were too vulnerable. This is why we actively engaged in promoting our agenda in the other social sciences departments. We actively lobbied the head of the social sciences faculty (a sociologist at the time and then a statistician – both very open-minded). We also forged alliances with other student groups, as well as with labour unions and other organisations. Thanks to them and their networks, we were interviewed by the most-watched news in our part of the country. We also published a couple of articles in the media. Student representatives also mentioned the point systematically at the opening ceremony of the University in front of hundreds of academics and so on. One last piece of advice: if the establishment refuses to do something, do it yourself. For example, this year, we directly and unilaterally invited heterodox professors to give courses/conferences. Heterodox professors are (most of the time) very happy to help, most of the time for free. To summarise: 1. Think creatively about what you can use as leverage, 2. Understand the various types of power relations that exist inside and outside the university and seek to utilise them to pressure the establishment. 3. Act by introducing directly heterodox thinking yourselves, even if this must occur in a cave, hidden from retaliations.

Go for it – the movement is strong, and the tide is shifting. There are alternative economic theories out there and they are worth fighting for. The importance of economic pluralism is not just better learning, creating better understanding – it is vital to achieve a shift towards a new economy that we so desperately need.

Try to find friends amongst the staff within your department/college. The department/college seems to be a lot more open to new ideas when they come from members of staff.

We first started by convincing the director of the school of economics and management that he allow us to impart elective subjects like Marxist economics, political philosophy, epistemology, and the economic history of our country, and that these subjects would count as credits for the Grade Point Average of the student. So, we had four or five elective subjects running in one semester in parallel. When the Dean and the lecturers noticed this, they started to understand that we were setting up a 'parallel curriculum', so they decided to incorporate many of these subjects in a new curriculum, so they could have control of the content of each subject. They also took a stronger control of the elective subjects. But in spite of all this recent reform, all the pluralism that was embedded in the form of new subjects was taught by external teachers, not by teachers of the economics department (where a lack of pluralism persists). The way we are seeing the strategy is in the form that Marc Lavoie proposes [see Lavoie 2015], that is, creating a Department of Political Economy in the Faculty of Social Sciences, and for that we need PhD graduates in political economy or heterodox economics capable of doing research and publishing. This is what we are trying to achieve now.

Providing interested students with alternative seminars, lectures and others.

Campaigning should be at the heart of any student society. Lobbying the department and building capacity.

Be prepared to take direct action. Departments are incredibly resistant to change and you need to grab and maintain their attention as best you can. Show you have student support, keep up a presence and if necessary find ways to annoy them. Discussions would be fine if they actually listened, but generally, they don't – you have to do something more.

The local level is insufficient. Many of the obstacles that prevent economic pluralism in education and research are intertwined with other requirements made of universities, or arise from the general competition among universities, the education policies of the country, and politics in general.

The word heterodox seems to imply some crazy voodoo, so I prefer political economy. I believe political economy is best situated under different management than economics. I have found conversations with the University hierarchy unproductive.

A general observation can be made that the survey results are a mix of the encouraging and discouraging. A lot of the common difficulties in pursuing pluralism were evident in the survey results. However, it is encouraging that students groups are generally growing, increasing their activity and supporting one another. Discussions that students had undertaken at various levels of the university were a bit better than one might expect. That political economy staff and their students had been mutually supporting was also a positive. The comments made by students also illustrates that they have quite developed understandings of the general issues that constrain pluralism. It would be worth exploring whether there could be more formal alliances and joint events between established political economy organisations and ISIPE. A more detailed, and larger, survey of students groups would also be desirable.

References

Agnew, S. 2015, 'Current Trends in Economics Enrolments at Secondary and Tertiary Level', *New Zealand Economic Papers*, vol. 49, no. 1, pp. 33–43.

Flynn, P. M. & Quinn, M. A. 2010, 'Economics: Good Choice of Major for Future Ceos', *The American Economist*, vol. 55, no. 1, pp. 58–72.

Guest, R. & Duhs, A. 2002, 'Economics Teaching in Australian Universities: Rewards and Outcomes', *Economic Record*, vol. 78, no. 241, pp. 147–61.

Kay, J. 2014, 'Angry Economics Students Are Naive – and Mostly Right', *Financial Times*, p. 1.

Lavoie, M. 2015, 'Should Heterodox Economics Be Taught in or Outside of Economics Departments?', *International Journal of Pluralism and Economics Education*, vol. 6, no. 2, pp. 134–50.

Millmow, A. 2002, 'The Quiet Death of Australian Economics', *Arena Magazine*, vol. 16, no. 2, pp. 16–18.

Millmow, A. & Tuck, J. 2011, 'Did the Global Financial Crisis Have Any Impact on Economics Degree Enrolments?', *Economic Papers*, vol. 30, no. 4, pp. 557–67.

Round, D. K. & Shanahan, M. P. 2010, 'The Economics Degree in Australia: Down but Not Out?', *The Journal of Economic Education*, vol. 41, no. 4, pp. 425–35.

Siegfried, J. J. 2014, 'Trends in Undergraduate Economics Degrees, 1991–2013', *Journal of Economic Education*, vol. 45, no. 4, pp. 387–91.

Stilwell, F. J. B. 2006, 'The Struggle for Political Economy at the University of Sydney', *Review of Radical Political Economics*, no. 30, Fall, pp. 539–50.

Stilwell, F. J. B. 2011, 'Teaching a Pluralist Course in Economics: The University of Sydney Experience', *International Journal of Pluralism and Economics Education*, vol. 2, no. 1, pp. 39–56.

Ward, I., Crosling, G. & Marangos, J. 2000, 'Encouraging Positive Perceptions of Economics: The Effectiveness of the Orientation Tutorial', *Economic Papers*, vol. 19, no. 3, pp. 76–86.

6 Economics textbooks

This chapter examines economics textbooks, looking at why textbooks are important, the problems with currently dominant texts, and the difficulty of establishing progressive textbooks. The chapter includes a case study of *Principles of Economics*, a textbook by Greg Mankiw, which is a good representation of the contemporary orthodox textbook – and everything that is wrong with it. There is also a case study of an alternative textbook, *Principles of Economics in Context* by Goodwin et al. that covers all the orthodox economics content that is normally in a first-year text, but does so in a manner that is a significant and welcome improvement on the dominant textbooks. The chapter concludes with an examination of the Institute for New Economic Thinking's CORE Econ Project, which is currently producing open-access teaching materials that are mildly reformist in nature.

The importance of textbooks

Textbooks are fundamental to explain the inertia in the curriculum. They are an important means to establish and maintain Kuhnian 'normal science', promoting reproduction of the dominant paradigm, defining the thinking and behaviour of the community of researchers and making up an important part of the disciplinary matrix. Economics textbooks are full of prescriptive instruction on how research is to be conducted and what the acceptable observations, questions and puzzles are that can be investigated. Textbooks also supply exemplars: seemingly powerful solutions to particular problems which allow the paradigm to attract and maintain followers and to also assist in demonstrating the acceptable processes via which research is conducted (Boumans et al. 2010).

It also needs to be explicitly pointed out that economics textbooks do not just exert a strong level of influence over the discipline; they also exert a strong level of influence over society. This reality is seldom lost on textbook authors. For example, Samuelson once stated, 'I don't care who writes a nation's laws – or crafts it advanced treatises – as long as I can write its textbooks' (cited in Skousen 1997, p. 150). This social engineering dimension of textbooks becomes obvious when one considers their huge circulation levels. As Lamm notes:

> At the peak of their sales, both Paul Samuelson's Economics and Campbell McConnell's Economics exceeded in a single year the lifetime sales to date

of Keynes's General Theory. Every year, six or seven introductory textbooks achieve sales of 60,000 copies or more. The market, variously estimated at a million and a half to two million students per annum, is immense.

(Lamm 1993, p. 104)

Because textbooks are part of the disciplinary matrix and provide exemplars, they are a necessary, though not sufficient, requirement for a school of thought to reproduce itself. The fate of a school rests in no small part on the ability of its proponents to provide good textbooks for their students. King (1995) argues that the inability to supply timely, coherent, well-written Post-Keynesian textbooks in the 1960s and 1970s carries significant weight in explaining why Post-Keynesian economics was unable to usurp the orthodoxy:

> We could speculate on the reasons for this Cambridge aversion to textbook writing, but the consequences are clear enough. The neoclassical synthesis filled the gap left by the exponents of Keynes, from the elementary level right up to the graduate courses, and beyond. When first Weintraub, then Davidson and Minsky, rebelled against 'Bastard Keynesianism' there was no counter-text to which they could refer their students, or their colleagues, and they had to write their own. If economists' thinking is shaped much more by the books they read than by articles and papers, as Victoria Chick believes ... then Robinson's 1937 'Essays' must be put down as an immense missed opportunity. To put it another way, 'Money and the real world' is the book that Joan Robinson should have written, a quarter of a century before Paul Davidson.
>
> (King 1995, p. 22)

While good textbooks are not sufficient in themselves to achieve curricular reform, they are certainly one of the necessary ingredients. On this basis, there is merit in supplying them to the market in the absence of immediate demand for them.

Reflecting the fact that better textbooks are an important ingredient to create a better economics, the World Economic Association launched the Textbook Commentaries Project in 2014. This worthy initiative, created though the exemplary efforts of Stuart Birks, Edward Fullbrook and others, is an excellent open-access resource that is suitable for both students and their teachers. It offers a range of resources including detailed commentary on the dominant economics texts. For example, all thirty-six chapters of the seventh edition of Mankiw have been analysed from a pluralist political economy perspective. The project also supplies a list of alternative texts and links to other teaching resources, along with providing the opportunity for academics and students to contribute to the textbook commentaries themselves (Birks 2014).

It is often emphasised how the publication of Samuelson's *Principles of Economics* in 1947 defined the nature of the modern economics textbook. This is largely correct, but Samuelson's *Economics* should not be seen as being *entirely* revolutionary and ground breaking as there is significant continuity of content with textbooks published earlier. This fact is made quite apparent by Lee's survey of the content in US textbooks in the twentieth century (Lee 2009, p. 3), which shows that Samuelson's textbook had significant commonalities in content. This continuity is not that surprising when one considers how monolithic, rigid and fragile neoclassical economics is. It is hard to modify its key features without the entire structure collapsing like a house of cards. The extreme doggedness of some economists thus becomes more intelligible: to give up one thing may endanger everything (Galbraith 1992).

The importance of pluralist introductory textbooks

This emphasis in our analysis here is on introductory textbooks. There is good reason for this. The path-dependent forces within human cognition mean that the sequence in which ideas is introduced is important. Habitual patterns of perception and thought once established can be hard to shift. Fuller (2010), drawing on the literature of contemporary neuroscience (Graybiel 2008; Lally et al. 2009), explains that as a habit is acquired, it transitions from largely conscious processing in the cerebral cortex to less conscious, deeper structures of the brain. The process of habituation can vary (depending on the habit and the context) from between as little as 18 days up to 250 days. Once this process is complete, habits can be strikingly automatic, constant and resistant to revision (Graybiel 2008). Such findings help to explain why many economists, having been severely habituated into neoclassical thinking, have trouble escaping from this thinking, even as a temporary exercise. The difficulty in shifting habits of thought has long been recognised within economics. As Samuelson once quipped, 'funeral by funeral, economics is making progress' (Samuelson 1997, p. 159). In the preface to the *General Theory*, Keynes talks about his own long and difficult path of escape from established habits of thought; indeed his *General Theory* is sometimes accused of failing truly to break free from such habits. Given that Keynes was such an agile and creative thinker, the admission of his own difficulty in breaking free from habitual thoughts emphasises the challenge involved.

The neurological research on the fixity of habits helps explain why institutionalists have long argued that habits are central to understanding human behaviour and why they are a key source of economic and social stability. Habits of thought can easily take on being understood as 'common sense'. William Blake's 'mind forged manacles' (cited in Erdman 1982, p. 27) and C. S. Pierce's point that the 'essence of belief is the establishment of habit' (Pierce 1878, p. 29) support this point, as does Mandler's point that economic theory derives part of its legitimacy from habitual thought and practice:

> [E]conomic theory explores the logic of assumptions and models that seem natural. These constructs are not invented anew with each article and monograph, but are partly conventional; they derive their plausibility from the past practices, or perceived practices, of the discipline.
>
> (Mandler 1999, p. 13)

All this strongly suggests that a plural and critical approach should be pursued from the very outset of an education in economics. The central importance of this point has been made by several prominent economists:

> The catalyst for my escape from this dogma was extremely simple: my first-year microeconomics lecturer pointed out a simple but glaring error in the application of conventional theory ... Had I come across that fragility in my honours or postgraduate education, which is when students normally learn such things, I would quite possibly have been willing to gloss over it, as most economists do. Instead, because I learnt it 'out of sequence', I was immediately suspicious of the simplistic statements of economic principle.
>
> (Keen 2001, pp. xii–xiii)

> The student who comes to economics for the first time is apt to raise two rather obvious questions. The first relates to the economist's habit of assuming that agents can be treated as rational maximisers ... by the time that students have advanced a couple of years, this question is forgotten. Those students that remain troubled by [it] have quit the field; those who remain are socialised and no longer ask about such things.
>
> (Sutton cited in Ormerod 2003, p. 72)

> There is a standard conditioning technique that puts off children who question a received orthodoxy by claiming that all will be revealed later. But when that question is asked in a more advanced course it is dismissed as childish.
>
> (Binmore 1998, p. ix)

Incoming data is made sense of through a conceptual framework that is the result of historical experience. As Beinhocker points out, people learn within the context of a mental model and established mental models can often get in the way of gaining new understanding and insights. One of the consequences of this is that resistance to change is 'a deep feature of human cognition' (Beinhocker 2006, p. 357), which often requires an economist to explain a theory in terms which are reasonably familiar to an audience (Dow 2002, p. 15). People can hold tenaciously to established ideas, even in the face of new evidence that would otherwise suggest these established ideas warrant modification, or even outright rejection. None of this is to say that new incoming sense data cannot potentially change an established conceptual framework. However, what is being emphasised is how difficult that might be and how long it might take.

Mankiw's *Principles of Economics*

Greg Mankiw is a prominent US economist and a former economic advisor to US President George W. Bush. He is currently the lead author of the world's largest-selling introductory textbook, *Principles of Economics* with many versions customised by co-opted authors to fit the requirements of particular countries. The book exhibits many objectionable aspects from a political economy perspective and is certainly vulnerable to nearly all lines of criticism in many of the well-known and detailed critiques of standard teaching content (Fullbrook 2004; Keen 2001; Keen & Lee 2004).

The section on microeconomics is very neoclassical, and accordingly ducks issues of historical and institutional specificity. The section on macroeconomics adopts a new-Keynesian approach that emphasises sticky prices and the long-run neutrality of money, and eschews any mention of uncertainty, all the while promoting itself as a Keynesian textbook. The text is built around Mankiw's '10 lessons of economics'. Some of these ten lessons (or are they commandments?) are quite dramatic in their overstatement and degree of simplification. Such an approach is consistent with a general pattern amongst introductory economics textbooks where the exposition of neoclassical economics has become more simplistic and less qualified and nuanced over the past two or three decades.

One could easily produce an *Anti-Mankiw* – a line-by-line attack on this textbook as per Linder's and Sensat's *The Anti-Samuelson* (1977), though given constraints of time and space, the focus will be on just two areas. The first concerns the underlying approach of the book, the second concerns the book's clumsy and superficial attempts to incorporate the orthodox research frontier.

The guiding approach of the book is made explicit in Mankiw's foreword. He states that 'an economic textbook should remove the "ifs and buts" and teach the "rule rather than the exception"' (Mankiw, Gans & King 2009, p. xxviii). For Mankiw, economics is very much a nomothetic, rather than an idiographic, undertaking. To quote from the preface:

> I had grown up in a family that often discussed politics over the dinner table. The pros and cons of various solutions to society's problems generated fervent debate. But, in school, I had been drawn to the sciences. Whereas politics seemed vague, rambling and subjective, science was analytic, systematic and objective. While political debate continued without end, science made progress.
>
> (Mankiw, Gans & King 2009, p. xxii)

There is a strong, obvious and sustained desire to tie economic and social reality into a neat bow. It conforms to a general pattern in economics education identified by Garnett (2009), where scholarly dispute is trivialised and downplayed, thus giving a false sense of consensus. Chapter 1 of the text draws on the survey work of Anderson and Blandy (1992) to assert '10 propositions with which most economists agree' (Mankiw, Gans & King 2009, p. 32). This is an all-too-early attempt to foreclose debate and persuade the student on many controversial questions simply by resorting to the authority of majority verdict (rather than by an application of reason or evidence to the question at hand). The only chapter that makes any attempt to portray economics as a contest of ideas is the final chapter, 'Five debates over macroeconomic policy'. However, the debates are between centrist and extreme right-wing policy positions: whether policymakers should try to stabilise the economy; rule versus discretion in monetary policy; whether to aim for zero inflation; whether budgets should be balanced; and whether tax laws should encourage greater saving. The analysis is conducted within the boundaries of the neoclassical paradigm. In general, the book reflects Mankiw's own ideological leanings. One edition of the book features a photograph of a large bee: obviously channelling Mandeville's extreme perspectives on the social virtues of individual self-interest. (For an important critique of Mandeville's position see Bowles 2005.)

As was explained in Chapter 3, to ignore or play down disputes is to miss an opportunity and to duck a responsibility. It is argued here that an economics education should concentrate on why economists disagree, not create a false sense of consensus. It is just as important to emphasise the weaknesses and well as the strengths of particular theories. As Robinson argued, 'the purpose of studying economics is not to acquire a set of ready-made answers to economic questions, but to learn how to avoid being deceived by economists' (Robinson 1955, p. 3).

How does Mankiw's textbook deal with the orthodox research frontier? Chapter 23, 'Frontiers of Microeconomics', provides some coverage of behavioural economics, but it is tokenistic and superficial. Significantly, there is no attempt to discuss whether behavioural economics can be incorporated into the integrated framework presented in earlier chapters. Such an omission could easily suggest to a student that these 'frontier' areas can still be part of the old integrated neoclassical framework; indeed we have seen in Chapter 4 that some of the 'new' behavioural economists understand behavioural economics in this way. If one wished to be generous it could be argued that the textbook's minor mention of behavioural economics means that it exhibits 'soft' pluralism of the type described by Dow (2007), though basic incoherence is probably a better description in this instance. The embrace of pluralism needs to be explicit and reasoned; in the absence of this it is better understood not as soft pluralism, but as cognitive dissonance (a situation where a person holds contradictory ideas but does not recognise them as contradictory).

The 'Frontiers of microeconomics' chapter is a good example of a syndrome identified by Earl (2010) whereby the 'new' behavioural economics is couched in such a way that it does not threaten the legitimacy and existence of the neoclassical hard core. Even the title of the chapter can be seen as being defensive: why would a school of economics established in the 1950s be referred to as 'frontier' if not to denote its provisional and uncertain nature? The sheer brevity of coverage is also consistent with a defensive orientation. Only three findings are really discussed, and each of them is given only a paragraph each: people are over-confident, people give too much weight to a small number of vivid observations, and people are reluctant to change their minds. The section is then wrapped up by asserting that the rationality assumption, 'even if not exactly true, is still a good approximation' (Mankiw, Gans & King 2009, p. 531) and that rational choice theory is 'not perfect, but it is good enough' (Mankiw, Gans & King 2009, p. 531). The neoclassical hard core is thus defended and business as usual can continue in all other chapters of the book. It certainly *is* business as usual. Consider lesson three of Mankiw's ten lessons of economics: 'rational people think at the margin'. This is not much of a 'lesson' in that it evades the question of whether these rational people that Mankiw speaks of actually exist; thus it is more of a clumsy attempt to defend marginalism than a general lesson about real people that students should uncritically absorb.

Have events such as the global financial crisis had an impact on recent editions of the book? No, or at least not in the way one might think. Recent promotional literature for Mankiw's textbook featured a promotional flyer entitled 'Economics Saves the World', with a cartoon of a single male student, taller than buildings, ripping back his shirt to reveal a super hero suit with a large 'E' ensign blazed across his chest. The promotional text read:

> Right now, you have the most important job in the world. See those teenagers sitting in your lecture room texting their friends? If you get it right, they will grow up to save the world from mayhem, anarchy and on-going financial crises. Using superb teaching materials you can turn your students into world leaders. Some of them, anyway. And even if that doesn't work out, they can all learn the curiosity and analytical skills that makes good economists.
>
> (Cengage 2011, p. 1)

Responding to accusations that neoclassical economics is imprisoned in a false paradigm, and that it could not adequately predict or explain the GFC, one of the co-authors of the Australian edition of Mankiw, Joshua Gans, argued 'everything that has happened in the global financial crisis was economics 101' (cited in Matchett 2009, p. 9). This illustrates how empirical evidence that one might assume would cause at least some review of one's beliefs is interpreted in a manner where the evidence simply functions to confirm existing beliefs (Varoufakis 1998).

Part of the explanation for this stalwart defence of neoclassical economics, and the absurd marketing material that is used to promote it, is that neoclassical economics is the only approach being covered, it therefore raises the stakes for it to be presented as a product that can meet all needs well. It is somewhat like a hardware store that only stocks hammers feeling the strong requirement to sell, and defend, the ability of a hammer to saw wood and drill holes.

Given all these problems, why do Mankiw's textbook and other similar textbooks, dominate? The initial and most basic answer is that they are successful because they meet the current preferences and needs of the economists who teach these subjects. It is not a case of market failure. David Colander, who has himself authored several textbooks, argues that publishers place a lot of pressure on authors to follow a '15 per cent rule',' whereby if any textbook has more than a 15 per cent difference from other textbooks in its subject area it will not be published. If it is published it will not prosper (Colander 2003, p. 1). Gintis argues that the strong preference for the established textbooks exists in spite of the knowledge of deep problems within their content, asserting that orthodox economists 'consistently *choose* textbooks that teach material that they *know* is false and/or completely out of date' (Gintis 2004, pp. 92–3; emphasis added).

Alternative textbooks

An early attempt to usurp the Samuelsonian textbook in the Post-Keynesian guise was *An Introduction to Modern Economics* (Robinson & Eatwell 1973). However, the intrinsic difficulty of the task, and also some lack of knowledge about what was really required, meant that the book failed to make any impact (King & Millmow 2003). It is argued that 'its lack of success marked something of a turning point in the history of economics, since it symbolized the collapse of the radical attempt to challenge orthodox theory at the pedagogical level' (King & Millmow 2003, p. 105), though it is argued here that the failure of this particular textbook is better seen as just one setback in a longer, and ongoing, campaign for progress. The World Economic Association's Textbook Project shows that alternative textbooks continue to be produced and that some have achieved multiple editions. The advent of desktop publishing, the internet and on-demand printing also create new opportunities for economists to produce their own textbooks. Print-on-demand may also promote the reissue of old textbooks. Self-publishing in electronic form could also be a viable option.

Principles of economics in context

The textbooks just mentioned seek largely to replace the dominant textbooks and to offer a political economy curriculum. Thus, they are not consistent with the conservative reformist advice to work within the economic orthodoxy. What then of progressive texts that are more consistent with their advice? Consider the textbook *Principles of Economics in Context* by Neva Goodwin, Jonathan Harris, Julie Nelson, Brian Roach, and Mariano Torras (2014). The textbook, written for first-year university students, covers both microeconomics and macroeconomics. It was first published in 2004 by Houghton Mifflin. It is now in its third edition, and is now published by Routledge. The authors have established backgrounds in areas such as feminist economics, ecological economics or radical political economy. In other words, they should be understood as being political economists. However, they have struck an artful balance within the textbook: on the one hand, they manage to cover all the standard content in a first-year economics course; on the other hand, they avoid many of the problems that afflict the dominant textbooks. As Goodwin states:

> Neoclassically minded instructors, and instructors constrained by the requirements of the larger curriculum, can be assured that neoclassical tools are presented in full. Economics instructors who are frustrated by the lack of attention to history, institutions, gender, social divisions, ethics, ecology, or poverty in other textbooks will find much to be enthusiastic about in our treatment, because these topics are integrated throughout the book. Even some instructors who prefer the market-focused approach of other texts will appreciate this text for way in which its exposition of the market's strengths and weaknesses encourages students to engage with the subject manner.
>
> (Goodwin et al. 2004, p. xiii)

These textbooks offer a useful resource for the very common situation within traditional centres of economics teaching where the prospects of radical or rapid change to the first-year curriculum often appear to be, at best, some way off in the future. As Nelson points out, lecturers may be under very direct departmental instruction (or at least pressure) to cover all the standard economics content. The content that is stipulated is usually material required for upper-level economics courses — even though most students are not majoring in economics and won't be doing such upper level courses (Nelson 2009).

Having decided to pursue an incrementalist strategy, the book's authors have gone to considerable lengths to be able to compete with established economics texts. All the supporting resources that are now *de rigueur* amongst the big selling textbooks are provided: slides for the lecturer, a student study guide, student website, a teacher website and exam questions. Notably, and in contrast to the main economics texts, all these extra resources are provided free of charge. Because the book is now published and promoted by a major publisher, there has been the capacity to draw upon the distributional and promotional resources that such publishers possess. The book is also relatively cheap, under US$100.00 and under US$60.00 each for *Microeconomics in Context* and *Macroeconomics in Context* – extracts of the book that can function as stand-alone textbooks for microeconomics and macroeconomics. The publisher also provides free examination copies.

The book is written with diplomacy and care. It would only seriously antagonise the most intolerant neoclassical economist, or perhaps more accurately, it *should* not antagonise anyone but the most intolerant neoclassical economist. The authors have not only managed to smuggle in many of the 'ifs and buts' excluded in Mankiw's best-selling text, but they have also flagged many important concepts from the non-neoclassical schools, even if they are structurally constrained from pursuing them in much detail.

The text avoids a combative tone towards neoclassical economics, which appears to be a reflection the authors' underlying philosophy and position. For example, Julie Nelson was one of the few political economists to respond in the affirmative when a special edition of the *Post-Autistic Economics Review* asked the question 'is there anything worth keeping in standard microeconomics?' The substance of her argument was that if the content is taught carefully, with a critical eye and with due acknowledgement of the 'ifs and buts', then it is defensible.[1] In other words, the authors were not writing the textbook through gritted teeth, which was most likely to be a prerequisite to being able to carry it off as well as they have.

It is quite hard to think of anything else that these authors could have done to create a textbook that has some prospect of displacing the established and narrow textbooks that currently dominate the market. Given this, it provides an excellent test case for this type of incrementalist reform strategy. So, what success has *Principles of Economics in Context* had to date? In November 2008, I asked Julie Nelson for an assessment of what has been achieved. Julie reported that the first edition, published with Houghton Mifflin, didn't sell enough copies to make the publisher happy. However, another publisher, M. E. Sharpe, had been found for the second edition. In December 2009, I followed up on how sales of the second edition were faring. Julie responded:

> I would have to say that the textbook is not exactly taking the profession by storm. New sales of the second edition over the 2009 fiscal year were only a little over 1,000 copies. (Used copies of both the 1st and 2nd editions, of course, now circulate as well.) That's not terrible, but it's not great either ... I would guess that it is both recalcitrance on the part of many individual economics faculty members, and institutional barriers (such as textbook adoption being a department decision), that prevent sympathetic instructors from adopting, that are behind the low numbers.
>
> (Nelson in Thornton 2009, p. 1)

It is worth noting that Nelson felt that the resistance was not coming from the students themselves, as the text seemed to work well in an educational sense. To their credit, the authors persisted and produced a third edition which ended up being published by Routledge (due to their takeover of M. E. Sharpe in November 2014). As of November 2015 sales of the current editions of the textbook are as follows:

Principles of Economics in Context: 689 copies.

Macroeconomics in Context: 2,578 copies in total.

Microeconomics in Context: 2,731 copies in total.

The sales display a trajectory of growth from the second edition. However, given all the criticisms of economics teaching that have occurred in recent years, particularly the global protests by students, it is does seem a little shocking that large numbers of economics departments around the world have not reached out for this textbook (and any similar textbooks) in the manner that a drowning person grasps for a life-preserver. One could not fault this particular group of political economists for trying to work within orthodox structures, nor for the skill with which they have done so. The lack of support they have received in return is a stark illustration of the level of indifference and inertia within economics.

What to do? This book, and any similar books like it, might benefit from organised, collective activities on the part of political economists and students. It is not hard, risky or time-consuming for any staff member or student to suggest an alternative text. It is just a matter of saying 'I think this book looks better than the one we use, it covers the same content, but does so in a much better way. Have a look at this preview copy and all the student and staff support materials'. A collective campaign, called the 'minimum ask', could be taken by all staff and students who subscribe to the *Real World Economics Review*, or the *Heterodox Economics Newsletter* as well as all ISIPE groups. The campaign could run for three months with people reporting back any wins they have made by filling out an online form. The results could then be published and circulated to see what has been achieved via worldwide collective action. Obviously, to be even handed, the campaign would also have to make people aware of other similar textbooks so they could then choose to advance the textbook they think is best. If such a campaign were successful, it could perhaps become the template for other collective campaigns to promote pluralism. I give a commitment here to try to push the idea forward – please keep an eye out for any campaign that might be developed and support it if you can.

It is relevant to report on my own very modest attempts to promote this book. In 2007, whilst a member of a Department of Economics and Finance, I tried to persuade the senior staff responsible at my own university to adopt this book. The lecturer at that time was unhappy with the Mankiw text and was looking around for alternatives, but in the end stuck with Mankiw due to the trouble involved in changing lectures slides. The Mankiw text continues to be used at this department. I have also suggested the text to other universities. In the first instance, staff were sympathetic and seemed to have a very poor opinion of the text they did use, but they too were put off by the work involved in changing over the lectures slides, assessment, etc.

In both cases above, the problem was not primarily intellectual; it was an aversion to doing any extra work. This is a recognised problem. Maxwell notes that even if a textbook impresses a lecturer, this may not be enough to get them to adopt it. A change of textbook will only occur 'after much reflection and often with reluctance because such decisions involve major investments of time and effort to reorganise lecture notes, tutorial presentations and other areas of course assessment' (Maxwell 1999, p. 128).

Maxwell is entirely correct in noting the reluctance of staff to invest time and effort in changing a textbook. However, it is questionable that the amount of work involved is really that major. In any case, it is a weak justification for two reasons. First, staff are knowingly using an inferior textbook when better textbooks are available for the same price. Second, introductory economics classes are typically very large, with many hundreds of students. In many universities the subject could easily bring in a million dollars per semester in student revenue. Accordingly, universities have an obligation to put a level of resourcing back into such a subject to make it reflective of best practice.

If staff or students can get an acknowledgement from the academics responsible for teaching first-year economics that there are superior textbooks available, then they are in a strong position to request the change be made by virtue of gross revenue the university receives for offering the subject and the relatively minor costs in changing the text. If necessary the university could be requested to provide an itemised account of the costs of changing the textbook. The minor costs involved can then be compared to the gross revenue the university receives in enrolment fees. The economics department can employ suitably qualified casual staff such as PhD students to expedite the necessary work if the lecturers concerned claim that they don't have the time.

Companion pieces

An alternative approach to remedy problems with the standard economics textbook is to create companion readers to fill in the gaps the textbooks leave and to reveal their limitations. A good example of the companion reader is *Foundations of Economics* by Varoufakis (1998). This book adopts a structure whereby each section of the textbook provides a chapter that is a reasonably succinct exposition of some major facet of neoclassical content, the next chapter explains the history and origins of the theory just described, followed by a chapter that exposes the theory and concepts to heavy critique.

A book such as this is a good counter to the problems created by Samuelsonian textbooks. It is worth noting that, because the first chapter of each section of the book is a neutral exposition of neoclassical theory, it can function as a way of reviewing and clarifying the standard first-year economics content (a second textbook is a useful resource when one is unclear about what is being said in the first). Furthermore, the whole essence of pluralism is that one should encounter a range of voices and the use of a single textbook, any single textbook, cannot really do that. The only issue with the text is that its candid and lively analysis of the deficiencies of orthodox economics would require a certain intellectual openness on the part of the teaching staff and this is not currently common among many orthodox economists. However, it would be a very good option in instances where teaching staff are stuck with a particular textbook due to departmental edict.

The CORE Project and INET

The final resource to be examined is an open-access textbook that has been produced under the auspices of the CORE Project, an initiative of the US-based Institute for New Economic Thinking (INET). The CORE project is described as 'an open-access, interactive eBook-based course for anyone interested in learning about the economy and economics' (INET 2015).

Before analysing CORE, it is necessary to understand INET. This organisation was founded in 2009 in response to the Global Financial Crisis. Funding initially came from a US$50 million grant from financier George Soros. It has subsequently been augmented by various philanthropic individuals and organisations such as the Carnegie Corporation and David Rockefeller. The details of INET's formation and nature have been well documented by others (see Morgan 2014; Sheehan, Embery & Morgan 2015) and their analysis is drawn upon here. The establishment of INET originates with Soros who consulted a range of high-profile economists and commentators on why economics was in such a mess and why it was so resistant to new ideas. This led to a meeting between Soros and twenty-five leading economists which has been described as having a confessional air to it, 'many well-known and ostensibly powerful economists expressed their dissatisfaction with the "dysfunctional" state of the discipline, including the inability of even some leading economists to move the discipline forward' (Morgan 2014, p. 4). INET describes itself and its mission as follows:

The Institute for New Economic Thinking is a nonpartisan research and education nonprofit organization based in New York, NY. Created in response to the global financial crisis of 2007 and 2008, the Institute accelerates the development of a new field of economic thought. By funding academic research, building communities of innovative scholars, and spreading the word globally about the urgent need for change, we are creating real-world solutions to the great challenges of the 21st century. Our work supports the efforts of scholars all over the world as they change the way economics is studied, considered and taught. The global financial crisis made it clear that the world needs new economic thinking, and it needs it now.

(INET 2015)

This stated purpose and motivation of INET has been questioned by Haering (2014) who ponders whether INET may perhaps be a 'Trojan horse' that is designed to control, steer and limit the existing momentum for change in a manner that will serve the interests of a financial oligarchy.

INET's analysis of the lack of innovation and conformity within economics emphasises two main factors. The first is that the economics establishment is unwilling or unable to fund genuinely innovative research. Second, the curriculum is in need of reform (Morgan 2014; Sheehan, Embery & Morgan 2015). Consequently, INET has sought to foster what it has determined to be innovative research by giving grants, by publishing papers and staging events. Second, it has developed CORE Econ, an open access online textbook.

The CORE programme team is candid about some of the more glaring failures of the curriculum. As Sheehan, Embery and Morgan (2015, p. 215) state:

[T]he team acknowledged that much of the teaching of economics focuses on the technical; that this resonates with few undergraduates; and that it renders them unable to express an opinion of any greater insight regarding economic affairs than a member of the general public. Put succinctly, the content of mainstream economics curricula is small in great things and great in small things.

For all this, CORE is not sufficiently pluralist. At the time of writing, no member of four-person steering CORE Econ Steering Committee has signed the ISIPE petition for pluralism in economics, nor have any of the twenty-six other economists, who either have either written material for Core Econ or are members of the Core Econ Teaching and Learning Committee. It is possible that some of these people had not heard about the ISIPE letter, though the ISIPE's website illustrates that the open letter did receive a high degree of coverage around the world. At best one could say CORE embraces a soft pluralism that recognises such things as diversity of method – for example that both qualitative and quantitative methods have their place. Key figures in the CORE project such as Wendy Carlin and Dianne Coyle have been keen to distance the project from heterodox economics. For them, the central task is the closing of the gap between what has occurred in orthodox economics research in the last two or three decades and what is taught to students; in other words, to update, rather than remake the curriculum (Lavoie 2015; Sheehan, Embery & Morgan 2015).

Given its approach, it is unsurprising that the CORE project has attracted some marked criticism from political economists, who have argued that CORE, as it has developed thus far, is inconsistent with INET's mission statement to bring about genuine change and improvements in economics. Whilst acknowledging that CORE is a work in progress that may improve, Sheehan, Embery and Morgan (2015, p. 215) argue that the project currently demonstrates a 'highly constrained perspective regarding what would constitute real change within the discipline'. They go on to point out that students are directed to confirm that they have understood CORE content when they should instead be gaining an appreciation that it can be possible to understand particular economic and social problems in more than one way and that analysis in economics tends to be contested. As they go on to note, the fact that it is technologically innovative does not change the fact that it is an essentially didactic instruction that has considerable continuity with the orthodox texts to which CORE is supposed to offer an alternative. Furthermore, the CORE project is criticised for exuding a general atmosphere of 'conservatism' where:

> [T]he failures of economics have been gradually side-lined, becoming somehow conditional successes. All that is needed is for economics to assimilate a few aspects of history and deviations from optimality, with a nod to some 'real world' examples, coupled with, perhaps, recognition of some alternative positions, such as Minsky's work on financial instability.
>
> (Sheehan, Embery & Morgan 2015, p. 216)

CORE can be seen as an instance of what Palley (2013) calls 'Gattopardo economics, a phrase derived from the Italian movie *Il Gattopardo* where one of the protagonists muses that to preserve his power and privilege some minor changes will need to occur so as to create the *impression* of substantive change and thus provide the necessary cover essentially to maintain the existing state of affairs. As a main character in the movie states 'things must change if they are to remain the same'. In this vein, the CORE project has attracted criticism from some student groups such as Rethinking Economics, the largest of the individual student networks within the International Student Initiative for Pluralism in Economics, who argue that:

> The CORE Curriculum is not an answer to our demands for reform. CORE is more engaging in its teaching style, but falls short of creating broader content … What we are looking for is curricula that embody the three pluralisms: pluralism in methodology, pluralism in schools of thought, and pluralism in disciplines. This means at least a key role for the history of economic thought in a way that encourages debate over different schools of thought.
>
> We believe it is important to introduce students to a critical approach to social science in general, meaning that students can engage in debate over

schools of thought, rather than be introduced to one narrative. CORE does not supply this in its present state.

Rethinking Economics welcomes progress in economics education, a small part of which CORE has achieved, but we believe firmly there is still much more to be done in economics education reform.

(Rethinking Economics 2014, p. 1)

These criticisms of CORE Econ are reasonable, though looking carefully at the resource, it is has a few saving graces. Some of the material has obviously been written by Samuel Bowles, who is an eclectic combination of radical political economist and leading researcher in the orthodox research frontier. This material is allowed to shine through at times. Core Econ, was always going to face a basic issue that no single resource was ever going to satisfy all constituencies, and economists and political economists are markedly different constituencies. It seems that one of the unfortunate legacies of Samuelson's Economics' (and its imitators) domination of the field of economics for so long is that the profession is still looking for *the* book, or *the* resource, to replace it. It may simply work better to let such conceptions go and encourage diversity.

In any event, it is reasonable to assume that any genuinely pluralist resource that was developed by INET that exhibited a fulsome embrace of political economy would surely be ignored by the majority of orthodox economists. Indeed, there is the possibility that CORE is already too different. I contacted CORE to ask for information on what universities had adopted it, but at the time of writing I have received no information about the uptake of the resource. The other issue is that we can hardly be surprised that an organisation largely funded by a financial oligarch might have constrained notions about what transformative change is. Given all this, perhaps the best path forward is not only to maintain some co-informing dialogue with the CORE team, but also to also encourage INET to consider producing a *range* of online textbooks and teaching resources in an even-handed manner, so that political economy orientated texts get the same level of resourcing. This probably represents the outer limits of what we can expect from the CORE project. In any event, Sheehan, Embery and Morgan (2015) are entirely correct in pointing out that political economists should hardly let INET define what should and should not occur.

This chapter commenced by stressing the importance of textbooks. They are a necessary, but not sufficient, condition for progress. Introductory textbooks are particularly important because of issues such as cognitive path-dependence and because a narrow introduction will simply cause potential political economy students to pursue other disciplines. Mankiw's *Principles of Economics* was analysed and shown to be badly lacking as any sort of satisfactory introductory text. The focus then turned to progressive texts where it was shown that well-crafted mildly reformist textbooks such a *Principles of Economics in Context* are being largely ignored. Finally, INET's core programme was examined. It was found wanting in terms of its pluralist credentials. An appropriate response by

INET would be to produce a range of curriculum materials rather than a single resource that is meant to satisfy all.

Note

1   Nelson is still arguing that economics needs significant reform. To get a fuller sense of Nelson's stance towards economics see Nelson (1995).

References

Anderson, M. & Blandy, R. 1992, 'What Australian Economic Professors Think', *Australian Economic Review*, vol. 100, pp. 17–40.

Beinhocker, E D 2006, *The Origin of Wealth: Evolution, Complexity, and the Radical Remaking of Economics*, Harvard Business School Press, Boston.

Binmore, K. 1998, *Game Theory and the Social Contract: Just Playing*, Massachussetts Institute of Technology, Cambridge, MA.

Birks, S. 2014, *Teaching Economics: The Wea Textbook Commentaries Project* Massey University, Palmerston North.

Boumans, M., Davis, J. B., Blaug, M., Maas, H. & Svorencik, A. 2010, *Economic Methodology: Understanding Economics as a Science*, Palgrave Macmillan, Basingstoke.

Bowles, S. 2005, *Microeconomics: Behavior, Institutions, and Evolution* Princeton University Press, Princeton.

Cengage 2011, *Principles of Economics* Cenage [online] http://www.cengage.com/economics/mankiw/edition_6/economics.html viewed 20 June 2011.

Colander, D. C. 2003, Caveat Lector: Living with the 15 Per Cent Rule, Discussion Paper No. 03–26, Department of Economics, Middlebury College, Vermont.

Dow, S. C. 2002, *Economic Methodology: An Inquiry*, Oxford University Press, Oxford.

Dow, S. C. 2007, 'Pluralism in Economics', in J. Groenewegen (ed.), *Teaching Pluralism in Economics*, Edward Elgar, Cheltenham, pp. 22–39.

Earl, P. E. 2010, 'Economics Fit for the Queen: A Pessimistic Assessment of Its Prospects', *Prometheus*, vol. 28, no. 3, pp. 209–25.

Erdman, D. V. (ed.) 1982, *The Complete Poetry and Prose of William Blake*, University of California Press, Los Angeles.

Fullbrook, E. 2004, *A Guide to What's Wrong with Economics*, Anthem, London.

Fuller, J. 2010, *Promoting Good Choices: Patterns of Habit and the Role of Government*, Per Capita, Melbourne.

Galbraith, J. K. 1992, *The Great Crash, 1929*, Penguin Books, Harmondsworth.

Garnett, R. F. 2009, 'Rethinking the Pluralist Agenda in Economics Education', *International Journal of Economics Education*, vol. 8, no. 2, pp. 59–71.

Gintis, H. 2004, 'Herbit Gintis', in D C Colander, J B Rosser & R P F Holt (eds), *The Changing Face of Economics: Conversations with Cutting Edge Economists*, University of Michigan Press, Ann Arbor, pp. 77–106.

Goodwin, N., Harris, J., Nelson, J., Roach, B., and Torras, M. (2014) *Principles of Economics in Context*, Routledge, London.

Goodwin, N. R., Nelson, J. A., Ackerman, F. & Weisskopf, T. 2004, *Microeconomics in Context*, Houghton Mifflin, Boston.

Graybiel, A. M. 2008, 'Habits, Rituals, and the Evaluative Brain', *Annual Review of Neuroscience*, vol. 31, pp. 359–87.

Haering, N. 2014, 'George Soros' Inet: An Institute to Improve the World or a Trojan Horse of the Financial Oligarchy?', *Real-World Economics Review*, no. 67, May, pp. 90–6.

INET 2015, *The Core Project*, London, Institute for New Economic Thinking [online] http://www.core-econ.org viewed 1 November.

Keen, S. 2001, *Debunking Economics: The Naked Emperor of the Social Sciences*, Pluto Press, Annandale.

Keen, S. & Lee, F. S. 2004, 'The Incoherent Emperor: A Heterodox Critique of Neoclassical Microeconomic Theory', *Review of Social Economy*, vol. 62, no. 2, pp. 169–99.

King, J. E. 1995, The First Post Keynesian: Joan Robinson's Essays in the Theory of Employment (1937), Discussion Paper, School of Economics and Commerce, La Trobe University, Bundoora.

King, J. E. & Millmow, A. 2003, 'Death of a Revolutionary Textbook', *History of Political Economy*, vol. 35, no. 1, pp. 105-34.

Lally, P., van Jaarsveld, C. H. M., Potts, H. W. W. & Wardle, J. 2009, 'How Are Habits Formed: Modelling Habit Formation in the Real World', *European Journal of Social Psychology*, vol. 40, no. 6, pp. 998–1009.

Lamm, D. S. 1993, 'Economics and the Common Reader', in D. Colander & A. W. Coates (eds), *The Spread of Economic Ideas*, Cambridge University Press, Cambridge, pp. 95–106.

Lavoie, M. 2015, 'Should Heterodox Economics Be Taught in or Outside of Economics Departments?', *International Journal of Pluralism and Economics Education*, vol. 6, no. 2, pp. 134–50.

Lee, F. S. 2009, *A History of Heterodox Economics: Challenging the Mainstream in the Twentieth Century*, Routledge, London.

Linder, M. & Sensat, J. 1977, *The Anti-Samuelson*, Urizen Books, New York.

Mandler, M. 1999, *Dilemmas in Economic Theory: Persisting Foundational Problems of Microeconomics*, Oxford University Press, Oxford.

Mankiw, N. G., Gans, J. & King, S. 2009, *Principles of Microeconomics*, Cengage Learning Australia, South Melbourne.

Matchett, S. 2009, 'Dismal Science of Economics Faces Dilemma', *The Australian*, Sydney, 25 March, p. 1.

Maxwell, P. 1999, 'The Economics Principles Text: Its Evolution and Influence in Australia', *Journal of Economic and Social Policy*, vol. 3, no. 2, pp. 117–32.

Morgan, J. 2014, *Pluralism, Heterodoxy and the Prospects for a New Economics Curriculum*, Association for Heterodox Economics, London.

Nelson, J. A. 1995, 'Feminism and Economics', *Journal of Economic Perspectives*, vol. 9, no. 2, pp. 131–48.

Nelson, J. A. 2009, 'The Principles Course', in J Reardon (ed.), *The Handbook of Pluralist Economics Education*, Routledge, London, pp. 57–68.

Ormerod, P. 2003, 'Turning the Tide: Bringing Economics Teaching into the Twenty First Century', *International Review of Economics Education*, vol. 1, no. 1, pp. 71–9.

Palley, T. I. 2013, 'Gattopardo Economics: The Crisis and the Mainstream Response of Change That Keeps Things the Same', *European Journal of Economics and Economic Policies*, vol. 10, no. 22, pp. 193–206.

Pierce, C. S. 1878, 'How to Make Our Ideas Clear', *Popular Science Monthly*, no. 12, January, pp. 286–302.

Rethinking Economics. 2014. *Press Release: Rethinking Economics Position on CORE Curriculum*, Rethinking Economics, 27 October. http://www.rethinkeconomics.org/

news/2014/10/press-release-rethinking-economics-position-on-core-curriculum/ [accessed 29 March 2016].

Robinson, J. 1955, *Marx, Marshall, and Keynes*, Delhi School of Economics, University of Delhi, Delhi.

Robinson, J. & Eatwell, J. 1973, *An Introduction to Modern Economics*, McGraw-Hill, London.

Samuelson, P. A. 1997, 'Credo of a Lucky Textbook Author', *Journal of Economic Perspectives*, vol. 11, no. 2, pp. 153–60.

Sheehan, B., Embery, J. & Morgan, J. 2015, 'Give Them Something to Think About, Don't Tell Them What to Think: A Constructive Heterodox Alternative to the Core Project', *Journal of Australian Political Economy*, no. 75, Winter, pp. 211–31.

Skousen, M. 1997, 'The Perseverance of Paul Samuelson's Economics', *The Journal of Economic Perspectives*, vol. 11, no. 2, pp. 137–52.

Thornton, T. B. 2009, *Email Correspondence with Professor Julie Nelson*, 17 December.

Varoufakis, Y. 1998, *Foundations of Economics: A Beginner's Companion*, Routledge, London.

7 Economics departments

This chapter examines the economics department, the entity that makes most of the decisions concerning how both orthodox economics and political economy are taught (or not taught). It is also the main entity determining who is hired, fired or promoted, thus affecting what research in orthodox economics and political economy is undertaken. The chapter provides the foundations for the five case studies that follow in later chapters. The analysis is structured around how economics departments go about the two central tasks they are required to perform: teaching and research. It is revealed that there are strong signals and incentives that often induce academics to prioritise research effort over teaching and curriculum development. The bias against political economy research is also discussed. The final part of the chapter is focused on the overall regulatory environment that exists in countries such as the United Kingdom and Australia. In particular, it examines how deregulation of student enrolments and greater competition can easily lead to an erosion of the range of degree and subject offerings within non-elite universities, which is where political economy is usually given some opportunity to develop.

Teaching

There is a very basic and important problem that afflicts curricular innovation and teaching in general: it is not highly rewarded in comparison to research. As a result, many individuals, departments and universities give a priority to research over teaching. This is a general problem within the university systems of most countries and is not confined to any particular discipline, though it is reasonable to assume it affects economics as much as any other discipline.

Universities will seldom admit to a bias of teaching over research, and most offer some minor incentives or rewards for teaching. However, an intense preoccupation with raising or maintaining their research standing is the norm. This is not to suggest that many academics do not often have quite heavy teaching loads, or that they do not wish to do a good job as teachers. Rather, the issue is that their career security and advancement are usually largely dependent on their research achievements. Given this, there are strong incentives to prioritise research after some minimum satisfactory level of teaching performance has been reached.

Some academics may give greater priority to teaching and research, but in Darwinian terms this is likely to be a poor survival strategy in an employment market that is usually competitive, with hundreds of academics applying for permanent positions.

Another issue is that it can be difficult to determine reliable measurements for teaching effectiveness. This makes it difficult to rank universities against each other for their teaching quality. Rankings, whether done privately or by government, cannot be decisive and may vary wildly, depending on small changes to the criteria and weightings used and on the different socio-economic profiles and intellectual aptitudes of the students enrolled. Unlike high school leaving exams, there are usually not common exams that all university students studying a subject would sit. If no university in the country can reliably claim to be significantly better at teaching than any other university, and no university can really be identified as being significantly worse than any other university at teaching, then there is little incentive for universities to invest in or worry too much about teaching. It is true that if teaching were particularly under-resourced or teaching performance scandalous, then that would be a liability. But provided such situations are avoided, universities tend to conclude that it is best to concentrate on other matters, such as research, marketing and promotion.

Economics departments do prioritise research over teaching (Guest & Duhs 2002; Hellier et al. 2004). Coyle (2012) emphasises the insufficient incentives for academics to focus on curriculum and teaching. Rather candidly, a current Professor of Economics and also a former Dean of Business and Economics states that focusing on teaching is 'a career disaster', as 'promotion depends on research not teaching'. Further, it is rational and unsurprising for academics to 'devote as little time as possible to teaching' and that the current incentive structure can only impair the quality of teaching (King 2012, p. 9).

Incentives matter, but so do underlying preferences. Most academic economists are primarily interested in research, and doing research is what attracted them to academic life. Survey work indicates that 'many economists want a quiet life in their teaching' so as to maximise their research output (Economics Society of Australia 2004, p. 29). This helps give rise to a culture that looks down on teaching. Ward recalls that, in a department in which he previously worked, an elite group of staff referred to those who concentrated on teaching as 'hacks'. When asked to elaborate, he explained that 'a hack means you are not doing enough research, you spend too much time on teaching. Students like you, that's what they meant' (Ward in Thornton & Millmow 2008, p. 6). The creation of such informal norms can have an effect that is as powerful as a formal institution; indeed Ward went on to recall how the labelling of one staff member as a 'hack' had a strong impact on that staff member:

> When he retired they made the mistake of holding a dinner for him. We were all sitting there and he gave the best speech I have ever heard; he stood up and said 'welcome, I'm the number one hack in the economics department', and it went on from there. He absolutely castigated them. That was the last

time he ever had any contact with them. It shows how deep the depth of feeling was.

(Ward in Thornton & Millmow 2008, p. 12)

Publications in highly ranked journals are the central criterion for promotion. Recruitment advertisements generally emphasise its importance.

The poor incentive structure and culture affect both curriculum content and the approach taken to teaching. Freedman and Blair (2009) point out that, as a consequence, academics often opt for something that is easy to teach and easy to test (the two Ts). In certain respects the established orthodox economics curriculum is relatively easier to teach than a political economy curriculum, though the mathematical content can be demanding for a proportion of students. The closed-system, fully determinate and rationalistic nature of economics is much tidier conceptually. There are few shades of grey, and students can quickly sense when they have fully understood something and when they have not. Also, the standard orthodox economics content means that most academics can simply teach the same content they were taught. They can also do so in the same way, via the same established methods, habits and routines with which they were taught. There is also the advantage of accumulated supporting resources (lecture slides, learning guides, etc.) that have been gradually developed and honed to support the established way of doing things. By contrast, political economy is in fact a relatively demanding area to teach. Stretton (1996) emphasises that practical, historical and institutional content relies less on simplifying abstraction and deductive theory. Instead it requires detailed and careful evaluation of diverse situations. Such analysis is necessarily longer and more involved in exposition. Because it is not as neatly constructed, it is also harder to grasp and genuinely to internalise into one's thinking. It is a content and approach that 'can put off, confuse or mislead many average or below-average students' (Stretton 1996, pp. 1577–8).

Vocationalism

Another factor affecting the curriculum, particularly the breadth of the curriculum, is a growing concern among students that they enrol in degrees having a very sharp vocational focus. A vocationally focused degree is not a problem in itself: society clearly needs to provide its citizens with technical and vocationally specific knowledge. Economics, to some extent, is one example of this. The challenge is to maintain a balance and plurality between different types of knowledge. Too much emphasis on narrowly vocational knowledge becomes self-defeating, even in terms of meeting workplace needs, let alone as a way of meeting larger social objectives. Students, wisely or unwisely, are often attracted to very specialised degrees, such as a degree in tourism, or a degree in sport and recreation management. It is not hard to see why this is so: if you want to work in a particular industry, having a degree that ostensibly equips you to work in exactly that industry sounds astute. However, it is only astute if there is evidence that such a degree is recognised by employers in that industry as being more vocationally useful than other more general degrees. Whether most students seek such evidence before enrolling is less than certain.

As will be explained in Chapter 11, there is evidence indicating that a significant proportion of employers are not so much interested in highly focused degrees, as in graduates possessing generic skills, such as the ability to communicate clearly and think critically. These generic skills are at least as likely to be developed in more generalist degrees as in more vocational degrees. It is worth noting that excessive vocational focus is not just limited to degree choice, but extends to the choice of individual subjects and can cause students to shun subjects they are otherwise interested in. Ward recalls:

> One of my best students in introductory micro (which was taught in a broadening way) came to see me after the semester and said he loved the subject, but could not do my other subject, Comparative Economic Systems, because 'it would look embarrassing on my CV.' I said, 'well that's your choice'.
> (Ward cited in Thornton & Millmow 2008, p. 16)

Ward responded to declining enrolments in comparative economic systems by changing the name of the subject from 'Comparative economic systems' to 'Economics systems and globalisation'. The inclusion of the rather amorphous buzz-word of 'globalisation' gave the subject a contemporary, vocational and business aura. Enrolments immediately rose significantly, even though course content remained almost the same.

The problem of excessive vocationalism needs to be also understood as a larger university-wide problem. Universities need to be more committed and become better skilled at making a case for the value of studying the arts and social sciences, explaining why broader knowledge actually has a synergistic relationship with more vocational and technical knowledge (Armstrong 2011). A broader sectoral push from the social sciences would support both political economy and orthodox economics as students would not feel the pressure of having to make every single subject conform to misplaced concepts of what will bring them career security, personal success and personal fulfilment.

The narrow vocational obsession that can dominate student choice raises important questions about how much choice students should be given and how much universities should cater to students' initial preferences and prejudices (as opposed to seeking to alter those prejudices and preferences). In matters of educational choice, it seems foolish, passive and lazy to assume that customers are always well informed about the options in front of them. Varoufakis goes so far as to say that, not only is the customer not always well informed, but also is wrong by definition:

> Good education is expensive. The trouble is that those who do not have it cannot possibly value it. 'Its customers are', by definition, 'always wrong'. It is like wisdom: its value cannot even be approximated by the foolish. In this

sense, a good education may be the ultimate good, but, alas one that cannot possibly be a viable commodity.

(Varoufakis 2009, p. 48)

While this may overstate the problem, it is true that universities, and society itself, run obvious dangers in relying on the 'collective wisdom of seventeen year-olds' to determine their subject offerings (Johnson cited in Cervini 2011, p. 3). The transformational nature of learning means that student preferences and beliefs can evolve rapidly. When properly conceived, restricting choice and mandating subjects can be a good thing. McCalman *et al.* in their assessment of a new breadth/subject at Melbourne University, assert that:

> Education is a domain where customer preferences, while important, cannot be permitted to rule. Discipline experts, in professional and general education, are expected by society to be able to decide what it matters to know. That does not mean that the customers' responses are not essential to the task of improving teaching and learning. However, at some point, despite student hostility, we have to say that 'this is something that you need to know if you are to function in a complex, difficult world'.

(McCalman, Muir & Soeterboek 2008, p. 18)

Similarly, when Ward reflected on his own undergraduate education at Melbourne University in the 1950s, graduate education at Berkeley University in the 1950s and 1960s, and his forty years of teaching economics, stated that:

> The point is you have to have some restriction on people's choice. Educators do know more than the students and their parents. There are quite often subjects that you would never have chosen, I mean I was compelled to do virtually everything when I was at Melbourne, there was very little choice. Even when I was a post-graduate student at Berkeley I had to study economic history. If you never get exposed to it before university how do you know what it is? You are thus likely come to university and study something like management, which lacks analytical rigour, or marketing. The economics that is covered is narrow and technocratic. They will do all right in life, but I don't think they are going to be visionaries. I do think we do need a bit of restriction on choice for an 18 year old as they just can't make informed choices.

(Ward cited in Thornton & Millmow 2008, p. 14)

Of course, the case for imposing a curriculum regardless of its popularity becomes much weaker if the curriculum is intellectually problematic and lacking in any real degree of pluralism.

Given that students are often not well placed to know which courses might turn out to be best for them, it would be desirable for universities to make more effort to explain the merits of more general and less narrowly vocational courses. This is not an unreasonable ask given that the contemporary university often has extensive marketing departments that spend big budgets taking out block ads that usually stay focused on trying to establish a 'brand' for the university. Some of this money and effort could be allocated to conveying meaningful ideas and persuading students of the professional and personal enrichment that results from studying broader subjects.

The curriculum

The focus will now turn to examining trends in the economics curriculum. Currently, there is no global survey evidence available on the economics curriculum. It would be desirable to develop such information, as a means to gauge progress, or lack thereof, in advancing political economy in the curriculum. Nevertheless there is survey work undertaken for Australia for 1980 and 2011 in Thornton (2013) and this will now be reviewed.

In 2012, the websites or academic handbooks, of all Australian universities were examined for the years 1980 and 2011. A total of 2,565 subjects in economics were identified and categorised as subjects in economics (936 subjects for 1980 and 1,629 subjects for 2011). The subjects were classified basically in accordance with positions developed in Chapter 4, though the orthodox research frontier was categorised as 'modern hybrid economics' and a fifth category of 'comparative economics systems' was included. Three broad categories and twelve subcategories were created. To avoid the problem of double counting, each subject was categorised on the basis of what its main emphasis was. For example, if a subject was primarily an economic history subject it was classified as economic history, even if it contained some minor component of, say, development economics. The categories are presented in Table 7.1 with additional explanations about each category to follow. The findings for each category and subcategory are presented in tables 7.2 and 7.3.

Two of these categories require specific explanation. Eclectic (ECL) was a category reserved for a tiny group of subjects (21 out of a total of 2,565) that were at risk of otherwise becoming unfairly pigeonholed. These subjects were in areas

Table 7.1 Subject categories

Category	Subcategory
Orthodox economics	Neoclassical economics Econometrics Mathematical methods
Political economy	Economic history History of economic thought Heterodox economics Development economics Comparative economic systems
Other	Modern hybrid economics Eclectic Open

Table 7.2 Economics and political curriculum, 1980–2011

Category	1980	1980%	2011	2011%	% change
Orthodox economics	621	66.3	1307	80.2	+13.9
Political economy	288	30.8	229	14.1	−16.7
Other	27	2.9	93	5.7	+2.8
Total	936		1629		

Table 7.3 Economics and Political Economy Curriculum in 1980 and in 2011 via subcategory

Subcategories	1980	%	2011	%	% change
Comparative economic systems (CES)	22	2.4	3	0.2	−2.2
Development economics (DE)	39	4.2	32	2.0	−2.2
Economic history (EH)	181	19.3	84	5.2	−14.2
Heterodox economics (HE)	24	2.6	94	5.8	3.2
History of economic thought (EH)	22	2.4	16	1.0	−1.4
Total political economy	288	30.0	229	14.1	−16.7
OPEN	19	2.0	68	4.2	2.1
Eclectic	8	0.9	13	0.8	−0.1
Modern hybrid economics	0	0.0	12	0.7	0.7
Sub total other	27	2.9	93	5.7	2.8
Neoclassical economics	404	43.2	1015	62.3	19.1
Econometrics	163	17.4	216	13.3	−4.2
Mathematical methods	54	5.8	76	4.7	−1.1
Total orthodox economics	621	66.3	1307	80.2	13.9
Grand total	936		1629		0.0

such as Islamic banking and ethical practice, or were obviously interdisciplinary. A subject was classified as open (OPEN) if it was a directed reading subject, or similar type of subject. Such subjects (19 instances in 1980 and 68 instances in 2011) could conceivably focus on any area of economics that the student and the lecturer wished to pursue.

The central finding emerging from Table 7.2 is that orthodox economics, already dominant in 1980 (66.3 per cent of the curriculum), has increased its dominance (constitutes 80.2 per cent of the curriculum in 2011). By contrast, political economy has declined from 30.8 per cent to 14.1 per cent. The curriculum is clearly not plural and is becoming less so.

Neoclassical economics

Neoclassical economics is defined as it was in Chapter 4. To recap briefly: it is a category that has a level of internal diversity and its boundaries are somewhat hazy. However, it has a very distinct core: fully rational and informed individuals with exogenous preferences who engage in constrained optimisation to reach equilibrium outcomes. It can be considered as being ontologically distinct from political economy by its presupposition of a complicated, rather than complex system (Potts 2000).

Table 7.3 shows that neoclassical economics, already dominant in 1980 (404 subjects, 43.2 per cent), had increased its dominance (1,015 subjects, 62.3 per cent). It is extremely rare for core subjects such as microeconomics and macroeconomics to be taught from anything other than a neoclassical perspective.

The degree to which a neoclassical subject might be informed, even to a small extent, by other perspectives has also decreased. In 1980 there were more instances of an essentially neoclassical subject being broadened by at least some content from the history of economic thought, political economy or economic history. For example, *Economics 1* at Flinders University was the compulsory introductory subject in economics, yet only half of it was neoclassical; the other half was political economy. Its full subject description captures its pluralist nature:

> This topic is designed for students taking Economics as a basic discipline in either the Arts or Economics degree, or taking Economic History as a basic discipline in their Arts degree. It is designed also to be suitable as a cognate topic for other disciplines and as an elective topic. One section of the topic is a study of the contemporary capitalist economy through an analysis of modern theories of price and income determination. In a second section, Capitalism is considered in a broader historical context through an examination of contemporary perceptions of the economy since the late eighteenth century in the light of economic history. The classical political economists' model of the economy is considered against the background of the Industrial Revolution and later shifts in emphasis in economic thought are placed in a context of economic change.
>
> (Flinders University 1980, pp. 202–3)

Economics 1 was a full-year (two-semester) subject. It is possible that the general move in universities to eliminate full-year subjects and replace them with half-year (one-semester) subjects has also contributed to the narrowing of the curriculum. When a subject like *Economics 1* is converted into a one-semester subject, the neoclassical component is not the content that is discarded. It is the political economy component that gives way, either being moved into a different subject or, more likely, dropped from the curriculum entirely. It is worth noting that the first-year subjects at Flinders University today are nothing like *Economics 1*. They are standard orthodox economics subjects: *Economics for Business, Foundation for Quantitative Methods, Quantitative Methods* and *Introductory Macroeconomics*.

There are many other examples similar to that of Flinders University. In 1980 at La Trobe University, both first-year microeconomics and macroeconomics had as textbooks Lipsey's *Introduction to Positive Economics* and Samuelson's *Economics*, yet this was balanced by also utilising Hunt and Sherman's *Economics: An Introduction to Traditional and Radical Views*. In 2011, there was a single text for both micro and macro, the Australian edition of Mankiw's *Economics*. Another example is that in 1980, second-year microeconomics had both Samuelson and Lipsey as textbooks, but this was counter-balanced by Stilwell's *Normative Economics: An Introduction to Microeconomic Theory and Radical Critiques*. In 2011, the set textbook was Varian. A further example is that second-year macroeconomics in 1980 utilised Kregel's *The Reconstruction of Political Economy*, Kalecki's *Selected Essays on the Dynamics of the Capitalist Economy 1933–1970* and Keynes's, *General Theory*. Today these have been simply replaced by a single stock standard neoclassical text: Blanchard and Sheen's *Macroeconomics*.

Econometrics and mathematical methods

Mathematical and econometric methods have been grouped under the category of orthodox economics. It is conceded that such methods can also be used within political economy. However, in this instance they have been grouped under orthodox economics because the particular mathematical and econometric methods taught are generally support subjects for neoclassical economics.

Econometrics increased in absolute terms (163 to 216) but decreased in percentage terms (17.4 per cent to 13.3 per cent). Mathematical methods increased in absolute terms 54 to 76, but decreased in percentage terms (5.8 per cent to 4.7 per cent). It is hard to draw any firm conclusions about such small changes. These slight relative declines may well be counterbalanced by an increasing amount of mathematical content in neoclassical economics coursework, particularly at the postgraduate level, but some finely detailed survey work would be needed to test this hypothesis properly.

Political economy

It has already been pointed out that political economy is now only 14.1 per cent of the curriculum, a 16.7 per cent decline since 1980. We will now examine the status of each of political economy's constituent parts.

Economic history

Economic history looks at change, including institutional change, in specific economies. It usually has a strong qualitative dimension to it, though descriptive statistics and some quantitative analysis can also occur. The survey results indicate that economic history has experienced the largest single decline of any sub-discipline. In 1980 there were 181 subjects (19.3 per cent); by 2011 this had fallen to 84 subjects (5.2 per cent) – a 14.1 per cent decline. Such a finding signals that the problems of marginalisation are not just with the heterodox traditions, but with political economy more generally.

Economic history is not a sub-discipline to which most economists are actively hostile, though it is not usually seen as an essential subject to have on the curriculum, nor is it seen as essential to have economic historians on staff. It is a respectable, rather than prestigious, area of economics. On this point, it is relevant to note Samuelson's argument that for economics to become a true science it had to break with history and embrace the ergodic axiom (Samuelson 1970); the increasing dominance of such an avowedly ahistorical economics has not helped the status of economic history. While economic historians are not as marginalised as other groups such as heterodox economists, they usually hold little institutional power within the discipline.

Economic history subjects are now rarely offered as a cumulative sequence. Another issue is that, even when there is more than one economic history subject on offer, it is very rare that subjects will require another as a prerequisite. Indeed, it is more common for such subjects to have no prerequisites at all. While it would be desirable to have a sequence, it is usually too damaging to enrolments. Unfortunately, this creates the problem identified by Dean and Dolan whereby 'so-called upper-level courses that lack the core prerequisites will almost inevitably become geared to the lowest common denominator. In such cases, the depth of learning for the major is clearly compromised' (Dean & Dolan 2001, p. 23).

A notable feature of how economic historians have responded to the decline of enrolments is that they have sought to name and rename subjects that are more in keeping with the vocational preoccupations of their students. The word history has regularly been purged from economics history subjects, or at least, leavened with something carrying suitably business or vocational connotations; the words 'modern', 'global', 'globalisation', 'business' and 'contemporary' are all standard words used to rebrand economic history in the curriculum. Once students are enrolled in these subjects they generally find them rewarding; the issue is of working around their initial prejudices against subjects that are explicitly historical. At Monash University, a subject that looked at the economic history of East Asia since 1945 was rather amorphously titled *Business in Asia.* When I enrolled in this subject in 1998 it had 330 students. La Trobe University also achieved good results by labelling its offerings in economic history as follows: *History of globalisation* (1st year), Second-year economic history *Modern world economy* (2nd Year), *Growth and decline in the global economy* (3rd Year). Obviously, such measures are a short-term fix and there is a point at which descriptive accuracy simply becomes too compromised. Furthermore, the subject description must include an accurate account of the actual content of the subject so as to not mislead students. In the long term, the prejudice against explicitly badged historical subjects needs to be countered in some way, unless the student zeitgeist autonomously switches towards historical study. Of course, introducing some economic history as part of any first-year subject (subjects which generally have hundreds of enrolments) would probably be a sufficient way to restore a healthy student constituency to economic history.

History of economic thought (HET)

History of economic thought studies the evolution of economic and political economic thought from antiquity to the present. It is a subject that can be taught by orthodox economists or political economists, though by virtue of its nature it tends often to be taught by those with at least some political-economic sympathies. Practitioners of this sub-discipline usually see it as the foundation stone for any sensible understanding of economics. In arguing this they are not entirely alone. For example, Lawrence Summers, whatever his other shortcomings, still recognises that the problem with economics is as much to do with what it has forgotten, than with what it is yet to know (Delong 2011).[1]

In 1980 there were twenty-two subjects in HET (2.4 per cent of the curriculum); by 2011 this had fallen to sixteen subjects (1 per cent of the curriculum). HET can suffer from students (and their parents) having misconceived notions of vocationalism or anti-intellectualism. One head of department remarked to me, only half-jokingly, that 'a key problem with HET was that it contained three words that do not appeal to the contemporary business student: history, economic and thought'. This is an exaggeration and may be even less true of social science students. In any case, one way of responding to this problem might be to use subject names such as 'evolution of economic theory'. Such a name is not compromising in its descriptive accuracy, but may be slightly more in tune with the prejudices and preconceptions of certain types of students. The same point made in relation to economic history applies to HET: introducing some HET content into first-year courses would have good prospects for supporting enrolments in upper level courses in HET.

There are few young scholars who have pursued HET. Part of the explanation for this is the fact that it is seen as folly from a career perspective. HET is usually seen as a peripheral subject within economics departments, or as a type of self-indulgent luxury good that most economics departments are not in a position to afford. The idea that it could potentially strengthen a department (if it was set up in right way) is not an idea that can be easily sold within traditional centres of economics teaching.

Lodewijks (2002b) places some explanatory weight for the decline of HET on the ever-growing use of mathematics in orthodox economics, which he views as having squeezed HET out. Lodewijks also makes the point that HET may well be damaged by being perceived as becoming overly aligned with heterodox economics. This perception of HET by the economists might not be so wide of the mark. Blaug, for one, notes that HET conferences have a disproportionately high representation of heterodox economists (Blaug 2001).

Heterodox economics (HE)

As discussed in Chapter 4, heterodox economics is the umbrella term for various Marxian, old institutionalist, Post-Keynesian, feminist, ecological and Austrian schools. It has already been argued that it is not an ideal term in many respects, but it can still function as an umbrella term for these schools and is used here in that capacity. However, it is worth noting that the term 'heterodox economists' or heterodoxy was not used in any subject title of the 936 subjects surveyed in 1980 or the 1,629 subjects surveyed in 2011 (i.e. 2,565 subjects in total). Heterodox subjects had subject titles denoting them as being one of the heterodox schools (for example Post Keynesian). Alternatively, the subject title denoted the subject as 'political economy' or as being issue based (e.g. ECOP2618 Neoliberalism: Theory, Practice, Crisis).

Looking at the basic figures in Table 7.3, the situation for heterodox economics seems to have improved, as the number of heterodox economics subjects has increased from 24 (2.6 per cent) in 1980, to 94 (5.8 per cent). However, there are some important things that need to be considered in the interpretation of this figure.

First, ninety-four subjects in heterodox economics is still far too small a presence across an entire country's university curriculum. Such a minuscule profile cannot provide these heterodox schools with the level of recognition and understanding they require to reproduce themselves, let alone to exert sufficient influence over areas such as policy analysis. Many of the subjects are single stand-alone subjects and it is not usually possible to build a stream or major in heterodox economics. This means that graduates are unlikely to develop sufficient depth of knowledge to be able to undertake heterodox analysis.

Second, thirty-nine of the ninety-four subjects (41.5 per cent) were taught in a single department (the Department of Political Economy at Sydney University), currently the only place in Australia where it is possible to specialise in heterodox economics. As will be shown in Chapter 9, this department was established as a breakaway department from the university's established orthodox economics department precisely because it was too difficult to teach and do research in heterodox economics from inside the economics department (Butler, Jones & Stilwell 2009).

Of the remaining fifty-five heterodox economics subjects that are not taught in the Department of Political Economy at Sydney University, twenty of these subjects are taught outside economics departments and business faculties. This leaves a total of thirty-five heterodox economics subjects within traditional centres of economics teaching — this is just 2.2 per cent of the curriculum.

At this point it is worth briefly digressing into other survey evidence from 2005 and 2009. This information is presented in Table 7.4. The small presence of heterodox economics in the curriculum does not appear to be due to a lack of student interest.

Argyrous (2006) examined enrolments in introductory heterodox economics in 2005 and found that most of these subjects were taught outside economics departments and faculties of business. A table from Argyrous's article is reproduced below as Table 7.5, but with an extra column on the right where the current author has updated enrolments for 2009. The 2009 data shows that, while two of these subjects were cancelled, overall there was a 50.8 per cent increase in enrolments. This increase outperforms the national 21.3 per cent increase in all undergraduate enrolments in economics that Millmow and Tuck (2011) document for the period 2005 to 2009.

Notably, the Department of Political Economy at the University of Sydney has large enrolments in its heterodox economics courses. In 2009 the department had a total of 2,083 enrolments, which is an average of 53 students for each of the

Table 7.4 Economics outside business faculties and traditional economics departments in 2011

Subject Name	Code	Outside	University
Money, Power, War	POLS1004	Sch. Politics & Intl Relations	ANU
Classical Marxism	POLS2061	Sch. Politics & Intl Relations	ANU
Ethics, Capitalism and Globalisation	PHIL615	Faculty of Theology and Philosophy	ACU
Economy and Society	SOC 182	Dept. of Sociology	MQU
The New Spirit of Capitalism	SOC 346	Dept. of Sociology	MQU
Political Economy for Social Policy and Research	SOC 865	Dept. of Sociology	MQU
Avoid Economic Deception: Study Political Economy	POLS306	Politics and International Studies	UNE
State and the Economy	SLSP2000	Faculty of Arts & Social Sciences	UNSW
Society, Economy and Globalisation	58123	Faculty of Arts & Social Sciences	UTS
Political Economy in the New Millennium	POL 319	Politics & History Dept.	UOW
Politics and the Economy	POLS2401	Pol. Science & Intl studies	UQ
Economic Analysis and Public Policy	POLS5740	Pol. Science & Intl studies	UQ
Politics and the Economy	POL2PAE	Faculty of Social Sciences	LTU
Politics and the Economy	POL3PAE	Faculty of Social Sciences	LTU
Australian political economy	PLT2910	Dept. Politics Faculty of Arts	MON
Ecological Economics	ENVI1160	Global Studies Social Science and Planning	RMIT
Economics for the Social Sciences	POLI1050	Global Studies Social Science and Planning	RMIT
Economics for the Social Sciences	HUSO2163	Global Studies Social Science and Planning	RMIT
Ecological Economics – Economics of Sustainability	HES4722	Faculty of life and social sciences	SWIN
Political Economy	POLS20031	Arts Faculty	MELB

39 courses offered. The first-year elective course *ECOP1001 Economics as a Social Science* had 647 enrolments in that year.

These are encouraging findings. It shows the demand that is there for heterodox economics and political economy more generally. Such a finding should not ever be forgotten when one is pondering whether political economy can again establish itself as a vibrant and flourishing area of teaching and research. In particular, universities are often looking to increase enrolments and so it can be useful not only to make the intellectual case for pluralist political economy but also to be able to point to findings such as this to illustrate that there is also a strong business case. The generally strong growth in enrolments evident in Table 7.5, combined with the fact that these subjects are usually taught outside economics departments, suggests that if heterodox economics subjects are not offered from within economics departments they may simply continue to develop from outside traditional centres of economics teaching. The case studies in Chapters 9 and 10 extensively explore this pathway for heterodoxy and political economy in general.

Table 7.5 Introductory heterodox economics subjects in Australian universities, 2005 and 2009

University	Courses	Enrolment 2005	Enrolment 2009
ANU	Money, Power, War POLS1004	102 (10,929)	145 (12,816)
Charles Sturt	Economic Philosophy and Policy ECO310	9	Cancelled
Macquarie	Contending Perspectives in Contemporary Economics ECON385	15	39 (subject moved to UTS)
Monash	Australian Political Economy PLT2910/3910	40 (49,426)	130 (51,689)
Ballarat	Economic Policy in Australia BE703	17 (9,782)	20 (12,888)
New England	Political Economy POLS306	74 (18,146)	71 (17,817)
New South Wales	Political Economy ECON3119	30 (38,292)	50 (46,302)
	Introduction to Political Economy PECO1000	55	72
	State and the Economy SLSP2000	120	170
Queensland	Political Economy and Comparative Systems ECON1100	125 (37,177)	120 (40,582)
	Social Aspects of Economic Issues SWSP2244	15	Cancelled
	Politics and the Economy POLS2401	35	35
South Australia	Political Economy and Social Policy POLI1009	190	Did not respond
Sydney	Economics as a Social Science ECOP1001	350 (45,966)	647 (47,775)
Western Sydney	Political Economy 200065.1	70 (35,372)	90 (37,409)
Wollongong	Political Economy in the New Millennium POL319	37 (22,907)	25 (26,614)

Sources: Argyrous (2006) Thornton (2012).

Note: The numbers in brackets in the final two columns are the total enrolments in all subjects of study at each university in 2005 and 2009. The combined increase from these bracketed totals is 267,997 to 293,892 students (a 9.67 per cent increase).

Comparative economic systems (CES)

CES compares different types of economic system. Such systems include idealised or actual versions of command socialism, market socialism, feudalism and capitalism. There is usually a strong focus on institutions and history. Returning to the 1980–2011 survey results, CES has fared very badly since 1980. Table 7.3 shows that in 1980 there were twenty-two subjects (2.4 per cent) and nearly all universities taught CES. By 2011 there were only three subjects in the entire country (0.2 per cent).

It is sometimes thought that the collapse of command socialism in Europe has made the study of comparative economic systems redundant. For example, Ward (in Thornton and Millmow 2008) recalls being told by his head of department in 1991 that, following the collapse of socialism, it was now pointless to teach CES. Such thinking is misconceived. One of the advantages of looking at different systems, such as command socialism, market socialism or feudalism, is that doing so deepens one's understanding of capitalism: to understand something properly often involves comparing it to something else (as already noted, this is also one rationale for pluralism in general). The other advantage of CES is that its 'systems view' of the economy allows students to understand the interrelations between particular institutions, rather than simply the characteristics of individual institutions.

In the last two decades there have also been developments in comparative economics, such as the varieties of capitalism approach (Coates 2005; Soskice & Hall 2001) or the social structures of accumulation approach (Kotz, McDonough & Reich 1994). This material could easily be incorporated into a contemporary CES subject. Capitalism has, and continues to take, diverse forms and so it provides an ongoing going relevance for CES. A further reason to look at the study of alternative systems of economic organisation is provided by the ongoing, often serious, problems with capitalism itself. CES offers an important resource in determining what possibilities there might be (and might not be) for creating better economic and social systems. If students do not understand this diversity, and the sources of its persistence, it constitutes a gap in their knowledge. The revival of CES under a revived and renewed political economy would be desirable.

Development economics (DE)

Development economics is a sub-discipline that looks at problems of developing countries. It can be studied in a neoclassical fashion where it can sometimes be seen as merely applied neoclassical microeconomics. This accounts for it often having a more legitimate status within economics departments than other areas of political economy. However, the emphasis on the political, historical, social and geo-political ultimately anchors it within political economy and the social sciences in general.

In 1980 there were thirty-nine development economics subjects in Australian Universities (4.2 per cent), by 2011 this had fallen to 32 (2.0 per cent). Part of the explanation for the decline of development economics is in the growth of development studies within social science and arts faculties since 1980. Many students who are specifically interested in development now enrol in undergraduate or postgraduate degrees in international development. These degrees do not generally require the study of development economics; indeed, development economics may not even be available as an elective. Students enrolled in these programmes are not often naturally drawn to doing development economics or economic history. They either do not see it as important to understanding global poverty or are generally prejudiced against economics and/or unsure about their abilities or appetite to deal with any quantitative work. However, it is reasonable to hypothesise that if development economics was taught within a social sciences faculty as a branch of political economy, this type of student might more willingly embrace it.

Modern hybrid economics (MHE)

As noted in Chapter 4, the orthodox research frontier (behavioural economics, experimental economics, evolutionary game theory and complexity economics) is initially puzzling to categorise. These schools are different from neoclassical economics, yet they are not usually perceived as dissident or heterodox by most neoclassical economists and consequently have much higher institutional standing. A key part of the explanation of this acceptance by orthodoxy is that modern hybrid economics appears to divide significantly on ontological lines. For example, there is a 'new' behavioural economics that is now a respectable part of the profession. Its ontology is close to the 'complicated' ontology of neoclassical economics discussed earlier. The agent is still a calculator, albeit an imperfect one. By contrast, there remains the 'old' behavioural economics that was pioneered by Herbert Simon. It is much closer to the 'complex' ontology of political economy and the social sciences in general. The agent is less a calculator and more a follower of rules and a creature of habit. Given this, it seemed warranted at the time the survey was conducted to classify this area of economics as 'modern hybrid economics'. 'Modern' denotes its recent development; 'hybrid' denotes its bifurcated ontological foundations.

With the benefit of hindsight, and when one considers the subjects in question (see Table 7.6 below) this category of modern hybrid economics could have been called the 'orthodox research frontier' – which would have made it more consistent with the taxonomy for economics and political economy argued for in Chapter 4. However, it seems inappropriate to tamper with the survey results in this manner at this time. In any case, it serves as a good reminder of the challenges of categorising complex objects like social science disciplines.

A surprising result of the survey is how little modern hybrid economics (in any of its forms) has been incorporated into the curriculum. Table 7.6 reveals that in 2011 there were only twelve subjects (0.7 per cent of the curriculum) that could be classified under this category. While it was not entirely uncommon for some neoclassical subjects to have some content from modern hybrid economics, it was nearly always only a minor or tokenistic coverage, and such subjects were essentially neoclassical in nature.

Table 7.6 Modern hybrid economics in Australian universities in 2011

Subject name	Code	Year Level	University
Behavioural Economics: Psychology and Economics	ECON2013	2	ANU
Experimental Economics	ECON 2126	2	UNSW
Experimental and Behavioural Economics	ECOS3016	3	USYD
Experimental Economics	ECON6027	PG	USYD
Applied Behavioural Economics	EFB332	3	QUT
Behavioural and Evolutionary Economics	ECON2060	2	UQ
Experimental Economics	ECON3060	3	UQ
Behaviour, rationality and organisation	ECC2600	2	Monash
Integrated economic modelling	ECC3860	3	Monash
Information, incentives and games	ECC5840	5	Monash
Behavioural Economics	ECON30019	3	Melbourne
Experimental Economics	ECON30022	3	Melbourne

Graduate education

Graduate subjects and undergraduate subjects have been aggregated in this survey. This has been done because they generally face the same dynamics and problems. However, it is worth saying something specifically about the evolution of graduate education. Graduate coursework subjects in economics were not common in 1980. Extensive coursework was the exception; indeed some honours programmes were 100 per cent research. The situation in 2011 was quite different. There has been a significant increase in the number of graduate diplomas, masters by coursework and doctorates with a significant coursework component.

Doctorates with a significant coursework component were not offered in Australian universities in 1980 but have sprung up in the last decade or so, mainly within the 'elite' 'Group of Eight' universities. The content of these coursework-orientated programmes is strongly influenced by US coursework degrees. A good example of the US-style coursework-orientated doctorate is that offered by the University of Melbourne. Students enrolled in this degree are required to undertake a Masters degree by coursework for two years and then do a 50,000-word thesis over the next two years (four years in total). The coursework component is heavily quantitative and areas such as HET, economic history, CES and development economics are either not offered or are at least not part of the required core. The curriculum appears to be designed so as to maximise one's chances of publishing in elite journals and thus establishing an academic career within economics.

That doctorates are increasingly going in a direction where there is more economics coursework makes any pluralism of content more difficult. The 100 per cent research doctorate allowed a certain degree of flexibility and specialisation that benefited the social science wing of the discipline. For example, at the Australian National University in 1980, one could undertake a doctorate in economic history (and thus gain employment in an economics department) and not even necessarily have an undergraduate degree in economics. This is definitely not possible today.

Within economics the establishment of these degrees is seen as improving the education of students and also as a way of responding to competition from US universities and other universities in Australia. For example, the Head of Department at the University of Melbourne described their doctorate programme as 'international best practice. It's the standard model in Canadian and US universities and increasingly the standard model in European universities' (Olekalns cited in Jones 2010, p. 9). However, the intellectual limitations of the US-style coursework-orientated doctorate have been criticised, notably, by the Commission on Graduate Education in Economics (Krueger 1991). They have also been criticised, to varying degrees, in an Australian context (Groenewegen & McFarlane 1990; Lodewijks 2001, 2002a). The essential limitation of these degrees is well summarised by Lodewijks:

> Students may obtain their doctorates without any appreciation of economic anthropology or economic psychology or evolutionary economics or the law

and economics literature, or indeed the history and philosophy of their discipline. The technocratic narrowing of the discipline, most notable in the American context, crowds out the more applied, institutional and empirical investigation of pressing public policy issues. We note the sparsity of academic economists in public economic debate in Australia in the last five years or so. The narrowing of economics training may mean that the training is not meeting a full range of desirable goals of a university education, nor allowing postgraduates to contribute in a broader sense to Australian society.

(Lodewijks 2001, p. 9)

The narrowness of the postgraduate curriculum deepens, rather than rectifies, all the problems of the undergraduate curriculum. The reform of graduate education seems more important than reform of the undergraduate curriculum, as the former is the precondition for the latter. It would be desirable to broaden graduate coursework,[2] but this seems a particularly tall order, given that the programmes seem currently designed to produce graduates who can publish in highly ranked mathematical journals. A more plausible strategy would be to see if departments could still be persuaded to continue to offer a 100 per cent research PhD for students wishing to undertake research in political economy. This, while limited, keeps a pathway open. The key limitation with this strategy is that it is only short term: eventually economics departments, or some other department, will have to employ such PhD graduates or there will be no academics to supervise incoming doctoral students.

Research

The way research in political economy is evaluated is currently highly problematic. The situation has been extensively analysed and documented by political economists who rightly point to a problem of bias against political economy research and a bias in favour of orthodox economics (Bloch 2010, 2012; Lee 2006, 2009; Lee et al. 2010; Lee, Pham & Gu 2013). The most basic problem in many ranking systems is the weighting given to raw citation counts. Such systems of assessment struggle not to penalise those who do research where the absolute number of researchers is small (Lavoie 2015). Obvious examples of this are in the history of economic thought or in the heterodox schools. If such research is penalised for being small, it is then likely to become even smaller over time, thus being further penalised: a process of vicious circular and cumulative causation. An area with many researchers producing many publications is large and is more likely to grow even larger: *virtuous* circular and cumulative causation (or at least for the researchers themselves). The dynamics of circular and cumulative causation just described help to explains Caldwell's observation that the business logic of diversification, specialization and niche marketing is often ignored by economics departments because 'everyone is trying to be a little MIT or a little Harvard, and look exactly the same because that's the way you get scientific prestige' (cited in Manson, McCallum & Haiven 2015, p. 18).

Highly ranked journals generally place a premium on formal economic analysis. The long-term trend in the top journals has been towards greater and greater use of mathematical reasoning and quantitative analysis. Robert Frank's analyses of 'arm's races' in nature may have some relevance here. Frank points out that the antlers on male deer are of a size that is far in excess of what helps them to survive from predators: large antlers exist and persist primarily to insure superior access to female deer. This dynamic is obviously applicable to Frank's own observations of the economics profession:

> Economists like formal models, that's true, but what's also true is that the more complicated they are the better. Formal analysis is a way to demonstrate how smart you are. If you're one of a pair of competing candidates for an economics opening, the most important thing for you to know is that it will be in your interest to be the more formally qualified of the two. Economists have responded to that incentive by becoming ever more formal in their approach to how they write about economic decisions.
>
> (Frank in Sloan Wilson & Frank 2015, p. 3)

The process by which research is assessed has also been accused of being captured by the leading US economics departments. As Lee (Lee 2006, p. 16) puts it, 'the ranking process essentially ensures that top departments publish in quality economic journals and quality journals publish economists from top departments'.' As Lavoie (2015) points out, this essentially circular process that has been foundational in preserving the quasi-monopoly position of economics over political economy. The leading journals have also been accused of upholding Kuhnian normal science, rather than being open to genuinely new developments. As one US academic stated:

> I am currently trying to bring another discipline into understanding economics and the results we're seeing, and I am getting a huge pushback. The editor one of the major journals said, 'Well, there's nothing empirical in this,' but I said, 'I know, but I'm looking at how we think about what we see in our empirics, and this is very important.' So, at least from my perspective, that's been frustrating. It's just a challenge for me to improve the quality of what I'm doing in order to reach that audience. But to be successful right now, if you're a junior person trying to get tenure, you have … being innovative in that sense is probably not going to be helpful, you're going to have to publish just like the standard has been.
>
> (cited in Harley et al. 2010, p. 335)

Another problem is that the top-ranked journals cannot even keep up with current research. This is because the processing of submitting papers is characterised by slow turnaround times. This is then combined with a slow-moving process of multiple revisions. The outcome is one where it can easily take five or more years to publish in a leading economics journal (Harley et al. 2010). The internet has meant that working papers are now the platform for the most recent research and journal articles have become an archival version of working papers (Harley et al. 2010). As another US academic has stated:

> People show up to conferences, they read papers, they teach papers. All of us are trying to push our field forward. We're still writing and doing research ourselves and the journals are so pathetically slow that they are frequently seven years out of date from where the field is, so if we relied on the journals, we wouldn't know anything.
>
> (cited in Harley et al. 2010, p.339)

The institutional economist Thorstein Veblen made somewhat of a distinction between instrumental versus ceremonial institutions. Instrumental institutions were seen as making a positive contribution to the task of social provisioning. By contrast, he saw ceremonial institutions as being primarily orientated to upholding status and privilege. Of course, one cannot be too dualistic about this as particular institutions may have elements of both these characteristics. However, it seems the leading journals are tending towards the ceremonial, upholding and signifying status, being of little practical use and being detrimental in some senses.

Another issue with rankings is their tendency to discourage interdisciplinary research. Departments are primarily orientated to the standing of their discipline and department. Indeed, given that individual departments compete for internal funding and prestige, boosting the research standing of another department could be seen as a bad thing. This dynamic has added to the isolation of economics from the other social sciences.

Another problem with research assessment exercises is that they easily function as winner-take-all systems, as many of the processes behind research success are characterised by circular and cumulative causation. The strong become stronger by making the others weaker:

> In a government-based university system where salaries are fairly equal the best academics will filter into the best-funded universities where research externalities are greatest. These master-of-the-universe universities then stack ... Grant-giving committees and take turns each year handing out the bulk of research grants to each other. Even if these grants produce little in the way of output they continue to flow with only token offerings to the 'serf' class of researchers ... The injustice of comparing research outcomes from those who do not teach at all and are blessed with abundant research budgets with those who have heavy teaching loads and negligible research budgets is obvious ... Even the meagre pickings given to the research 'drones' should be transferred to their better-off prima donna colleagues who can make better use of the loot. It's the Matthew effect – to him that hath more shall be given but to him that hath little, take that little away.
>
> (Clarke 2010, p. 1)

The prestige and publicity generated by strong research performance then makes it easier to conduct more research. Universities can consequently be extremely anxious about raising and protecting the quality and amount of their research output. The strong universities are anxious to hold their gains and build upon them; the weaker universities are even more anxious about slipping behind further (the case studies in the chapters ahead illustrate this very clearly). This can all add to the pressure to employ orthodox economists over political economists.

There is also an important linkage between good research performance and teaching performance. Good research outcomes by a university can be used to attract larger numbers of students, and attract students of a higher calibre. This is because a good research profile raises the overall prestige and profile of the university. It is not hard to see how students might assume that a world-class research university must also be a world class teaching university. If universities are admitting high-calibre students they will be easier to teach and they will probably be more knowledgeable graduates; this will reflect well on the university. Winning research grants brings in income, raises morale and denotes a university as being either dynamic or a backwater. This then affects the research and teaching quality of the academics that a university can recruit and hold. In summary, the dynamics of circular and cumulative causation are pervasive. The dynamics are virtuous for the strong and (mostly) vicious for the weak.

How should we address the problems raised in research assessment? It would help considerably for political economy to be assessed by other political economists, not by orthodox economists. Such arguments have already been made by others (Lee 2006, 2012; Lee et al. 2010; Lee, Pham & Gu 2013) but in such cases the argument has been made in terms of a separate assessment for heterodox economists within the discipline of economics; i.e. that they seek an *alternative* ranking because economics 'is a contested discipline'. To argue that a single discipline needs two regimes of research measurement seems an ambitious idea to advance. Following the arguments of Chapter 4, it may be better for research in political economy to be assessed as a separate academic discipline, or perhaps *as if* it were a separate academic discipline for the purposes of research assessment. This may create a stronger case for political economy research to be assessed by other political economists and not become tangled up in the assessment of orthodox research. Just as finance research is usually assessed as a separate discipline from economics, so can political economy be assessed as separate discipline from economics. As a strategy it is not without some risks (just as the status quo carries significant risks). At the very least, consideration of this strategy might benefit from further discussion amongst political economists.

To summarise, there are clearly problems in the way that economics teaching and research is currently practised within universities. Teaching is too often seen as existing primarily to cross-subsidise research that allows orthodox economists to try and impress each other (rather than the world at large). As the historian of economic thought Tony Aspromourgos notes:

The large number of students doing low-level economics provides a funding base for academic departments of economists who, along with that teaching (and some higher level teaching), are able to undertake all sorts of high-level ('neoclassical' if you like) research, about which maybe nobody but them gives a damn. That research might be the most precious thing in their self-understanding of their professional activities; but in a wider functional sense it's rather incidental in the scheme of things.

(Aspromourgos cited in Thornton 2011, p. 1)

The survey evidence examined in this chapter highlighted a narrow curriculum and an overall trend away from pluralism. However, more encouragingly, a pluralist political economy, denied a place in traditional centres of economics teaching, has increasingly found a home for itself in faculties of arts and social sciences. The focus then moved to how research was assessed. Drawing on the arguments of Chapter 4 it was argued that greater differentiation of political economy (at least for the purposes of research assessment) might provide part of the solution to the ongoing bias against political economy research and the ongoing problems this then creates in academic appointments, economics teaching and economic policy advice.

Notes

1 It is indeed a good point, though listening to Summers's address at The Institute for New Economic Thinking where this point was made, it seemed to present, wittingly or unwittingly, a prime example of an economist engaging in what Vernengo calls a double discourse,

> 'that allows some economists to sound reasonable under certain circumstances, rejecting the worst parts of orthodoxy, while being able to never break with the mainstream. In other words, one may argue that the authors of the edge of the profession profess principles that they have no intention of following. They seem non-orthodox in many ways, but they have no intention of taking their ideas to full fruition, if that means breaking with mainstream economics. That is a form of what has been called, in other contexts, organized hypocrisy.'

(Vernengo 2010, p. 389)

2 One example of such an approach is the PhD programme that was established at the University of Athens (see Varoufakis 2010).

References

Argyrous, G. 2006, 'Alternative Approaches to Teaching Introductory Economics Courses in Australian Universities', *Australasian Journal of Economics Education*, vol. 3, nos. 1 & 2, pp. 58–74.

Armstrong, J. 2011, 'Reformation and Renaissance: New Life for the Humanities', *Griffith Review*, vol. 31, Autumn, pp. 13–51.

Blaug, M. 2001, 'No History of Ideas, Please, We're Economists', *Journal of Economic Perspectives*, vol. 15, no. 1, pp. 145–64.

Bloch, H. 2010, 'Research Evaluation Down Under: An Outsider's View from the inside of the Australian Approach', *American Journal of Economics and Sociology*, vol. 69, no. 5, pp. 1530–52.

Bloch, H. 2012, An Uneven Playing Field: Rankings and Ratings for Economics in Era 2010, Working Paper 04042012, School of Economics and Finance, Curtin University of Technology Centre for Research in Applied Economics.

Butler, G., Jones, E. & Stilwell, F. J. B. 2009, *Political Economy Now! The Struggle for Alternative Economics at the University of Sydney*, Darlington Press, Sydney.

Cervini, E. 2011, 'Unis Enter an Age of Uncertainty', *The Age*, Melbourne, 25 October.

Clarke, H. 2010, 'Era Fiasco', *Harry Clarke on Economics, Politics and Other Things*, [online] http://www.harryrclarke.com/2011/02/05/era-fiasco/ [accessed 2 September 2011].

Coates, D. 2005, *Varieties of Capitalism, Varieties of Approaches*, Palgrave Macmillan, Basingstoke.

Coyle, D. (ed.) 2012, *What's the Use of Economics? Teaching the Dismal Science after the Crisis*, London Publishing Partnership, London.

Dean, D. H. & Dolan, R. C. 2001, 'Liberal Arts or Business: Does the Location of the Economics Department Alter the Major?', *The Journal of Economic Education*, vol. 32, no. 1, pp. 18–35.

Delong, J. B. 2011, 'The Crisis in Economics', *The Economist's Voice*, May, pp. 1–2.

Economics Society of Australia 2004, *A Survey of Student Standards in Economics in Australian Universities in 2003*, ESA, St Ives.

Flinders University 1980, *Calendar*, Flinders University, Bedford Park.

Freedman, C. & Blair, A. 2009, 'Silver Linings: Teaching Economics in Times of Crisis', *Australasian Journal of Economics Education*, vol. 6, no. 1, pp. 1–20.

Groenewegen, P. D. & McFarlane, B. J. 1990, *A History of Australian Economic Thought*, Routledge, London.

Guest, R. & Duhs, A. 2002, 'Economics Teaching in Australian Universities: Rewards and Outcomes', *Economic Record*, vol. 78, no. 241, pp. 147–61.

Harley, D., Krzys Acord, S., Earl-Novell, S., Lawrence, S. & Judson, K. C. 2010, *Assessing the Future Landscape of Scholarly Communication: An Exploration of Faculty Values and Needs in Seven Disciplines*, Center for Studies in Higher Education, University of California Berkeley.

Hellier, P., Keneley, M., Carr, R. & Lynch, B. 2004, 'Towards a Market Oriented Approach: Employer Requirements and Implications for Undergraduate Economics Programs', *Economic Papers*, vol. 23, no. 3, pp. 213–21.

Jones, A. 2010, 'Doctoral Program Adds Fourth Year', *The Weekend Australian*, Sydney, p. 38.

King, S. 2012, 'Are Graduate Economists Still Fit for Employment?', *Core Economics*, [online] http://economics.com.au/?p=9033&utm_source=feedburner&utm_medium=feed&utm_campaign=Feed%3A+com%2FJUlM+%28CoreEcon%29 [accessed 3 November 2012].

Kotz, D. M., McDonough, T. & Reich, M. 1994, *Social Structures of Accumulation: The Political Economy of Growth and Crisis*, Cambridge University Press, Cambridge.

Krueger, A. O. 1991, 'Report of the Commission on Graduate Education in Economics', *Journal of Economic Literature*, vol. 29, no. 3, pp. 1035–53.

Lavoie, M. 2015, 'Should Heterodox Economics Be Taught in or Outside of Economics Departments?', *International Journal of Pluralism and Economics Education*, vol. 6, no. 2, pp. 134–50.

Lee, F. S. 2006, 'The Ranking Game, Class, and Scholarship in American Mainstream Economics', *Australasian Journal of Economics Education*, vol. 3, no. 1 & 2.

Lee, F. S. 2009, *A History of Heterodox Economics: Challenging the Mainstream in the Twentieth Century*, Routledge, London.

Lee, F. S. 2012, 'Heterodox Economics and Its Critics', *Review of Political Economy*, vol. 24, no. 2, pp. 337–51

Lee, F. S., Cronin, B. C., McConnell, S. & Dean, E. 2010, 'Research Quality Rankings of Heterodox Economic Journals in a Contested Discipline', *American Journal of Economics and Sociology*, vol. 69, no. 5, pp. 1409–52.

Lee, F. S., Pham, X. & Gu, G. 2013, 'The UK Research Assessment Exercise and the Narrowing of UK Economics', *Cambridge Journal of Economics*, vol. 37, no. 4, pp. 693–717.

Lodewijks, J. K. 2001, 'Educating Australian Economists', *Journal of Economic and Social Policy*, vol. 5, no. 2, pp. 1–10.

Lodewijks, J. K. 2002a, 'Economics: The Doctoring of Economics', *Journal of Australian Studies*, pp. 73–92.

Lodewijks, J. K. 2002b, 'The History of Economic Thought in Australia and New Zealand', *History of Political Economy*, vol. 34, Annual Supplement, pp. 154–64.

Manson, A., McCallum, P. & Haiven, L. 2015, *Report of the Ad Hoc Investigatory Committee into the Department of Economics at the University of Manitoba*, Canadian Association of University Teachers, Manitoba.

McCalman, J., Muir, L. & Soeterboek, C. 2008, *Adventures with Breadth a Story of Interdisciplinary Innovation* Melbourne University, Melbourne.

Millmow, A. & Tuck, J. 2011, 'Did the Global Financial Crisis Have Any Impact on Economics Degree Enrolments?', *Economic Papers*, vol. 30, no. 4, pp. 557–67.

Potts, J. 2000, *The New Evolutionary Microeconomics: Complexity, Competence, and Adaptive Behaviour*, Edward Elgar, Cheltenham.

Samuelson, P. A. 1970, 'Classical and Neoclassical Theory', in R W Clower (ed.), *Monetary Theory*, Penguin Books, Baltimore, pp. 1–25.

Sloan Wilson, D. & Frank, R. H. 2015, 'We Had It All Wrong: Adam Smith Isn't the True Father of Economics', *Evonomics*, [online] http://www.evonomics.com/is-charles-darwin-the-father-of-economics-a-conversation-with-robert-frank/ [accessed 15 January 2016].

Soskice, D. W. & Hall, P. A. 2001, *Varieties of Capitalism: The Institutional Foundations of Comparative Advantage*, Oxford University Press, Oxford.

Stretton, H. 1996, 'After Samuelson?', *World Development*, vol. 24, no. 10, pp. 1561–78.

Thornton, T. B. 2011, *Interview with Professor Tony Aspromourgos*, Coogee, 5 December.

Thornton, T. B. 2012, 'The Economics Curriculum in Australian Universities 1980 to 2011', *Economic Papers*, vol. 31, no. 1, pp. 103–13.

Thornton, T. B. 2013, 'The Possibility of a Pluralist Economics Curriculum in Australian Universities: Historical Forces and Contemporary Strategies', PhD thesis, La Trobe University.

Thornton, T. B. & Millmow, A. 2008, *Interview with Assoc Prof Ian Ward* La Trobe University, 23 May.

Varoufakis, Y. 2009, 'Where the Customers Are Always Wrong: Some Thoughts on the Societal Impact of a Non-Pluralist Economic Education', *International Journal of Pluralism and Economics Education*, vol. 1, no. 1/2, pp. 46–57.

Varoufakis, Y. 2010, 'A Most Peculiar Success: Constructing Uadphilecon – a Doctoral Program in Economics at the University of Athens', in R. Garnett, E. K. Olsen & M. Starr (eds), *Economic Pluralism*, Routledge, New York, pp. 278–92.

Vernengo, M. 2010, 'Conversation or Monologue? On Advising Heterodox Economists', *Journal of Post Keynesian Economics*, vol. 32, no. 3, pp. 389–96.

8   Reform from within

Given the sometimes challenging findings in previous chapters, it is tempting to conclude that attempting reform from within economics departments will *always* be futile and that efforts are best directed outside traditional centres of economics teaching in departments of social science, or departments of management. However, the existence of pluralist economics departments provides empirical refutation of the ultra-pessimist position that all contemporary economics departments must of necessity be irredeemably monist. Given the clear reality of pluralist departments, there are three lines of inquiry that seem important to pursue. First, how have such departments developed? Second, how do they manage pluralism in practice? Third, do such departments have any prospects for becoming the norm or are they just special cases that are only likely to develop, and persist, in very special circumstances?

Two departmental case studies are undertaken that seek to offer some responses to the questions just posed: the Department of Economics at Kingston University in the United Kingdom and the former School of Economics and Finance at Western Sydney University in Australia. Both departments are to be considered pluralist rather than exclusively heterodox departments or dedicated departments of political economy. This contrasts with hundreds if not thousands of exclusively orthodox economics departments that exist.

Economics at Kingston University

Kingston University is located in Southwest London in the UK. It is a former polytechnic that became a university in 1992. It has three campuses, all based in the Kingston area. It conducts teaching and research across five faculties: Arts and Social Science, Business and Law, Health Sciences, Art and Design, and Science and Engineering. The Department of Economics is based in a School of Economics, History and Politics within the Faculty of Arts and Social Sciences. This institutional setting has been of some assistance in advancing pluralism. For example, the current dean, a continental philosopher, is described as 'helping a great deal' by the head of department (Keen in Thornton 2015). There is not as yet a particularly developed relationship with the Faculty of Business and Law – they are on a different campus and cater to a more MBA-orientated audience. However, stronger connections in the near future are hoped for and there is no obvious barrier to prevent this occurring. The department's pluralist direction currently enjoys clear support from the Vice Chancellor and Deputy Vice Chancellor levels. As we shall see in the Western Sydney University case study, such support for pluralism from senior management cannot be naturally assumed, so economics at Kingston is fortunate in this respect.

The department became an avowedly pluralist economics department in mid-2014. As such it is one of a handful of UK departments that have explicitly embraced pluralism, the other departments being Greenwich and to some extent, Leeds, and West England – and also SOAS – which has a long history of pluralism. That Kingston has become one of the first UK Departments to embrace pluralism is partly a result of its established history of having some political economists on staff. For example, Engelbert Stockhammer, Paul Auerbach, Ali Shamsavari and Julian Wells were all members of staff prior to the official embrace of pluralism in 2014. Furthermore, political economy subjects like 'Capitalism' and 'Contemporary Economic Issues' were also already established, as was Kingston's Masters programme in Political Economy and its Political Economy Research Group (PERG) – note that political economy is the preferred term to heterodox economics. Given the history just described, the department's embrace of pluralism in 2014 might best be seen as a gradual (and ongoing) evolution rather than a sudden revolution that emerged out of a vacuum, or in response to the actions of a particular individual or particular event.

It should also be noted that Kingston's pluralist staffing profile and subject offerings are not so very far removed from the *historical* norm within UK economics departments. Up until the last two or three decades, many departments employed at least some political economists and had some breadth in their subject offerings. What then is atypical about Kingston is that has been able to *preserve* this norm where most other departments have actively sought to expunge it. The movement away from plurality commenced in the 1980s, and it has been particularly evident in the highly ranked UK universities. For example, Cambridge has changed from being a hothouse of Post-Keynesian thought to being a notably standard economics department with barely a trace of its earlier self. It is obvious that in more highly ranked universities, individual departments will be under more pressure for their department's research to be highly ranked (regardless of the question of how meaningful or accurate such ranking processes are). Lee's (2009) history of heterodox economics in the UK makes it very clear how significantly, and how quickly, the introduction of biased research assessment exercises damaged heterodox economics and political economy in general, having rapid effects on who was (or was not) hired. Because Kingston was a polytechnic until 1992, remains outside the elite 'Russell Group' of universities, and retains a strong emphasis on teaching, there has not been the expectation from senior management that each department in the university is to be ranked in the upper band of their respective disciplines. The benefit of this is that the pressure to pursue conformity, and to purge diversity, is simply not as strong as exists in more 'elite' economics departments.

Notwithstanding the long-term presence of some pluralism at Kingston, the decision to identify and promote Kingston as a pluralist department was a significant development. It occurred when Steve Keen, a high-profile Post-Keynesian economist from Australia, was appointed Professor and Head of the School of Economics, History and Politics in May 2014. When Keen applied for the position of head of school, his central (and successful) pitch to the selection committee, and also the department's staff, was that Kingston's status as a relatively young university meant that trying to compete with economics departments at Cambridge or Oxford on the standard metrics was unlikely to be a successful strategy. The smarter approach was to exploit a niche by becoming an explicitly pluralist department, thus tapping into the growing student demand for economic pluralism that has continued to build since the economic crisis of 2008. It was also argued that pursuing a greater pluralist staffing profile would provide the department with a more distinctive and innovative research direction, thus generating a higher level of interest amongst policymakers, the media and business.

In contrast to the Sydney University case study that will be examined in the next chapter, student activism does not appear to have been significant in explaining the *emergence* of pluralism at Kingston. Pluralism has been primarily advanced via the initiatives of academic staff rather than as a result of student agitation. However, the support of students is important and their role in supporting pluralism is likely to increase. In November 2014, students established the Kingston branch of Rethinking Economics, the largest of the international networks of student groups that form the International Student Initiative for Pluralism in Economics (ISIPE). Kingston has become very well known amongst pluralist student groups all around the world. This awareness is a source of both enrolments and potentially important alliances should the pluralist direction at Kingston come under threat. No such threats can currently be identified. However, much evidence exists which suggests sustaining a pluralist department over the long-term can be difficult (indeed, several case studies in the chapters ahead directly attest to this). The existence of an established and well-organised student support base can become very important in such circumstances. The presence of a pre-existing student group acts a disincentive to attack a pluralist department in the first place and also allows for organised support to be mobilised *quickly* – something that is often required for an effective response.

The pluralist strategy at Kingston is being implemented at a fair pace. Since May 2014, the department has appointed six new staff with strong pluralist credentials in both research and teaching. There has been a particular focus on recruiting for research capabilities in economic development, nonlinear dynamics, complexity and multi-agent modelling, as well as the capacity to teach Post-Keynesian and Evolutionary Economics. Those appointed have strong technical skills, but this technical expertise is in areas that can be considered less traditional: complexity theory, dynamics, multi-agent modelling, high-level mathematics and computing. However, those appointed are not just technicians or mathematicians. This is unsurprising given that Keen himself has raised concerns that technical work being done in areas of complexity is being undertaken by those without a sufficient background in key methodological and theoretical debates within economics (see Gallegati et al. 2006; Keen 2003).

Currently about 50 per cent of staff could be described as being standard economists, though Keen has found these staff members to be of an open, rather than closed, intellectual orientation. Relations between orthodox economics staff and political economy staff are described by Keen as collegial and friendly. Such an environment is partly the product of the long-term open and pluralist culture within the department, with figures such as Paul Auerbach playing a friendly 'founding father' role for such a culture. Keen identifies perpetuating collegial relations as a key responsibility for the head of school. This conclusion arises from his many years of experience at Western Sydney University (WSU), working under four consecutive heads of school committed to promoting pluralism. The experience allowed Keen to observe how pluralist departments were established and run (see the WSU case study later in this chapter for further information). In particular, it allowed Keen to recognise the value of those who can teach orthodox economics well. The latter is important not just so that these economists know their expertise is respected within the department, but because the department needs such staff to deliver a well-rounded economics education.

Whilst collegiality is important, in itself it is insufficient to sustain pluralism. A strategy of differentiation via pluralism not only needs to be well understood and accepted across the department, it also must deliver tangible benefits to all. What then have been the benefits of the pluralist strategy thus far? It is too early in the process to make a full assessment, but in terms of tangible gains, enrolments in the Masters programme increased from about thirty students in 2014 to forty-eight students in 2015. This increase was due to bringing greater pluralism to the degree, which then benefited from the significant levels of free publicity and media coverage the department received for explicitly embracing pluralism. This publicity also had a spill over benefit in providing positive publicity for the university as a whole, thus cultivating support for the department's direction within senior management. The department can also look at its successes in terms of outreach and impact with staff such as Keen providing over half a dozen seminars to organisations such as the Bank of England and speaking at conferences organised by the Financial Times.

The curriculum itself is about 50 per cent orthodox and Keen states that the intention is to maintain something like that ratio in the long-term. The view within the department is that it is imperative that orthodox economics is taught well, but by definition this requires a 'warts and all' coverage rather than the often uncritical treatment it gets at most universities. This level of support and legitimacy given to neoclassical economics illustrates that, if given any opportunity or institutional power, heterodox economists do not necessarily turn on neoclassical economists and exhibit the sort of anti-pluralism that they often experience. This level of legitimacy and curricular space allocated to neoclassical economic is all the more interesting when it is considered that it would be hard to nominate anybody who has been more critical of the dominance of neoclassical economics, and of the uncritical approach with which it is taught, than Steve Keen (see Keen 2009; Keen

2011; Keen & Lee 2004). One can safely say Keen is not a neoclassical economist. However, Kingston's approach to pluralism has clearly not been selective in regard to neoclassical economics and neoclassical economics in the curriculum.

In terms of the non-neoclassical content, the department is developing two strands in its undergraduate programme – one with a more technical orientation – teaching the basics of dynamic modelling, complexity, multi-agent modelling and so on – and one with a more descriptive emphasis. A similar, but more advanced, approach is being developing at the Masters level.

What are the key challenges facing the department? External ranking regimes are one. The department is ranked at the very bottom (67th) of the *Guardian* newspaper's League Table on Economics. As we shall see, this particular ranking system has a number of weaknesses, but is nonetheless influential with school leavers and other potential undergraduates who are poorly placed to understand the contested and diverse nature of economics. It is unfortunate that Kingston appears as if it is the worst place to study economics when its pluralist orientation means it is one of the best. The factors that have driven this ranking not only include the fact that some political economy research is being produced at Kingston (with the attendant bias problems that come with how that research is assessed) but also that Kingston is a former polytechnic rather than an elite university.

The Guardian League Tables also have a number of more technical problems. First, the rankings are based on lagged data that can be up to four years old, thus presenting a snapshot of performance that can be quite out of date. Another issue is the basic characteristic of any ranking process whereby the absolute distance between all the entities on key measures need not themselves be significant: even a microscopic difference between two entities is reason enough to establish a rank order. Table 8.1 Compares Kingston (ranked last in economics) with Oxford (ranked first).

There are no genuinely dramatic differences between some of the most important metrics (those focused on the quality of education received). The more disparate results are primarily generated on the metrics that are heavily dependent on funding (for example staff–student ratios) as well as reputational factors. From this perspective, the Guardian League Tables capture, but in some ways also perpetuate and deepen, some ugly disparities between UK universities that have been allowed to develop. There is particular need to reform these types of rankings given the fact that in 2015 the UK moved to a system where the government has removed caps on how many students individual universities can enrol on their degrees. This creates the possibility of more prestigious universities increasing their market share

Table 8.1 Guardian rankings of Oxford University and Kingston University

Institution	Guardian score/ 100	Satisfied with course	Satisfied with teaching	Satisfied with feedback	Student to staff ratio	Spend per student/ 10	Average entry tariff	Value added score/10	Career after 6 months
Oxford	100	92.9	93.2	64.3	14.5	–	598	8	85
Kingston	34.6	75.2	74.5	62.7	24.9	3	247	5	30

at the expense of less prestigious universities. Indeed, Kingston University has already noticed an across-the-board decrease in student demand.All this illustrates some of the general processes of circular and cumulative causation that often characterise relationships between elite and non-elite universities.

What to do? The uncapping of tertiary places makes it more, rather than less, important to have a distinctive teaching programme, so abandoning pluralism seems an ill-advised response to any fall in demand. The department is instead looking to develop a school's programme whereby it can tell its own story directly to students. In addition to this, it would be of obvious benefit to persuade *The Guardian* not to aggregate all its various measures into a single overall ranking metric. The tables would still be problematic, but considerably less so.

In general, the assessment of both teaching and research struggles to measure all the different variables involved in an accurate and fair manner. This problem is then compounded, sometimes dramatically, by combining already flawed measures (often in a quite arbitrary way) to produce a single metric. This single metric is then used to create league tables for departments and universities. It is this reductionism and aggregation that can be a particular curse.

Turning directly to the issue of academic rankings, the government conducted the Research Assessment Framework (RAF) in 2014, which sought to rank outputs in thirty-six disciplinary areas across 154 UK universities. Kingston submitted research under nine of the thirty-six disciplinary areas, of which 60 per cent were rated as world leading or internationally excellent. Economics was not one of the nine disciplinary areas submitted for assessment. This was a typical pattern across the UK with 82 per cent of universities being unwilling or unable to submit research under the RAF category of 'Economics and Econometrics'. Why might this be? The known biases against research in political economy are part of the explanation, but in addition to this, there are strong incentives for the majority of universities to avoid such exercises unless they are very sure they will be able to outrank nearly all their competitors given the strong winner-take-all aspects of the ranking process.

To see why universities would not be inclined to participate in the national rankings, we need only look at what occurred when Kingston submitted research under the previous 'Research Assessment Exercise' (ERA) that the government conducted in 2008. Under the ERA, Kingston was ranked 34 out 35 for its research outputs. Such a lowly ranking suggests a poor research performance, and as such, does the department no favours. However, when the results are examined on their own terms they read as being as something of which the department should be reasonably proud: 25 per cent of the research assessed was rated '1. Quality that is recognised nationally in terms of originality, significance and rigour', 55 per cent was rated '2. Recognised internationally in terms of originality, significance and rigour', 15 per cent was rated '3. Quality that is internationally excellent in terms of originality, significance and rigour but which nonetheless falls short of the highest standards of excellence', and the remaining five per cent rated '4. Quality that is world-leading in terms of originality, significance and rigour'. The old adage 'comparisons are odious' is indeed true, with single numerical rankings compiled into league tables being a particularly odious form of comparison.

Changing national level schemes like the Research Evaluation Framework is seen as being best addressed by working collectively with organisations such as the Association for Heterodox Economics. The plan to develop a programme for schools whereby they can communicate their appeal directly to potential undergraduates also makes sense. Within the university there is the additional task of persuading bureaucrats that it will probably continue to remain unwise for departments such as Kingston to play the rankings game, at least as the ranking regimes are currently designed. Indeed, this argument holds for most non-elite university economics departments regardless of whether they are monist or pluralist. Keen identifies one of his roles as shielding staff from pressure to abandon the research they themselves have identified as being important. Keen also emphasises that heterodox economists will often get a better hearing for their research in the media, government and business than they do within academia. The media in particular is seeking different explanations for economic phenomena with neoliberal policy prescriptions being more questioned since the financial crisis. The business and finance sectors are also seeking more realistic and relevant analysis, thus offering openings to heterodox economists and political economists in general. All this strengthens the department's position within the university and within academia more generally. It provides partial inoculation against problems generated by external research assessments. In fact, demonstrating research impact in media, business and finance should increase the 'impact' metrics that should form part of any research assessment exercise. Indeed, if they do not do so, it undermines the claims of such exercises to have any claim to have measured research impact.

Given that Kingston has sought to pursue pluralism from within a department of economics, Keen was asked for his opinion of the strategy of pursuing pluralism via establishing separate departments of political economy. Keen has no problem with such a strategy per se, but would take issue with any department that then decided to eschew formal (mathematical) methods of analysis. For Keen, mathematics is essential for exposing logical flaws within economics and as an important means to advance political economy, particularly in regard to complexity. Keen feels there is a strong basis for establishing 'Econophysics Departments', where students with strong backgrounds in mathematics and science can advance complexity economics. In arguing this, it may initially sound as if Keen is following Colander's 'inside-the-mainstream' approach that was explored in Chapter 2. There is the obvious commonality of enthusiasm for complexity. However, there are some important distinctions between Keen's approach and Colander's. It has already been noted that Keen has emphasised that those working in the area of complexity economics need to have a strong appreciation of theoretical lineages, issues and debates. Worrying less about methodological issues is not an edict to which Keen would subscribe. Furthermore, in terms of how to interact with the orthodoxy, Keen most certainly does not adopt Colander's advice for dissenting economists to 'give the mainstream their due' and to adopt an approach of deferential diplomacy. Keen's approach is notably non-deferential and direct; his high-profile intellectual clashes with Paul Krugman are but one example of this. Furthermore, Keen also advises students not to be deferential, stating that: 'students should give their lecturers hell unless they establish pluralist courses and to keep making nuisances of themselves until the university gives in' (Keen cited in Thornton 2015, p. 1).

Economics at Western Sydney University

Western Sydney University (WSU) is a relatively young, middle-ranked university, established in 2000. It was created out of a merger between a range of existing colleges and teaching institutions that existed in Greater Western Sydney. The School of Economics and Finance was formed in 2001 through a merger of existing departments of these colleges and teaching institutions. The school existed until the end of 2011, when it was merged into a newly created school of business (this merger will be discussed later in the chapter). The former school is now described as the Academic Programme of Economics and Finance.

Pluralist foundations

SEF's first head of department was Associate Professor Brian Pinkstone. Pinkstone, a Marxist economic historian with a strong interest in critical realism, was head of department from 2000 to 2006 and oversaw the amalgamation of previous offerings in earlier departments. In doing so, units in economic history and history of economic thought were revamped and units in behavioural finance and political economy were introduced. Several of these subjects were compulsory subjects in the Bachelor of Economics and the Honours programme in economics. That all this was possible is reflective of the fact that the department was diverse and there was a degree of tolerance:

> Although the new school included people from across the political spectrum and most were of a mainstream orientation, many were open to the idea that the students should be at least exposed to alternative perspectives. In addition I argued that as a new non-sandstone school of economics and finance, we would be better off pursuing a pluralist approach, which would permit us to stake out a unique identity rather than attempting to simply present ourselves as another run of the mill orthodox school. I put this to a school meeting in 2001 and received overwhelming support for the approach (even from key orthodox economists within the school). This pluralist approach was subsequently enshrined in the introduction on the school's website.
>
> (Pinkstone cited in Thornton 2011, p. 1)

It is worth quoting the introduction on the school's website, as the focus on pluralism and debate is explicit:

> In many of our units, we explore simplified models of the economy, and use deductive reasoning and available data, to try to understand how the

various economic variables interact and produce the outcomes that so concern society as a whole. Some of the issues we will examine are hotly contested and we introduce controversies among economists regarding economic theory and policy.

The school aims to provide students with an understanding of the theoretical and methodological variety that exists in approaches to understanding economic and financial phenomena, as well as the comprehensive technical skills in economic analysis and statistical techniques. Our school is committed to pluralism in theory and methodology.

(University of Western Sydney 2011)

The pluralist orientation was established via collegial means, rather than enforced from above by the head of school. It is true that there was a strong degree of initiation by senior leadership, but persuasion, collegiality and democratic determination were also central to achieving the required level of support. In 2001, rough proposals for the general structure of an economics degree, a bachelor of business (Economics and Finance) and the Bachelor of Business (Applied Finance) were developed. These degree proposals were then discussed in a series of school meetings and then put to a vote of all academics in the school.

The key task for Pinkstone was to persuade all economists in the school that a pluralist approach was legitimate. Five subject review committees were developed to develop subjects. The committees were in microeconomics, macroeconomics, finance, quantitative units and miscellaneous units, the latter covering history of economic thought, economic history, political economy, Asian economies, labour economics, development economics, international economics, managerial economics and economics of tourism. There was no limitation on staff membership of the committees so anyone could attend any of them to have a say about how a subject was to be developed and how it would fit into the general context of the department's offerings. Each review committee then made recommendations for the school to vote upon (Thornton 2011).

The school decided to offer three distinct degree programmes in economics and in finance. One reason for doing this was that having a diversified set of degree programmes meant that the department could create conventional-style degrees (to allay the concerns of economic staff) and pluralist degrees (to satisfy the political economy staff). Consequently the Bachelor of Economics was developed to be a pluralist degree, while the Bachelor of Business (Economic and Finance Major) and the Bachelor of Business (Applied Finance) were developed to be of a more conventional nature. This 'something for everybody' approach seems a wise way to manage a pluralist department as it meant that everybody was getting something they wanted, some of the time, rather than all programmes being the result of compromise and mutual accommodation by all concerned.

Another important reason for creating three distinct degrees was the belief that there were three distinct student constituencies. Bachelor of Economics students were considered more likely to have studied economics at high school and were more likely to be interested in becoming professional/academic economists, and they had a bias towards seeking alternative views and subjects in their study of economics. Those who took the Bachelor of Business double major in economics and finance were more business oriented and preferred a structured and more conventional programme. Those who took applied finance had clearly decided upon a career in the finance sector, most commonly in areas such as financial planning and also had their own particular needs. All three degree programmes expanded rapidly, to annual intakes of around 100 per year each. Subsequent moves by senior management to merge the programmes and restrict the majors on offer proved to be ill advised as the various specialised constituencies identified above appear to have largely decided to enrol at other universities.

The Bachelor of Economics was pluralist, yet it had a clear standard economics component: first-year and second-year microeconomics and first-year and second-year macroeconomics as well as an introductory quantitative unit. The remainder of the core was made up of political economy subjects (broadly defined): *Australia and the global economy*, *History of economic thought* and *Political economy*. Third-year micro and macro and second and third-year econometrics were available via the majors or as electives, and students were required to take these subjects if they wanted to do honours. The degree programme in the Bachelor of Economics was designed to be quite open-ended and interdisciplinary in terms of electives. Students could undertake a diverse set of majors that ranged from areas such as econometrics and management to history, politics and philosophy.

The essential nature of Bachelor of Economics remained pluralist during its existence. However, in 2006 senior management insisted that all business degrees have a common first-year curriculum. The school was also instructed to cancel any subjects that had fewer than thirty enrolments in units that were taught in the business degree programmes. This led to the cancellation of managerial economics, development economics, labour economics, and the economics of tourism. The removal of these subjects had a negative effect on the overall programmes and their cancellation may well have been a case of false economy: individual subjects with low enrolments, while not profitable in themselves, can sometimes play an important role in increasing the attractiveness (and thus profitability) of the entire degree programme, as well as supporting the reputation of the department as being well rounded. Enrolment numbers can also vary from year to year, meaning that low enrolment subjects can recover given time. In 2006, senior management also actively considered merging SEF and the School of Accounting, thus creating a School of Business. However, by working in coalition with accounting and in bringing external pressure to bear a merger was avoided.

In April 2007 Professor John Lodewijks was appointed Head of School. Lodewijks's interests encompass development economics, history, and philosophy of economics, and macroeconomics. He also has a strong interest in how economics is taught, being an award-winning teacher of economics himself. Lodewijks was in the first cohort of students in the political economy programme at Sydney University in the 1970s (a programme discussed in the next chapter), though he was generally not actively involved in the various episodes of collective struggle and protest that characterised the dispute. Lodewijks studied both economics and political economy, graduating with a first-class honours degree, before going on to a PhD at Duke University.

Under Lodewijks SEF continued to develop itself as a pluralist department. Indeed, at the time of its dissolution in 2011, SEF had the strongest representation of heterodox economists and political economists in the country. Lodewijks (2011) estimates that of the forty academic staff employed at SEF, approximately twenty would identify themselves as heterodox or as political economists. While the curriculum had only six subjects that are explicitly heterodox or political economic in nature, it is important to note that many predominantly standard economics subjects also had a political economy component, or were at least taught by staff who had a political economy orientation.

Lodewijks also shared the view that SEF's strategy for success was one of active differentiation. The focus was on the creative possibilities, rather than the limitations, of being outside the elite 'Group of Eight' Universities that hold most of the status and power in the Australian university system. This did deliver benefits. For example, SEF was able attract some excellent PhD students because of its range of supervisors and employed PhD graduates who could have worked anywhere in the world but were attracted to SEF's unique environment and expertise.

How did such a plural school function in practice? This is a critical question, given the obvious risk of intellectual difference leading to personal conflict and organisation dysfunction. The school seems to have functioned well enough and there is no indication of deep dysfunctionality. However, Lodewijks found that heterodox economists were actually more prone to argue *with each other* than they were to argue with the orthodox economists! This particular finding, if indicative of a general pattern elsewhere, suggests that heterodox/political economists have more challenges in front of them than just being marginalised by orthodox economists. For Lodewijks, it quickly became apparent that in a plural department, there is a particular responsibility for the head of school to take an active role in making sure that the culture of the school is collegial and respectful of difference. The clear criterion that he emphasised was that the individual staff member is to be a good exponent within their chosen field of economics and to respect achievements by other staff members in their chosen field. Lodewijks recalls early on in his appointment having to outlaw instances of 'death by email', whereby staff would launch withering broadsides at each other (Thornton 2010). Others, such as Steve Keen, who worked at Western Sydney University for many years before taking up his role at Kingston, would not subscribe quite as strongly to Lodewijks's view that heterodox economists are particularly prone to argue with each other, maintaining that it may have been more to do with the nature of particular individuals, rather than intellectual affiliation per se. Nonetheless, Keen, like Lodewijks and Pinkstone, emphasises the need for a pluralist department to foster and maintain a culture of collegiality and tolerance and consider that the head of school has particular responsibilities to encourage this.

Predictably, a major problem for the department was the biased nature of national research rankings. The School's annual reports document an impressive set of outcomes in teaching and research. However, in the 2010 Excellence in Research for Australia (ERA), SEF was given an overall ranking for economics of one out of five (against the national average for economics of 2.17 out of 5). A ranking of one is described as 'evidence of performance well below world standard presented by the suite of indicators used for evaluation'. The key indicators of success were publications in highly ranked journals that were nearly all orientated to orthodox economics. Given that approximately half of SEF's academics were heterodox economists or political economists, it could only have put it at a disadvantage that ERA journal rankings, and the ERA process generally, discriminated against these areas of research (Bloch 2012). In this, it was consistent with a pattern in the United States and the United Kingdom (Lee et al. 2010; Lee, Pham & Gu 2013).

The ERA process had a highly damaging impact on the School. Officially the result was seen as a 'disappointment' to the university, and not long after the rankings were announced research funding to the school was considerably restricted and redirected to areas of research concentration in the university that had achieved higher ratings. Of course, this made it harder to obtain a higher result in the next round of the ERA.

While the ERA process was neither kind nor fair to SEF, its dissolution was primarily due to a seemingly insatiable appetite by senior management for organisational restructuring. While SEF had survived the previous attempt to merge it with the School of Accounting in 2006, this time it was swept away in a restructuring that was university-wide and which occurred unexpectedly and at great speed. Administrative Blitzkrieg might not be too strong a term to use. The restructuring was announced in the latter half of 2011, with the restructuring to be in place by the beginning of 2012. Up until 2012, WSU had been structured around three colleges: Arts, Business and Law, and Health and Sciences. These colleges were essentially faculties, with five to six schools in each college. Under the restructuring, the college layer was removed and WSU is now structured around the existence of nine large schools. In the case of the School of Economics and Finance it was merged with the schools of marketing, management and accounting to create a single business school. The new business school is extremely large, with 132 permanent academic staff.

The rationale for such mergers appears to be due significantly to the belief that they will reduce administrative and managerial staff costs. The strategy to reduce degrees and subject offerings is again to do with maximising revenue. The aim, if not the reality, was a grand vision of having more students enrolling in a diminished pool of subjects and degree programmes. The faculty then delivers greater surpluses to cross-subsidise other aspects of the university's operations.

As will be clearly evident in the other two case studies in this book, this type of sudden and radical restructuring of departments is a general syndrome, at least in Australian universities, whereby growing corporate managerialism has replaced more collegial systems of administration (Lafferty & Fleming 2000; Lodewijks 2007). The pattern is one whereby incoming senior managers (be they deans, deputy vice-chancellors or vice chancellors) suddenly impose changes from above. The academics at ground level have little or no input into the decision and often struggle to see either the intellectual or practical justification. The new organisational structure is put into place and then within a few years (perhaps even a few months) it can be changed yet again. Such a state of permanent revolution consumes an enormous amount of time and energy and can be very disruptive and bad for morale. The changes also interfere with the 'learning by doing' processes that are at the heart of efficiency improvements. What is driving this process of constant change? In part, it is a reflection of federal government policy to make universities more self-sufficient and market-orientated. There is an increased intensity of competition between universities for research funding and for student enrolments. University management has generally responded to these pressures by becoming hyperactive, impatient and overly focused on the short-term. Appearance can become more important than substance. In such an environment senior managers with a demonstrated appetite and capacity for rapid organisational change will be more employable, thus creating an incentive for senior managers to earn their stripes playing the restructuring game.

By December 2012 this particular wave of change at Western Sydney University had played itself out. The Dean of the School of Business issued an Organisational Change Plan that cancelled the Bachelor of Economics and made eleven economics staff redundant, including four of the five professors. One of the key drivers of this change is a reduction in student preferences for the Bachelor of Economics that primarily arose as result of the deregulation of tertiary enrolments. Steve Keen, a Professor at WSU at that time, attributes much weight to this factor (Keen 2012, p. 2). Other documents and online blogs produced by WSU staff (authored anonymously) also argue that the budgetary crisis is in part the result of central administration drawing too much money away from the teaching units and investing it elsewhere. At one point it was proposed to cut subjects with fewer than 100 student enrolments which is well beyond the financial break-even point in most cases and is unduly constraining of student choice

A public campaign was mounted to oppose the level of cuts and various political economists and heterodox associations also wrote in support of economics at WSU. This has had no result other than the olive branch of allowing economics a major in the business degree with highly restricted student choice. Economics and finance at WSU is now defined simply as an 'academic programme' within the business school. There are still some pluralist staff working there. However, under the new arrangements it has lost its autonomy and thus much of its distinctive direction.

It does appear that the senior management never fully understood or appreciated the pluralist project at UWS. Pinkstone argues that a lesson that emerges from the WSU story is that getting, and maintaining, the support of senior management is vital:

> I failed to ever convince senior management that the pluralist strategy would be effective in raising the profile of the school and WSU or that the school would prove as successful as it did. There seemed to remain an underlying lack of interest which I could never break through … So one important lesson

from our experience for any economics group that tries to pursue such an approach in the future is that senior management needs to be convinced of the merit of the project from the very start and continually courted to ensure on-going support at senior levels.

(Pinkstone cited in Thornton 2011, p. 2)

With the exception of Kingston University, all the case studies undertaken in this book tell a story of senior management being insufficiently supportive of, or actively hostile to, economic pluralism.

The case study of Kingston and Western Sydney University shows that plurality within a traditional economics department is indeed possible to achieve. However, it is obviously not without its challenges, particularly in regard to research assessment. Indeed, both cases illustrate that the biases against heterodox economics and political economy in general are substantial. It is a problem that needs to be resolved, particularly if more 'elite' departments are ever to be attracted to go in a plural direction. If getting political economy research assessed as a separate discipline was pursued as the solution, then there would be a logic in departments such as Kingston's or WSU's then becoming known as departments of economics and political economy.

Comparisons

Some comparative observations are in order at this point. Both departments emerged in new non-elite universities that were former technical colleges or polytechnics. In such places the pressure to purge pluralism is simply not as strong. Furthermore, it is easier to sell pluralism in such circumstances as staff recognise that they have little to lose and much to gain by abandoning the conventional pathway to success. Heads of departments at both WSU and Kingston stressed the importance of collegial processes of decision-making and of creating and maintaining a culture of tolerance, with particular responsibilities assigned to the head of school in this regard.

WSU and Kingston both illustrate how certain types of deregulation pose challenges to non-elite universities. Previously, universities had an upper limit placed on how many students they could enrol, this provided lower ranked universities with some security that a certain proportion of students would enrol with them. The result of this is that more students are now applying to the elite universities on the basis of higher expectations of being admitted, and more significantly, elite universities are now enrolling more students (Keen 2012). If economies of scale are present and the marginal revenue of each new enrolment exceeds the marginal cost, and senior administrators see expansion as synonymous with success, then the temptation to expand enrolments is strong in both elite and non-elite universities.

Non-elite universities can respond to deregulation by lowering their admission requirements or lowering their fees. However, the former can run the risk of being counter-productive as the stigma of a course with a low entrance requirement becomes a further disincentive to enrol in a degree course; the latter runs the risk that reduced fee income will affect the quality of teaching and services provided. Vicious circles of circular and cumulative causation can occur, where elite universities enrol a larger and larger proportion of students who are both interested in, and capable of doing, intellectually demanding degrees and non-elite universities end up teaching more generic, less intellectually demanding degrees. In turn, this makes it more difficult for these non-elite universities to attract and maintain good teaching and research staff, which further damages their capacities and attractiveness. All of this is good for the elite universities, but it appears less than ideal to the university sector as a whole or to society in general. Why not just fund and support all the universities in a manner that allows them to prosper and to make a distinctive contribution? Previous policy settings in both countries allowed for this. Two-tier university systems are a false economy in that the non-elite universities still end up being very expensive to run but do not deliver anywhere near their potential to society.

The points of difference are that pluralism at Kingston, at least for the time being, has the clear support of upper management of the university, whereas at WSU this never seemed to be the case despite efforts at persuasion. The record of WSU's senior management is also generally poor, being too ready to engage in rapid top-down restructuring and being unable to allow SEF to exploit the pluralist niche it had identified and was pursuing.

References

Bloch, H. 2012, An Uneven Playing Field: Rankings and Ratings for Economics in Era 2010, Working Paper 04042012, School of Economics and Finance, Curtin University of Technology Centre for Research in Applied Economics.

Gallegati, M., Keen, S., Lux, T. & Ormerod, P. 2006, 'Worrying Trends in Econophysics', *Physica A: Statistical Mechanics and its Applications*, vol. 370, no. 1, pp. 1–6.

Keen, S. 2003, 'Standing on the Toes of Pygmies: Why Econophysics Must Be Careful of the Economic Foundations on Which It Builds', *Physica A: Statistical Mechanics and its Applications*, vol. 324, nos. 1–2, pp. 108–16.

Keen, S. 2009, 'Mad, Bad and Dangerous to Know', *Real-World Economics Review*, no. 49, pp. 2–7.

Keen, S. 2011, *Debunking Economics*, London, Zed Books [online] viewed 2 September.

Keen, S. 2012, 'A Fail Grade for Market Deregulation', *Business Spectator*, Melbourne, pp. 1–2.

Keen, S. & Lee, F. S. 2004, 'The Incoherent Emperor: A Heterodox Critique of Neoclassical Microeconomic Theory', *Review of Social Economy*, vol. 62, no. 2, pp. 169–99.

Lafferty, G. & Fleming, J. 2000, 'The Restructuring of Academic Work in Australia: Power, Management and Gender', *British Journal of Sociology of Education*, vol. 21, no. 2, pp. 257–67.

Lee, F. S. 2009, *A History of Heterodox Economics: Challenging the Mainstream in the Twentieth Century*, Routledge, London.

Lee, F. S., Cronin, B. C., McConnell, S. & Dean, E. 2010, 'Research Quality Rankings of Heterodox Economic Journals in a Contested Discipline', *American Journal of Economics and Sociology*, vol. 69, no. 5, pp. 1409–52.

Lee, F. S., Pham, X. & Gu, G. 2013, 'The UK Research Assessment Exercise and the Narrowing of UK Economics', *Cambridge Journal of Economics*, vol. 37, no. 4, pp. 693–717.

Lodewijks, J. K. 2007, 'A Conversation with Warren Hogan', *Economic Record*, vol. 83, pp. 446–60.

Lodewijks, J. K. 2011, 'Economics at the University of Western Sydney', paper presented to Society of Heterodox Economists 10th Annual Conference, Coogee, 6 December.

Thornton, T. B. 2010, Telephone Interview with Professor John Lodewijks, 14 April.

Thornton, T. B. 2011, Email Correspondence with Assoc Prof Brian Pinkstone, 30 December, pp. 1–8.

Thornton, T. 2015, *Email Correspondence with Steve Keen*, Melbourne, 4 October.

University of Western Sydney 2011, *University of Western Sydney School of Economics and Finance*, Penrith, UWS [online] http://www.uws.edu.au/economics_finance/sef viewed 20 July 2011.

9   Reform from without

This chapter is focused on a strategy whereby non-pluralist economics departments are left to their own devices and an alternative base for a pluralist economics is established elsewhere in the university. This strategy has a modest form whereby one or more pluralist subjects or majors are established in other departments. For example a political economy subject, or sequence of subjects, could be taught in a department of politics. The more ambitious form of the strategy is where dedicated political economy departments are created. The ambitious strategy of institutional separation needs to be understood as being separate from the idea of establishing pluralist departments with a clear political economy presence – such pluralist departments exist or have existed at the University of Missouri Kansas City, University of Amherst Massachusetts, and of course, Western Sydney University and Kingston University, as well as elsewhere. The point of differentiation between such departments and the strategy being analysed in this chapter is that these pluralist departments constituted the one and only department on campus that taught economics and political economy. In the cases studied in this chapter, a *second* department was created that existed in *addition* to that university's existing department of economics. For this reason it can be considered a 'reform from without' strategy, rather than the 'reform from within strategy' whereby political economy and orthodox economics are taught from within the same department.

The structure of this chapter is as follows. First, the modest form of institutional separation is considered and then two detailed case studies focus on the ambitious form of the strategy. The first case study is of the Department of Political Economy at the University of Sydney in Australia. It is shown that whilst creating and defending institutional independence has been a struggle, it can be successful. The second case study is of the University of Notre Dame in the United States. In this case, the situation is very different. Indeed, establishing a separate institutional base functioned as means to undermine pluralism at the university.

The modest form of separation and independence

Establishing individual political economy subjects in other existing departments within a university is, and is likely to remain, something many political economists are likely to entertain at some point because it may be the only option available.

The easiest fit for such a strategy is usually within departments of politics where such subjects can be taught as political economy. In such instances, one can again invoke the argument that it is possible and valid to frame political economy as being either a sub-discipline of politics or a cross-disciplinary subject that spans politics and economics. Given the fluidity of disciplines in the social sciences and the nature of modern categorisation that was discussed in Chapter 4, such framing is reasonable. Indeed, as Fine and Milonakis point out, for the classical economists such as Smith, Mill and Marx, political economy was 'a sort of unified social science' (Fine & Milonakis 2009, p. 3). From the classical economist's perspective, it would be entirely appropriate for political economists to work inside politics departments, or for political scientists to work inside political economy departments. In general, political economy can be legitimately described in a diverse number of ways to facilitate its ongoing existence and relationship with other social sciences. Some obvious examples would be institutionalism as economic sociology, economic history as history, history of economic thought as history of political economy, comparative economic systems as comparative political economy. The list could go on. Again, the basic point being made is that disciplinary boundaries (at least in the social sciences) are always unclear and somewhat arbitrary. In the light of this, political economists should not have their options limited by unreflective dictates about traditional disciplinary boundaries.

Working inside other departments to establish a single subject, major or full programme in political economy has a lot to recommend it (Argyrous 1996; Argyrous 2006; Argyrous & Thornton 2014a, 2014b). First, one does not have to endure the intellectual hostility and incomprehension towards political economy that often occurs in economics departments. Second, other disciplines can be more able to recognise that political economy can represent an opportunity for their department in terms of bringing in undergraduate and postgraduate students and new lines of research expertise. Third, other academics, particularly other social scientists, often recognise a need for students to have some basic knowledge of issues such as depressions, recessions, unemployment, inflation, etc., and political economy is often more readily recognised by them as a valid and appropriate introduction to these issues for social science students (Argyrous 1996).

Of course, one cannot assume that every academic, department or faculty will exhibit such attitudes and interest towards political economy. It is sometimes the case that individual staff or departments become highly focused on building their standing and size within narrow disciplinary boundaries and view related disciplines as being a threat or competition. As ever, particular institutional contexts and the particular individuals within them can be significant determining factors of what is and is not possible. However, it will become apparent in the case studies to come that other departments, particularly other social science departments, can offer assistance and support and are relatively more open to identifying mutually beneficial collaborations. Indeed, it possible that this 'modest' form of institutional separation could be built up into substantial teaching and research programmes in political economy.

Dedicated political economy departments

Turning to the strategy of full departmental independence for political economy, it must be admitted at the outset, it is a rarely used and controversial strategy with which to advance pluralism. Indeed, a key feature of this chapter's case study of the University of Notre Dame is that political economists strongly resisted the suggestion that they should be separated from the economics department via the creation of a new department. They were strongly of the view that it would *undermine* pluralism and time has proven their hypothesis to be correct in this instance. Similarly, political economists at the University of Manitoba in Canada are, at the time of writing, staunchly resisting the idea of institutional separation on the same basis (Manson, McCalllum & Haiven 2015).

Given the opposition by political economists at Notre Dame at Manitoba, one may initially conclude that setting up departments of political economy is a disastrous prospect that should always be actively resisted. It is not so straightforward: the University of Sydney case study illustrates that institutional separation can allow political economy to prosper strongly and to do so in a manner that would have been very unlikely had institutional separation not occurred. There is a line of literature that argues that it should be more often considered as a reform strategy (Argyrous & Thornton 2014a; Butler, Jones & Stilwell 2009; Lavoie 2015; Thornton 2013).

The most recent contribution to this literature concerning institutional separation comes from Lavoie (2015), who simultaneously ponders both the ambitious and modest forms of institutional independence. Lavoie's decades of experience as a heterodox economist have led him to ask whether it any longer makes sense for political economists to try to work within economics departments. For example, he states that 'there is a whole series of institutional barriers that makes it difficult, if not downright impossible to achieve an extended and substantial curriculum reform in economics' (Lavoie 2015, p. 135) and that there are many positive feedback loops, path-dependencies and self-reinforcing processes of circular and cumulative causation that make reform of the economics profession very challenging (Lavoie 2015). However, he also notes that institutional separation is not an easy or risk-free path: 'it is clear that to establish a distinct field outside economics proper is ripe with complex problems and potential negative effects' (Lavoie 2015, p. 145). This is true, but it must be remembered that working inside economics departments is also ripe with its own complex problems and potential negative effects.

Lavoie's somewhat tentative conclusions draw on his knowledge of the current situation in France. He points out that French heterodox economists, after decades of debate, have now established the Association française d'économie politique (AFEP) – the French Association of Political Economy – note the usage of the term political economy rather than heterodox economics. The majority of members have concluded that their future lies in a new intellectual field that they have tentatively titled 'Economics and Society'. Encouragingly, the French Government raised the prospect that they would establish a new field in the French university system called 'institutions, economics, territory and society'. This would have created a level of differentiation and independence for political economy. However, there was a backlash from orthodox economists and this pressured the government into backing down. The arguments used against the new field were that economics was already sufficiently pluralist (in that there are debates and different positions within the orthodoxy) and that creating the new field would function as a haven for 'leftists and misfits' (Lavoie 2015).

Lavoie then reflects upon his own experiences working at the Department of Economics at the University of Ottawa. When Lavoie started working there, six out of the eighteen staff were heterodox, but now there are only two heterodox staff in a department of twenty-five. He sees 'virtually no hope of improving or even maintaining this ratio in the future' (Lavoie 2015, p. 145). He then concludes that, in retrospect, it was a strategic error not to take up an offer made fifteen years ago by the Dean of his faculty for the four heterodox staff to move the university's School of Political Studies. Heterodox staff resisted because they viewed it as attempt to purge the discipline of heterodox economics and that it was not consistent with their self-identification as economists. However, he now concludes that 'had we accepted the offer, in all likelihood we would have had the independence to make hires and build a strong unit of political economy within the school of political studies' (Lavoie 2015, p. 146).

Can we expect support for separation from economists? There are reasons to suggest that they may support institutional separation, or at least not oppose it as 'a significant proportion of those in the mainstream of the profession regard the challengers as not really practicing the same profession and hence belong, not in the profession, but at best, in some other profession entirely' (Manson, McCallum & Haiven 2015, p. 14). However, much may depend on whether they would see the creation of a new discipline as representing serious competition or not. This in turn depends on the level of support and strength a new department may acquire. It is relevant to point out how the creation of a new field of study in France was prevented and that prominent economists were some of the loudest voices in opposition.

The evidence from the case studies and elsewhere indicates that there would be a range of perspectives within economics departments. Some orthodox economists will be elated or at least relieved at the idea and will actively encourage or initiate it. Others might be fearful of any increased competition for students and internal funding. Others might be complacent or indifferent, thinking such a department will never prosper or survive. Others might be able to grasp potential synergies and win–win relationships. Others will have an entrenched hostility towards political economy and will adopt the response that they feel is most damaging to its status.

It must also be added that some political economists, perhaps a significant number, might conclude that seeking to base political economy within economics departments is the most appropriate and strategically wise course for them to persist with. The cases of both Notre Dame and Manitoba universities illustrate such a viewpoint, and also provide some explanation for it. Political economists may also reject the idea of their research being assessed as anything other than research in economics. Obviously, the sometimes difficult and seldom risk-free business of deciding on (or persisting with) a strategy to defend or advance political economy is a finely balanced matter; thus wide discussion and careful assessment of context is desirable.

To summarise the analysis so far, institutional separation in the form of separate departments of political economy is a reform strategy that has demonstrated both real gains but also presents real dangers. The more modest form of the strategy (setting up shop in another department and perhaps also pursuing political economy as a sub-discipline of another discipline) will usually be easier and is likely to attract less opposition from orthodox economists. However, the more ambitious form of the strategy offers potentially much greater gains and requires serious consideration.

The University of Notre Dame

The University of Notre Dame is located near South Bend, Indiana, in the Midwest of the United States. The university was founded in 1842 by the Congregation of the Holy Cross and it maintains a stated commitment to the Catholic faith. Notre Dame is currently ranked in the upper band of US universities. For example, *Forbes* currently ranks Notre Dame at 13 within America's university system and the 2015, Times Higher Education University Rankings ranked Notre at 108 in the world.

Dating back to the mid-1970s, and until quite recently, the economics department at Notre Dame had been pluralist. Lee (2009) denotes it as one of a small number of US economics departments such as the New School for Social Research, American University, University of California-Riverside, Rutgers University, Colorado State University-Fort Collins, and the University of Utah that could be called heterodox in *some* manner. Some of the current and former political economy staff at Notre Dame have international reputations in their field. For example, Philip Mirowski and Esther Miriam Sent in the History of Economic Thought, David Ruccio in Marxian Economics and Charles Wilber in Social Economics. For most of the period in which the department was pluralist, the head of department was also a political economist. For example, Charles Wilber was head of department from 1975 to 1984 and played an important role in establishing Notre Dame's pluralist orientation. The department could at no stage be classified as predominantly 'heterodox' or as a being 100 per cent political economy in nature, for even during its most pluralist phases orthodox economists still constituted the majority within the department and political economists were in the minority.

That a pluralist economic department would emerge at Notre Dame is not wholly surprising given that it is consistent with the university's official mission statement, part of which contains an explicit commitment to intellectual diversity:

> The University is dedicated to the pursuit and sharing of truth for its own sake. As a Catholic university one of its distinctive goals is to provide a forum where through free inquiry and open discussion the various lines of Catholic

thought may intersect with all the forms of knowledge found in the arts, sciences, professions, and every other area of human scholarship and creativity. The intellectual interchange essential to a university requires, and is enriched by, the presence and voices of diverse scholars and students ...

(University of Notre Dame 2015, p. 1)

The university does appear to have once actively encouraged the development of a pluralist department. For example, a 2002 internal report on the economics department states that:

Many years ago the Department chose, in response to what appears to have been a clear mandate from the administration, to follow a heterodox approach to the study of Economics. Many of the current faculty were hired precisely because of their skill in this branch of Economics ...

(Hallinan et al. 2002, p. 3)

This pluralist orientation of the department held from the mid 1970s until the turn of the century. However, pluralism within the department came under growing pressure from the 1980s onwards. There was growing dissatisfaction within the university administration about the presence of political economists within the department, as well as there being tensions between the economists and political economists within the department about the correct path for the department to pursue and disagreements about curriculum, the value of some the department's research outputs and choices in staff recruitment. The issues were analysed in a 2002 internal report that concluded that the only adequate response was to split the department into two. This recommendation, which was opposed by the majority of the department and also the college council, was proposed and implemented by the university administration in 2003, creating on the one hand the purely orthodox Department of Economics and Econometrics (DEE) and on the other hand the pluralist Department of Economics and Policy Studies (ECOP).

Prior to the split, both the university administration and some of the orthodox economists expressed concern about the department's position within the established external ranking regimes that have become increasingly important to many economics departments as well as to universities in general. Notre Dame's position in the area of economics in some of the established ranking regimes was relatively low. It was also relatively low when compared to Notre Dame's overall ranking as a university. For example, in 2003 (the year of the split) the department was ranked 81 out of 108 for research-doctorate programmes by National Research Council (though the department was more highly ranked in specific sub-disciplines, such as development economics), whereas the University of Notre Dame as a whole was ranked at 18 out 108. Concerns about such rankings within Notre Dame appear to have existed for some time. For example, in 2004, the then provost Nathan Hatch stated that 'the economics department has been a quandary for the university for 20 years' (cited in Donovan 2004b, p. 2).

As has already been discussed in previous chapters, rankings are very problematic measures of academic worth, and do not deserve to be taken as seriously as they often are. This is particularly the case with economics because the methodology typically employed has been shown to exhibit systemic biases against non-neoclassical research (Lee, Grijalva & Nowell 2010; Lee, Pham & Gu 2013). Lee et al. (2010) evaluated Notre Dame's research output using less biased measures and determined a ranking of 45 out of 108 for overall productivity (Lee, Grijalva & Nowell 2010, p. 1368). The ranking methodology deployed in this instance was better able to account for what they defined as 'the contested nature of economics as a discipline' as well as better reflecting Notre Dame's strong performance within particular subfields such as heterodox economics and development economics.

A significant driver of the 2003 split was the already mentioned 2002 internal investigation of the department. The investigation was conducted by five academic staff from other disciplines within the university, with their analysis and recommendations being published as the 2002 *Report of Blue Ribbon Committee on the Department of Economics* (Hallinan et al. 2002). The report says nothing about the hostility of senior management towards political economy. The diagnosis is instead centred on problems of 'low morale', 'tensions' and 'problems' between staff within the department. It does not explicitly mention the issue of rankings, yet it appears to be an implicit concern. For example, it chastises the university administration for, at one stage, actively encouraging the development of a pluralist department whilst simultaneously expecting the department to achieve the level of 'scholarly visibility comparable to that of leading economics departments' (Hallinan et al. 2002, p. 3). The report is brief (only three pages long with a one-page appendix), but in many ways it is the key document in the demise of pluralism at Notre Dame because it recommended the split and also made a series of recommendations about the terms of this split that were mostly implemented. For some political economy staff such as Ruccio, a shortcoming of the Blue Ribbon Report is its heavy emphasis on problems within the department, rather than on determining whether senior administrators were opposed to a political economy presence within the department, and if so why. Ruccio acknowledges that there were tensions within the department, but argues that these tensions should not have been seen as unmanageable. In support of this view one could look to other pluralist economics departments such as that at the University of Amherst where an agreement (a *modus vivendi*) was eventually developed that allowed economists and political economists to coexist (Katzner 2011). In any case, Ruccio argues that internal issues were minor relative to the problematic agenda of senior management.

The major recommendation of the report was that the department be split in two. The report is unambiguous about this recommendation, arguing that no other solution was viable:

> [W]e regard the differences between the heterodox and orthodox economists to be so great that reconciliation within a single cohesive department is

wholly unrealistic. The differences in assumptions, methods; and paradigms are simply too great to overcome. Thus, while we did consider other possible solutions such as retaining the status quo, or putting the Department in so called 'receivership' we do not consider these to be viable long-term solutions.

(Hallinan et al. 2002, p. 3)

The idea of splitting the department is presented as a desirable decision for all parties. Indeed, the committee asserts that such a division of labour is consistent with the general development of scholarship within universities. The split is seen as an almost natural development that will be:

[S]imilar to many other divisions that have occurred in the Academy. Examples include the separation of statistics from mathematics, engineering from science; and, at Notre Dame and in much of the Academy, the separation of Anthropology from Sociology. Such separations can strengthen the Academy, leading to a broader set of course offerings and experiences for students at all levels.

(Hallinan et al. 2002, p. 2)

It is worth thinking very carefully about this particular statement. The first thing that must be said about it is that all Notre Dame's political economists (as well as significant number of its orthodox economists) were implacably opposed to this line of reasoning, arguing that for intellectual and strategic reasons it would be better to retain the established single pluralist department. It was conceded that this would not necessarily always be smooth sailing, but coexistence had previously been achieved at Notre Dame and had also been achieved elsewhere. The majority of staff also felt that splitting the department would not be advantageous to them personally, nor would it advance pluralism.

The concerns that the majority of economics staff had about institutional separation – which turned out to be justified in this instance – does not mean that separation, in *principle*, could not have been beneficial in just the way it is described in the Blue Ribbon report. A mutual flourishing through division is possible. It *could* promote economic pluralism. However, there is a crucial condition that must be met if independence and differentiation is to be pursued: both sides of a formerly unified discipline need to be given a fair opportunity to grow and prosper. In the absence of this condition, splitting an academic discipline can become an intentional or unintentional exercise in intellectual suppression.

The *Blue Ribbon Report* concluded that relations between political economics and orthodox economists had made coexistence untenable. We have previously noted that this claim has been rejected by some of the political economy staff. However, several of the department's orthodox economists have made statements indicating that *they* were dissatisfied with cohabitation. In fact, they complained of *exactly* the sort of persecution and marginalisation that economists usually complain of having to endure in economics departments. For example, the chair at the time of the split, Richard Jenson, complained of a hostile environment towards orthodox economics staff and claimed that his agenda to teach neoclassical economics was unwelcome. He described his chairing of the department at that time as having been 'very unpleasant' (cited in Donovan 2004b, p. 2). Similarly, Thomas Gresik, another economist, though one based in the Business School in the years leading up to the split, asserted that an 'unproductive and nasty politicization of the department' (Gresik 2003, p. 2) had developed and accused political economists of vilifying the orthodox staff members:

> At its core, the fundamental problems have been the long-standing and openly hostile treatment of economists whose teaching and research has been well-received by mainstream economists and the continuing attempt to portray mainstream economists as lacking the proper interest, perspectives, philosophies and techniques to address the important social justice issues the University consistently expresses the resolve to tackle ... Rather than supporting and objectively presenting diverse points of view in and out of the classroom, the tradition of the economics department has instead been to vilify those who have attempted to apply well-vetted mainstream techniques to the economic problems so important to all of us ... All of these are issues that speak directly to the human condition, especially in our modern, globally interconnected society. These are also very complex issues that require sophisticated theories and empirical methods to help us distinguish policies that only superficially address symptoms from policies that truly have a chance to improve social conditions.
>
> (Gresik 2003, p. 11)

Gresik asserts that all options to improve the department had been exhausted. For him, all possible attempts to work with political economy staff had been tried and failed; thus splitting the department was the only option left to resolve the situation (Gresik 2003, p. 2).

As well as stressing the antipathy that they felt was directed against them, some of the orthodox economists also raised the problem of external research rankings and the university's research reputation in economics. They did not appear to share the political economist's reservations concerning the inadequacies and biases that afflict the ranking process. Indeed, there are some clear instances where economics staff expressed a very poor estimation of the political economy research being produced in the department:

> The faculty [in the Economics and Policy Studies Department] are way behind the frontier and haven't done anything useful since they got their dissertations in the 60s and 70s. They're out of date and not doing very much.
>
> (Mark cited in Panhans 2009, p. 1)

> If the department were actually good, then the market would decide. If you're a football player and you're not getting any playing time, but really deserve to play, you ask for a transfer and other teams will want to pick you up. Same

with academia. If you feel like you're being dumped on, then send out your
vita and there are a lot of other departments that will want to pick you up.

(Mark cited in Panhans 2009, p. 1)

Gresik complained of difficulties the department had in recruiting 'high quality'
candidates because of its poor reputation. It was also argued that it was unfair to
students that they undertake their studies in an economics department that was not
highly ranked (Gresik 2003, p. 11). Mirroring the optimistic perspective on
splitting the department in the *Blue Ribbon Report* Gresik argues that the
split would be highly desirable for all concerned as 'the beauty of the current
proposal is that it allows both groups of economists to credibly co-exist' (Gresik
2003, p. 2).

It is important to understand that even if the economics staff did not have a
personal antipathy to the political economists (on either intellectual or ideological
grounds) some may still have concluded there was a strong self-interest incentive
to purge political economists from the department, if not from the university itself.
The incentive was that it would be best for their own career to work in a department
that was highly ranked and which enjoyed a high reputation within orthodox
economics. In other words, economists need not be *actively against* political
economists in any intellectual or ideological sense. Rather, economists may
conclude that they have grounds enough to oppose political economists simply
because they feel that their presence in a department is antithetical to their career
plans. In summary, the presence of political economists is something economists
can be acutely disturbed about for both intellectual and non-intellectual reasons.

Political economy staff had quite a different perspective on what had driven
problems in the department. Their view was that orthodox economics staff, and
the university, had become unreasonable and gone far too in what they were
asking for. For Ruccio, the most extraordinary aspect of the entire episode was the
length economists (and their allies within the university administration) were
willing to go to marginalise all forms of political economy within the curriculum,
research profile, and policy recommendations of the department. What then is the
record of compromises made? Political economists agreed to hire more orthodox
economists, removing the requirement for graduate students to study both political
economics and history of economic thought (in favour of choosing one or another).
Political economy staff also agreed to have an orthodox economist as chair of the
department. Ruccio argues that economics staff, short of completely capitulating,
did everything they reasonably could to accommodate administration demands to
make the department more orthodox.

Agreeing to have an orthodox economist as a head of department was a significant
concession. This is because of the analysis in the previous case studies that suggests
that the head of a pluralist department needs to take particular care to be even-
handed, understanding and appreciative of different schools of thought or relations
between staff will quickly unravel. Pinkstone (WSU), Lodewijks (WSU) and Keen
(Kingston) all emphasised this point. Their view was that the key task is to create an
environment where it is understood that academics are expected both to pursue

excellence in their own field, but also to respect the achievements and expertise of others in their chosen field. Such a philosophy is increasingly rare amongst orthodox economists and so it is not surprising that it had little currency in the period leading up to the split. Donovan (2004b, p. 2) cites a number of professors with ECOP who claim that 'Jensen's tumultuous leadership was responsible for much of the conflict experienced in the department over the last two years.'

A key issue in all this is what constitutes a reasonable compromise. Both parties stated, and probably believed, their own position was reasonable. There is a general problem that economists can simply become fearful, almost allergic, to any level of pluralism. As Lavoie argues, there is a general viewpoint that

> '[D]epartments of economics belong to mainstream economists. It is theirs. If there are already a couple of heterodox economists in the department, it is a generous concession, an anomaly; there is no way the department will hire a third one: the ratio is already much too high, as it is higher than elsewhere, so that the departmental assembly is not going to raise it. Also, several orthodox members fear that their department could be known as a heterodox outpost, especially if the heterodox members are active and publish a lot.'
>
> (Lavoie 2015, p. 141)

Lavoie goes on to note that in his own department at the University of Ottawa he came to learn that his economist colleagues held fears of the university being known as a 'Post-Keynesian stronghold' despite there being only three heterodox economists on staff. The Post-Keynesian Paul Davidson has also experienced the syndrome at Rutgers despite only four to five people out of eighty-one faculty being political economists. This small presence did not stop economists expressing concerns that Rutgers was becoming known as 'a weird place with Post Keynesians' (Colander & Davidson 2001, p. 102). If similar perspectives were shared by the economists at Notre Dame it goes some way to explaining why a mutually agreed compromise was difficult.

We should now examine the important question of why the majority of staff in the department were opposed to the split. The rationales for the opposition include the following:

1   Commitment to the idea that economics departments should not just be left to neoclassical economists.
2   That the former situation of pluralism that characterised economics at Notre Dame could be recovered and then protected over the long term.
3   That the university would not set the new pluralist department up in a fair and even-handed manner that would allow it to grow and prosper.
4   The university might initially set up a new pluralist department on a viable basis, but then subsequently change institutional arrangements, perhaps at the behest of economists, so that it gradually (or quickly) becomes unviable.
5   That the university will just dissolve the new department in a few years when the attention and controversy have died down.

The ranking of factors above would be different for each individual and would probably have changed over time. For example, Ruccio is of the view that leaving the discipline of economics to orthodox economists is problematic as any type of general proposition. Furthermore, he is of the view that it is viable for other academics and their students to resist any opposition that orthodox economists might wish to mount. Ruccio's general view of institutional separation is as follows:

> I don't think that's the solution in all cases. I think it cedes too much to mainstream economists, by abandoning the field entirely. I can teach economics and call myself an economist because I received a Ph.D. from an economics program (the University of Massachusetts-Amherst). And I don't think pluralism relies on the goodwill of mainstream economists, which in any case is thin if not (in most cases) non-existent. It relies, instead, on the demands of students and other scholars, who want colleagues in economics who can teach them and converse with them.
>
> (Ruccio in Thornton 2009, p. 1)

There may also have been additional reasons for opposing the split that are best known to those individuals themselves. However, what can be said with certainty was that there was a very strong general view amongst the majority of staff that splitting the department would marginalize political economy leading to its eventual disappearance. As ECOP staff member Jennifer Warlick stated in 2004, 'There's still lingering suspicion that the purpose of splitting us … is to marginalize us so that we will eventually be dissolved.' A hypothesis confirmed by events. Members of ECOP demanded written guarantees from the university that if ECOP were dissolved their employment elsewhere within the university would be guaranteed.

The graduate students were nearly all opposed, spending weeks drafting objections to the split. Only one student thought the split desirable (Donovan 2004a). Two graduate students, one of whom was earlier interviewed as part of a 2002 review into the department, argued that the department could have worked its differences out and that splitting the department was a violation of subsidiarity. The strong response against the split was indicative of the fact that many of the graduate students had been attracted to Notre Dame because of its pluralist programme. There was also opposition among undergraduate students – both to the split itself and also to the process by which the split occurred, with students complaining of the lack of input or sufficient levels of forewarning.

When the split was engineered in 2003, fifteen members of the original department (all of whom voted against the split) moved to ECOP and five staff (who voted in favour of the split) moved to DEE, which from the outset referred to itself as a 'neoclassical' department (Thornton 2012). Rather strangely, it appears that criterion for admission to ECOP was not theoretical, as there were at least two members of ECOP who self-identified as neoclassical; indeed Ruccio argues that, depending on how one defines orthodoxy and its sub-disciplines, one could argue that the majority of staff in ECOP could be defined as orthodox. In any event, the key point is that it was not by any means a purely heterodox department and was in fact quite pluralist. The division of staff between departments seems to have been based on, or at least correlates with, how faculty members voted on the split. Another alternative, or at least contributing factor, may have been whether a particular staff member had not only published orthodox economics research, but had published enough of their research in the 'right' orthodox economics journals.

ECOP were not allowed to recruit new staff or even replace staff who had retired or left. A staff freeze was recommended in the 2002 Blue Ribbon Report, but it was then only proposed as a short-term measure, which was to be removed when DEE had grown to equal size with ECOP. In general, there was a marked asymmetry in the resourcing, promotion and marketing between the two departments with ECOP being subject to relative neglect. Indeed, Ruccio argues that 'from the very beginning in 2003, ECOE received considerable support from the administration (from salaries to public relations) and ECOP was marginalized and undermined in every conceivable manner' (Ruccio in Thornton 2015, p. 2).

A notable feature of the split was that DEE was given effective ownership and control of the entire graduate programme in economics, with ECOP staff being prohibited from offering their own programme. The rationale for this given by the then Provost, Nathan Hatch, was that resourcing the programme would be problematic. Furthermore there was not enough 'quality and reputation in the field to warrant a full doctoral program' (cited in Donovan 2004b, p. 2). Such a rationale sits awkwardly with the international reputation of some of the political economy staff. Furthermore, given that there was demonstrated student demand for Notre Dame's pluralist postgraduate programme, the necessary resourcing would normally be expected to flow from student enrolment revenue (as is the case in most graduate programmes). Given these stated rationales of reputation and resourcing, it seems justified to wonder whether an ECOP graduate programme was forbidden for other reasons. For example, it would have meant ECOP would then be included in the influential National Research Council Rankings on Research Doctorate Programmes. Another possibility is that the university administration may also have simply disliked the idea of re-establishing a graduate programme that had a clear political economy orientation.

After the split, there was some discussion within ECOP about developing an MA programme, but again the administration refused to support such an initiative. ECOP was thus confined to having an undergraduate programme only, though ECOP staff often took on the responsibility of assisting graduate students who had enrolled in the previous pluralist incarnation of the graduate programmes and who needed a level of support and direction that DEE was unable and/or unwilling to provide.

ECOP had some input into the title given to their department. One option considered was the title 'Department of Public Policy'. However, because many staff wanted the term 'economics' to form part of the name, the compromise was 'Economics and Policy Studies'. 'Political economy' was also one of the names considered, but the Department of Political Science at Notre Dame objected to the use of that name. How strong that resistance was, whether negotiation was possible, or how indicative such resistance would be amongst more US political science departments is unclear at this point.

ECOP did not exhibit the interpersonal tensions that were apparent in the department before the split, and faculty and support staff worked well together. Economics staff within ECOP were able to go about their business: continuing to teach their courses, conduct their research, and be involved in service much as they did when we were all in a single department. ECOP was given primary responsibility for the undergraduate programme but both departments shared the teaching responsibilities.

There was little interaction between the departments from the very beginning and almost no interaction by the end. For example, there were complaints from some ECOP staff that, despite sustained efforts, they were not able to procure sufficient levels of information about seminars in DEE (Rakowski 2010). No ECOP staff member was able to teach courses in the DEE graduate programme. Initially one member of ECOP was selected to participate in graduate admissions in economics, but this eventually stopped.

The university dissolved ECOP in 2010. There does not appear to be any publicly available document that set out a detailed rationale for its dissolution. This lack of documentation contrasts with the 2002 *Blue Ribbon Report* that recommended dividing economics. There were some public statements made by John McGreevy, Dean of the College of Arts and Letters, but these are somewhat hard to understand. McGreevy argued that the move was to encourage economic diversity and to allow ECOP staff better to participate in the economic conversation, yet it is not explained how dissolving the department and scattering economists across other departments across the university would do this (Glenn 2009; Tierney 2010). In 2010 McGreevy made the forecast that 'in the long run, we're going to have more economic diversity, not less',' and 'In the new Department of Economics, we're going to want economic diversity' (cited in Tierney 2010, p. 2). Given all that had transpired at Notre Dame to this point (not to mention subsequently) such statements and explanations seem rather surprising. Ruccio recalls in meetings with the university administration that two rationales were mentioned to him. The first rationale was that ECOP, as it existed, was not viable. The second rationale was that ECOP was unnecessary as its staff could all be employed in other departments and centres.

What would the term 'unviable' mean? There were no claims made by the administration that the department was financially insolvent. Indeed, because ECOP was not allowed to replace staff who had retired or left, its demand on resources was getting smaller rather than larger. Perhaps it had become unviably small? Again, it appears not: the department was still of a reasonable size and this would have been likely to continue for at least a decade, even under the staff freeze. In any case, the obvious way to remedy the problem of inadequate size would have been to revoke the freeze on replacing staff.

What about the rationale that it would work at least as well to distribute ECOP staff across other departments? The issue with such reasoning is that once staff are allocated to other academic departments there is no longer any institutional base for political economists. Furthermore, once staff were placed with other departments they would most likely have responsibilities to teach in that department's disciplinary area(s) and to publish research within the disciplinary focus of that department. None of this means that some political economy research and teaching would not continue, just that it would be an inferior arrangement.

Perhaps research rankings were the underlying rationale for the dissolution of ECOP? This was denied as a rationale in a statement by McGreevy, yet in the same breath he pointed to the merits of ranking and stated that 'I think it's unacceptable for Notre Dame to have a major department ranked 109' (cited in Tierney 2010, p. 2). Was ranking then an issue? Ruccio (in Thornton 2013) asserts that ECOP was not officially ranked during its existence. Given this, McGreevy may be positing a ranking of 109 hypothetically. In any case, much depends on whether ranking regimes rank individual departments within a university, or alternatively, rank a university's overall performance in an academic discipline. If ranking is done by academic discipline, this creates an incentive for economists to purge the production of all political economy research not only from their own department but also from any other department in the university for fear that political economy research will drag down the ranking of economic research. Such issues further support the logic of establishing political economy research as a separate discipline of political economy – at least for the purposes of research. Biased research assessment regimes that aggregate political economy and economic research into a single ranking do appear to create strong incentives for orthodox economists to try to prevent political economy research occurring anywhere within a university.

Ruccio is of the view that the decision to disband ECOP was made at the very highest levels of the university with mid-level administrators then given the job of trying to justify a decision they may not have been involved in, or which they themselves may not have fully understood or supported. Ruccio's hypothesis is that upper administration simply didn't want any department where there was a concentration of political economists. His view is that this preference may have been driven by pressure from some of the university's existing wealthy financial donors, or as a ground-clearing exercise to attract more wealthy financial donors. It should be noted that there is no supporting documentation for this claim, though as a general idea it is hardly without precedent. Steinbaum and Weisberger (2015) point to cases of donor influence on economics departments at Florida State, Kansas, and numerous others, where the objective has been to rout out any challenge to free market orthodoxy. It can also be pointed out there is a broad alliance between economics and the business establishment that allows the discipline to procure funding far in excess of what is available to many other disciplines (Steinbaum & Weisberger 2015), thus making economics sensitive to any perception that it is not sufficiently pro-business. Similarly, Lee's history of heterodox economics in the United States and United Kingdom (Lee 2009) emphasises regular hostility to heterodox economists not only by orthodox economists, but also by university administration, business and government.

Notre Dame now has only a few remnants from its pluralist past. Former ECOP faculty have either now retired, found employment at other universities, or work in other departments and programmes where they have diminished scope to offer courses and conduct research in economics. Some faculty members have offered to cross-list their courses with the Department of Economics, but have been turned down. There are still two non-orthodox courses offered at the upper-undergraduate level. One is a writing-intensive seminar capped at twenty students; the other course is on Marxian Economics which has enrolments of fifteen to twenty students each time it's offered. However, these upper electives are marooned in that students receive no prior education in these traditions, nor can they undertake any subsequent coursework to build their understanding. Previously, first-year introductory economics at Notre Dame was able at least to flag clearly the presence of the various political economy traditions. This then supported enrolments in specialised political economy courses at second- and third-year level. Obviously, so much can subsequently hinge on whether the large first-year subjects are genuinely introductory economics courses or just introductory neoclassical economics subjects pretending to be introductory economics.

The department of Economics and Econometrics was renamed in 2010 and is now simply called the Department of Economics. Its mission statement is notable for the fact that it identifies itself solely as a neoclassical economics department:

> Our mission is to achieve and to sustain excellence in research and teaching at both the undergraduate and graduate levels. We are a neoclassical economics department committed to rigorous theoretical and quantitative analysis in teaching and research. Members of our department have specialties in the areas of micro and macro theory, econometrics, labor, monetary, international, and environmental economics.
>
> (Department of Economics 2015, p. 1)

The statement in general signifies just how much economics at Notre Dame is now just like nearly all other economics departments in the United States and elsewhere.

The case of Notre Dame will remain a relevant case study for those trying to understand the non-plural nature of contemporary economics and what might be done to reform it. Particular problems in this instance appear to have been the alleged hostile stance of senior management at Notre Dame towards pluralism and heterodoxy, the usual problem of research ranking regimes (which is of particular importance in status-conscious universities that have a high overall ranking) and incomprehension of political economists by orthodox economists. The Notre Dame case also illustrates that relations between orthodox economists and political economists can easily become strained. It adds weight to the idea that such departments require a head of school who is willing and able to embrace pluralism and who is able to promote a culture and other arrangements that actively supportive it.

Whilst the former members of ECOP were all implacably opposed to institutional separation, and time has warranted their opposition in this instance, it is nonetheless argued here that the *idea* of separation was not, of itself, the problem. A separate and prospering political economy department would appear to have been possible. The key issue seems to have been the inability of the university to set up the political economy department in a manner that gave it a reasonable opportunity to prosper and maintain itself. The university espoused the rhetoric of mutual flourishing through institutional independence without making the necessary institutional commitments to make it a reality.

Political economy at the University of Sydney

The University of Sydney, founded in 1850, is Australia's oldest university. It is a member of Australia's 'elite' Group of Eight Universities. In 2015 it was ranked 25th in the QS World University Rankings. The university has sixteen faculties and schools and has a total of nearly 50,000 students enrolled in its programmes. The University has an economics department but also a dedicated political economy department which was established as a breakaway department from the university's economics department. The Department of Political Economy (DPE) conducts teaching and research in institutional economics, Marxian economics, Post-Keynesian economics, ecological economics and feminist economics. It also provides some coverage of neoclassical economics, albeit from a largely critical perspective. For example, the second-year subject Economic Theories of Modern Capitalism provides a substantial coverage of neoclassical theory and the first-year subject Economics as a Social Science also provides some coverage. In other words, whilst being focused on heterodox traditions of political economy, some coverage of orthodox economics occurs, demonstrating a pluralist orientation.

The survey examined in Chapter 7 revealed that the department teaches 41.5 per cent of all political economy subjects in Australian universities. It has also played an important part in producing political economists who have then gone on to teach in other universities, triggering a process of circular and cumulative causation that has led to the teaching of political economy across the Greater Sydney area:

> Almost all the faculty involved in teaching these courses [throughout Greater Sydney] have a connection of a fairly direct kind (especially through PhD supervision) with the the University of Sydney Political Economy movement. In a manner resonant of the cumulative causation theory of industrialization, graduates of Sydney PE have often found jobs at universities 'close to home' and then have sought to introduce non-orthodox courses at these universities. The existence of this cluster of heterodox courses then provides a steady base of casual tutoring work for postgraduate students, and potential supervisors, who then further expand the pool of faculty pushing for the introduction of heterodox courses in the region.
>
> (Argyrous 2006, pp. 61–2)

The formation of the department was the result of a four-decade period of dispute about how economics should be taught within the university's Department of Economics. The complexity, intensity and duration of the dispute is demonstrated by the fact that it has its own extensive literature, including a monograph (Butler, Jones & Stilwell 2009), a symposium (Groenewegen 2009a, 2009b; Hawkins 2009; O'Donnell 2009), journal articles (Jones & Stilwell 1986; Stilwell 2006, 2011), a chapter in a vice-chancellor's memoir (Williams 2005), a discussion of the dispute in official histories of the Business and Economics Faculty (Groenewegen 2009a) and of the University of Sydney (Williams 2006), and several cubic metres of archival records on the dispute at the Fisher Library at the University of Sydney.

For all the abundance of material, the analysis of the dispute is highly polarised: a reflection of the fact that nearly all of the analysis has been undertaken by those who were directly involved in either side of what was a long and bitter dispute. In general, the protagonists have a poor opinion of each other's rendering of the dispute, and some would almost certainly have a poor opinion of how the dispute will be described here. A thorough analysis of the dispute that can adequately consider every claim and counterclaim within the dispute warrants an entire doctoral thesis. Given this, the focus here is not to provide the definitive account of the DPE story, but to instead focus on the factors that lead to the creation of a separate institutional base for political economy and to evaluate the possibility that what has occurred at USYD represents a general model of reform that could be replicated at other universities.

The origins of the dispute can be traced back to the late 1960s and 1970s when some staff members in the Department of Economics (this group is hereafter referred to as the political economists) sought to develop a greater presence for political economy. At this point they were not seeking to establish a separate department or a new degree, though they wanted political economy to be at the core rather than the periphery of the department's curriculum. This was a surprisingly bold ambition, then as much as now. Their ambition prompted them to reject a 1972 offer to develop a single second- or third-year elective in 'radical economics'. To accept a single upper-level elective was seen as insufficient and also as a strategic error that was likely to dissipate the momentum to achieve something more substantial. While this bold decision has turned out to be far-sighted, the rejection of an upper-level elective subject in radical economics antagonised the economics professors (Hogan 1974; Simkin 1975), who complained of 'there never having been a willingness to compromise or seek a measure of mutual accommodation' (Hogan 1974, p. 8).

The lack of success in establishing political economy in the curriculum led to a significant degree of sustained protest on the part of both political economists and their students (this group of staff and students quickly came to refer to themselves as the 'Political Economy Movement'), who staged various protests, conferences and also developed their own teaching materials. The most substantial of these materials was the 1976 two-volume *Readings in Political Economy* (Stilwell & Wheelwright 1976). The foreword, written by the Dean of the faculty, G. A. J.

Simpson Lee, variously seen as one of the political economists, or someone sympathetic to them, gives a sense of the sharpness of the conflict and the intensity of feeling:

> I should have liked to have been able to say in this 'Foreword' that it is a matter of pride and propriety that this highly innovative and important book should have originated in the oldest, largest and most illustrious university in Australia, but that would be to mislead the reader into believing that things are as they should be in such an institution. In fact, the book is born of a long and bitter struggle involving staff and students in the Department of Economics for the right to try and come to a better and fuller understanding of how the economic system really works and how it can be made to serve the welfare of mankind.
>
> One day the history of this struggle will be written, and its repercussions throughout the University of Sydney and the wider academic world will be documented. Until that time, the reader who gains enlightenment from this volume cannot know what efforts were made to deprive him of it.
>
> (Simpson Lee in Stilwell & Wheelwright 1976, p. v)

One of the first examples of significant collective action was the staging of a day of protest in 1973. The protests involved the boycotting of lectures and the staging of alternative workshops. A proposal to establish political economy subjects was also developed and put forward. Such actions contributed to the faculty establishing the first of three committees of inquiry (the Mills Committee). The committee issued a report which recommended establishing a separate department of political economy. The recommendation was approved by a majority of the faculty, but was opposed by the economics department and on this basis vetoed by the Vice-Chancellor, Bruce Williams (Williams 2005).

One of the key rationales for rejecting a separate department had been that there was no intellectual basis for separation (Hogan 1974; Simkin 1975). This was disputed by the political economists (Butler, Jones & Stilwell 2009; Stilwell 1988). That this occurred, illustrates the point made in Chapter 4: that categorisation in the social sciences is strategically important and that developing and articulating the case that political economy can be considered as a distinct discipline (or at least a distinct branch of economics) is important. In any event, it is quite significant to note that the university had *already* subdivided economics by creating a separate Department of Economic Statistics and a separate Department of Economic History. There appear to have been no arguments that these departments had not been able to integrate their teaching and other responsibilities with the Department of Economics, as required. Nor is there any record of long struggle and resistance to their establishment. Given this, even if the university did not view political economy as a separate discipline, the departments of economic history and economic statistics provide a clear precedent for establishing a separate department of political economy. The situation illustrates a point made in Chapter 4 that both the creation of disciplines and departments is significantly shaped by non-intellectual considerations such as administrative convenience, tradition, path-dependence and the distribution of institutional power within universities – something which is in turn affected by the distribution of power in society.

In 1975 the political economists established a first-year undergraduate course in political economy. This was followed by a second-year course in 1976. The courses attracted strong enrolments. Jones and Stilwell (1986) state that by the 1980s, the political economy subjects were approaching 50 per cent of all enrolments in the economics department. The fact that enrolments were so strong could only have hardened opposition from within the economics departments: generally a token political economy subject with minor enrolments can be tolerated, but these much larger political economy enrolments genuinely challenged the dominance of economics.

In 1976 the second committee of inquiry was established (the Ward committee). It recommended the establishment of an 'independent unit' of political economy within the Department of Economics, but this recommendation for a quasi-department was also rejected by the Department of Economics, with the Vice-Chancellor again supporting the economics department's decision.

Stilwell (2006) argues that the hostility towards political economy from economists, combined with the lack of support for political economy by the then Vice-Chancellor, meant that subsequent attempts to develop political economy further from within the economics department at the University of Sydney were very limited. A particular frustration was not being able to offer a third-year subject in political economy (thus establishing a three-year sequence or major). Another frustration was that political economy could not be offered at an honours or postgraduate level. The political economists also complained of discrimination in matters of hiring and promotion of staff (Jones & Stilwell 1986). The resistance that the political economists encountered in curriculum development, appointments and promotions was usually justified on the basis of protecting academic standards (Butler, Jones & Stilwell 2009). However, the determination of standards was a case of economists viewing political economy through the paradigm of orthodox economics.

In 1981 ongoing protest and agitation led to the establishment of a third committee of inquiry (the Wilkes Committee). The 1982 report produced by this committee recommended the establishment of a third-year undergraduate and honours course in political economy. It also recommended that the first-year political economy course be deleted from the curriculum and that the Department of Economics teach a single introductory economics course that contained both economics and political economy content. The rationale for this recommendation was that first-year students should not have to choose between approaches at such an early point in their university studies. The recommendation was implemented, and by 1984 all first-year students in economics were doing a course that was one-third Marxian and institutional, and two-thirds neoclassical (Butler, Jones & Stilwell 2009).

This jointly taught economics–political economic course subject is worthy of specific comment. From the standpoint of pluralism, an introductory subject of this nature is desirable. At least one of the political economists states that it could have provided the foundation for a lasting solution to the dispute, though he also points out that 'no one was enthusiastic at the time' (cited in Gilling 2010, p. 1). The lack of enthusiasm by the political economists is evident in the fact that they abstained from the departmental vote to establish the subject (Groenewegen 2009a). A key source of their ambivalence was that it involved the removal of the first-year political economy subject whose existence had been so hard-won (Butler, Jones & Stilwell 2009). While the political economists were not initially enthusiastic about the subject, they engaged with their responsibilities. They placed the blame for eventual removal of the subject upon the economists: 'in retrospect it worked well, and could have provided a lasting solution. Unfortunately, Hogan, Simkin and the then Dean ...were adamantly opposed to it, and eventually succeeded in scuttling it. Structural pluralism discomfited them' (Stilwell cited in Gilling 2010, p. 1). The political economists also claim that attempts were made to move political economy and other so-called 'softer' subjects to other faculties. The political economists resisted these attempts as the terms of the transfer were deemed undesirable. The political economists also argued that because the economics professors were not in a position to directly remove the PE subjects, they worked with the then Dean to prevent students who were doing a Bachelor of Economics from undertaking political economy subjects (Jones & Stilwell 1986). A new degree, Bachelor of Economics (Social Sciences), was established for students who wanted to do political economy. This degree, despite some very sharp press criticism from conservatives in and outside the university, turned out to be popular and was chosen by one-third of all students in the faculty (Butler, Jones & Stilwell 2009). Enrolments benefited from the fact that the political economists had managed to influence the structure of the degree, so that it was quite open to enrolments from students studying other social sciences (Butler, Jones & Stilwell 2009; Stilwell 2006).

The 1990s were not quite as dramatic as previous decades, and the political economists consolidated their previous gains by establishing both a Masters degree and a PhD programme. In 1999, as part of a university-wide initiative to restructure departments into schools, the new dean created the School of Economics and Political Science, in the process establishing political economy as a separate 'discipline' within that school. This outcome was less the result of collective action and protest and more to do with the faculty wanting to boost its image and credentials as a business faculty. The Dean of the faculty had previously complained that the profile of the political economists had made it more difficult for him to secure the support of business (Butler, Jones & Stilwell 2009). Thus, by delineating the political economists as belonging to a separate discipline from economics, the faculty could create an economics department that had more of the appearance of being business orientated. This is a very clear illustration of how political economy, with its generally more critical and reformist (rather than celebrationary), perspective on capitalism, can sit awkwardly and precariously inside a business faculty.

In 2008 the political economists, as part of a larger restructuring in the university, were transferred out of the Faculty of Business and Economics into the Faculty of Arts and Social Sciences. It was at this point that political economy finally became a separate department. Significantly, political economy has subsequently prospered in a way that was not possible previously. Enrolments boomed, which led to the appointment of additional staff (Thornton 2008). This has occurred despite little change to subject offerings or subject names. Part of the explanation for this appears to be that offering political economy subjects from within the Arts faculty has appeared to make them not only more accessible to Arts faculty students, but also more attractive generally (Thornton 2011b). It seems plausible to suggest that basing the subjects in a social science faculty may have had a framing effect upon students. It should also be noted that in the Arts faculty there have not been the same issues of having to play down the presence of political economy to cultivate the support of the business community.

In 2011, the future of DPE was challenged by a proposal to merge it with the Department of Government and International Relations (University of Sydney 2011). However, the combined efforts of the staff and postgraduate students managed to defeat the proposal. That the proposal was mooted in the first place appears to be, at least in part, a reflection of the fact that the Dean of the faculty was particularly enamoured of the 'Chicago Model' of a strong economics department, politics department and philosophy department (Thornton 2011b).

Another constraint is that DPE is currently not permitted to offer a dedicated Bachelor of Political Economy as there is a policy in place to limit the number of degrees being offered within the faculty. This has meant that the most specialised degree offered is the rather generic-sounding Bachelor of Political, Economic and Social Sciences. It appears that the challenges now facing DPE are as much to do with the uncertainties and vagaries of corporate managerialism within the university system as they are with intellectual and ideological hostility.

The focus will now turn to four aspects of the dispute that are most fundamental to our purposes here: the role of collective struggle; the basis for opposition to political economy; the role of marketing and networking; and the advantages and disadvantages of having a separate institutional base.

The establishment of DPE was characterised by collective struggle. Those involved in the political economy movement see the role of collective protest and struggle not as an incidental by-product in the goal of establishing political economy, but as a key driver of the changes that occurred (Butler, Jones & Stilwell 2009; Jones & Stilwell 1986). Such struggles included the on-campus protests, staff and students going on strike, and the Vice-Chancellor's office being occupied by students. There were also a few instances of graffiti and damage to university buildings, as well as graffiti to the private homes of one or two of those who opposed the political economists (Groenewegen 2009a, 2009b). There were also times when protest spilled over into mild violence, though there are differences of opinion on some of the details of such instances and how they should be understood (Groenewegen 2009a; O'Donnell 2009). Those who opposed the political economists described it as a serious issue (Groenewegen 2009b; Williams 2005,

2006), while those within the political economy movement considered instances of violence as regrettable, but relatively minor (Butler, Jones & Stilwell 2009; O'Donnell 2009).

It is necessary to understand that for most of the dispute, the power structures within the university were not geared towards democratic participation. The Vice-Chancellor and departmental professors had a very dominant position in what has been described as a 'master–servant structure' (Jones & Stilwell 1986, p. 30). If the current era is one of the 'God-Administrator', the previous era was one of the 'God-Professor'. A genuinely collegial and democratic structure has been elusive throughout. It was this absence of democratic structures within the university that led many within the political economy movement to conclude that mass protest and struggle were necessary:

> Between 1974 and 1976, often hundreds and sometimes thousands of students were active in the movement. It was not only positive personal experiences, but also mistakes I made that led me to assimilate the idea that change was crucially the product of mass action and militancy.
>
> (Kuhn 2009, p. 178)

> In its early years, the PE movement learned a vital lesson. One may have excellent intellectual arguments, but when power in a discipline or institution overrides reason, rational argument can make no further progress unassisted. Where reason is necessary but insufficient, people with resolve also campaign on the terrain of power and decision-making.
>
> (O'Donnell 2009, p. 91)

It is important to recognise that campaigning was not always dramatic or openly conflicting: it also involved steady and persistent efforts through more established channels. The importance of undertaking this more mundane and unglamorous work is evident in the reflections of one of the students involved in the earlier phases of the struggle:

> On reflection, the real learning from being in the PE movement was about how our society works and what levers can be used to effect change and mobilise people. It was about how to force your agenda, how to keep your issue alive and *not be taken out of the game in the process*. In practice, that meant taking action with the ombudsman, petitioning the Senate, soliciting the support of unions and journalists, and writing in the University newspapers, Honi Soit, the University News and Union Recorder.
>
> (Porteous 2009, pp. 74–5 emphasis added)

While the political economists themselves were not involved in any of the more dramatic manifestations of protest (such as the occupation of the Vice-Chancellor's office), their unwillingness to attempt to influence or restrain these incidents was a point of tension within the Department of Economics. It was felt that it was inappropriate to involve students in what was seen as being a dispute between academics. By contrast, the political economists themselves saw the role of students as being critical, arguing that, 'one lesson from the political economy struggle is clear: cooperative and sustained commitment by students and staff is an essential ingredient for turning concern into challenge and struggle into success' (Butler, Jones & Stilwell 2009, p. 191).

Why is cooperation between staff and students so essential? There are several reasons. First, staff and students can apply pressure and advance the agenda in different ways. There are simply certain activities that are suited, or even limited, to that which staff can undertake. For example, pushing the agenda in a departmental meeting is obviously limited to staff within that department. Pushing the agenda through the student union and student newspaper is obviously something that must come from students. Second, staff and students can take similar action in similar forums. This duplication can add weight and momentum. Third, staff and students can motivate, and learn from each other.

It is clear that the institutional structures of the university frustrated the political economists, but why were those who held the most power in this structure so opposed to their agenda? This is not a simple question to answer, for two reasons. First, within the economics department one can identify to two clear poles in terms of those who were strongly and consistently for and against, but there were also some economists who supported one side on some matters and were at least sympathetic to the other side on other matters. Thus, ascribing simple 'group think' opposition is not possible or fair. However, given the constraints of space, and the purposes of this book, it is best to focus on three key protagonists who most clearly opposed the agenda of the political economists and who also held the most institutional power: Professor Bruce Williams (Vice-Chancellor for most of the dispute), Professor Warren Hogan (head of the economics department for most of the dispute), Professor Colin Simkin (a professor in the economics department during most of the dispute).

The second reason for the complex nature of the opposition was that it not only involved intellectual and ideological motivations, but also non-intellectual motivations. For example there have been some claims that the dispute was partially about personality clashes. It has also been claimed that the dispute was partly about some individuals acting to promote or protect their career prospects; this particular claim has been made by both sides in the dispute, though no individual admits to it, nor is any individual explicitly and publicly named as being guilty of it (Jones & Stilwell 1986; Lodewijks 2007). It is quite difficult to evaluate precisely the role of non-intellectual motivations. However, ultimately it is quite clear that the dispute had a very strong intellectual and ideological component to it and that much of the explanatory weight can be placed here.

The Vice-Chancellor, Bruce Williams, argues that the dispute would never have occurred had it not been for the rise of student radicalism in the 1960s and 1970s. He ascribes the general rise of such radicalism to the Vietnam War (Williams 2005, 2006). Williams primarily justifies his actions and inactions in terms of respecting the wishes of the Department of Economics:

I was often asked why, having created a school of philosophy with two departments, I did not do the same in economics. That I did not do so was partly explained by the outcome of my discussions with staff, as outlined above, and partly because there was no danger of losing the best staff, as there had been in philosophy.

(Williams 2005, p. 121)

Such reasoning may well have been part of his motivation, but given that more than anyone involved, he had the power to impose a resolution, it seems reasonable to try to assess whether his motivation was quite as simple as this.

O'Donnell indicates that it should be remembered that both Hogan and Simkin were appointed under Williams's tenure as Vice-Chancellor and that he supported their vision of wanting to create a department that would be seen by the world at large as being modern and successful (Thornton 2011a). One can also see some indication of Williams having had a degree of methodological opposition to the political economists. For example, he describes political economy as 'politicised economics' (Williams 2005, p. 105), a term which suggests a belief that there exists some positive, objective, value-free, non-political economics. Williams is interesting from a methodological or ideological perspective in that he made a series of statements in his early career that can be plausibly read as being quite supportive of the type of vision for economics that the political economists were pursuing. For example, his 1953 article 'Economics and public policy' asserted, justifiably, that there were no distinct boundaries between the disciplines, no agreed definitions of economics or of other social sciences (Williams 1953). Williams also had an early dalliance with socialism (Williams 1943) which, ironically enough, was reproduced, in part, in the first textbook produced by the political economists (see Stilwell & Wheelwright 1976).

Despite such leanings in the early works of Williams, by the time of the dispute he was no ideological or methodological radical. Indeed, the political economists viewed him as a conservative, pointing to the fact that as well as serving as Vice-Chancellor, he served four terms as a member of the Reserve Bank Board of Australia between 1969 and 1981 (Butler, Jones & Stilwell 2009; Jones & Stilwell 1986; O'Donnell 2009). Holding multiple important roles in the existing economic and social order would hardly predispose him to the political economists who were, and generally remain, orientated to criticising and reforming or changing this order.

The head of department through most of the dispute, Warren Hogan had a strong belief that the dispute had its origins in the inability of the political economists (and the university as a whole) to accept the idea that the professors of economics in the department knew best. For Hogan, it was an issue of 'academic leadership' and it was 'the central issue in the academic debate on political economy' (Hogan 1974, p. 8). Hogan viewed younger members of staff, and those of lesser rank to professor, as only being able to make 'relatively minor contributions' and to have only 'limited grounds for pressing a viewpoint' (Hogan 1974, p. 3). Furthermore, Hogan strongly objected to the outside intrusion of both the faculty and the professorial board (Hogan 1974); these bodies were not seen as being in a legitimate position to dictate to the professors of economics how best to manage their department and what was taught. This rationale of academic leadership is made clearly enough, but in itself it does not answer *why* Hogan opposed the political economists, only that he felt entitled to reject their views and agendas.

Hogan never took the standpoint of the political economists as a serious intellectual challenge. He also argues that others should also not have taken it as seriously as they did. For example, when recalling his colleague Colin Simkin he states:

> He found Sydney a challenging experience. He was unable to grip the political economy dispute. He saw it as an academic issue while others, including myself, treated it as purely academic politics and not an academic issue per se. Simkin wrote any number of papers about issues in dispute in an effort to bring them into focus. The negative outcome of his efforts brought him disappointment.
>
> (Hogan cited in Lodewijks 2007, p. 451)

Hogan did not regard political economy as a distinct area of knowledge. For him there was 'no distinctive feature in 'political economy' that would substantiate academic claims for a separate discipline' (Hogan 1974, p. 10). He was resolute that the department needed to adopt the generally held view of academic economists (presumably its senior economists) about what ought to be taught. Hogan saw the political economy dispute as arising not out of inherent tensions or problems within economics and political economy, but because the political economists and their students were behaving opportunistically, being aware that the university had previously split the philosophy department following the intellectual schism that had emerged over feminist and continental philosophy, 'In my judgement the development of sustained opposition to the economics programme had its origin in the philosophy dispute in July 1973 ... It showed the possibilities for change in the economics department' (Hogan 1974, p. 7). The splitting of the philosophy department does have a role in providing one of the triggers or the initial inspiration for the dispute (see Keen in Butler, Jones & Stilwell 2009). But according to one of the protagonists in the philosophy dispute, Professor Paul Redding, the two disputes are not closely connected in any general sense (Thornton 2011c).

While Hogan was dismissive of the political economists on intellectual grounds, he did take the dispute seriously in political and ideological terms:

> The focus on quantitative work and the subsequent broadening into how to approach economics and what economics was about revealed what was at stake in terms of political and ideological confrontation. Social, economic and political developments in the past couple of decades have cast this challenge as some quaint academic posturing.
>
> (Hogan cited in Lodewijks 2007, pp. 450–1)

The quotation above seems to suggest that Hogan may have viewed the political economy dispute through the prism of the Cold War (something that was raging for most of the political economy dispute), or at the very least saw it as having clear implications for both economy and society. While none of the political economists advocated Stalinist-style command socialism, it is true that the majority were reformist-orientated institutionalists or Marxians: both groups are capable of being seen with considerable suspicion and fear by those who hold strong right-wing ideological positions.

Something of Hogan's ideological orientation can be gleaned from his association with the Centre for Independent Studies (CIS) a stridently classical liberal think-tank that views its role as being 'actively engaged in supporting a free enterprise economy and a free society under limited government where individuals can prosper and fully develop their talents' (Centre for Independent Studies 2011, p. 3). In the official history of the CIS, Hogan is praised for his role as an economist and for his work and dedication in building up the CIS profile in economic policy and philosophical and constitutional issues (Centre for Independent Studies 2011). A founding idea of the CIS was that what occurred in the intellectual sphere was of central importance to the libertarian agenda. For instance, the founding director of the CIS, Greg Lindsay, recalls that:

> [D]uring 1975 I had read Hayek's essay 'The Intellectuals and Socialism', which in one sense was the most important piece that I'd read. It made me realise that what I was seeing was an intellectual problem, not a political problem.
>
> (Lindsey & Norton 1996, p. 17)

Despite being largely dismissive of the political economists on intellectual grounds, Hogan nonetheless outlined a basic methodological opposition to the political economists:

> The most testing immediate issue [on his arrival in the department] was about the amount of quantitative work which should be required of all undergraduates taking the Bachelor of Economics (B.Ec.) degree. This caused the most turbulence initially which left me dumbfounded, given the requirements were rather modest by standards in other institutions. This feature emerged initially as the 'lightning rod' for disagreements on what Economics was about. If undergraduates cannot understand basic aspects of quantitative work, testing the applicability of theoretical constructs becomes very hard to resolve. A state of indeterminacy may well have been comfortable for some not wishing to seek preferences of one claim to validity over another in order to sustain unsubstantiated claims.
>
> (Hogan cited in Lodewijks 2007, p. 450)

Such a position is based on the received view of science within economic methodology. Hogan gives particular emphasis to quantitative methods for the testing of theory. This draws on a different philosophy of science from that of the political economists who were early adopters of Thomas Kuhn's work on scientific paradigms.

Colin Simkin was one of the Professors of Economics and was an active player in the dispute. His *Economics vs Political Economy* (Simkin 1975), a collection of his and the political economists' writings on the dispute, shows that he sought to engage with the political economists on intellectual grounds, though, as has already noted by Hogan, such efforts brought no resolution or mutual acceptance: the divide was just too deep. As one of the political economists wrote,

> [S]ince institutionalists and neo-classicists have basically different attitudes to knowledge, you might guess that they don't have much respect for each other. And you would be right. The tragedy is that the conflict stems from basic differences for which there seems little possibility of resolution.
>
> (Jones 1976, p. 278)

This statement by Jones captures much of the essence of the dispute. Indeed, reading through *Economics vs Political Economy*, it is clear just how opposed the two sides were and how small were the chances of their reconciling or compromising on their positions. Simkin did try to engage with the arguments put forward by the political economists, yet made no progress, viewing their arguments as 'shallow, mistaken and academically pernicious' and as being 'more personal and political than academic' (Simkin 1975, p. 1).

The strength and nature of Simkin's opposition becomes more understandable when it is considered in the context of his long and close association with Karl Popper, who had a 'huge' influence upon him (Hogan in Lodewijks 2007, p. 447). Indeed Popper's *The Open Society and its Enemies* (Popper 1966) was used as a text in one of Simkin's subjects (Lodewijks 2007) and Popper himself acknowledged Simkin's contribution to the development of his own ideas in the preface of *The Open Society and its Enemies* (Hogan 2007). On matters of methodology, Simkin was most concerned about the political economists' Kuhnian leanings. This is readily identifiable in his attack on frameworks or paradigms and his strong commitment to, and defence of, objective truth. He is critical of the Kuhnian framework approach as defeatist, declaring that it 'exaggerates a difficulty into an impossibility' (Simkin 1975, p. 5). He is also critical of the political economists for 'glorifying the intrusion of personal bias', particularly in the sphere of teaching. He seems particularly concerned with the deployment of a 'holistic method that both predicts and facilitates wholesale change' and that 'promotes both sympathy and activism in conflicts' (Simkin 1975, p. 5).

The mention of wholesale change and social conflict in the excerpt above illustrates that Simkin was also opposed to the political economists on both ideological and methodological grounds. Simkin was certainly of a different ideological persuasion, and was understood by prominent economists such as Fred Gruen to belong to a group of Australian 'radical right libertarian economists' (Groenewegen 1979, p. 207). Simkin also had some minor association with the

CIS (Butler, Jones & Stilwell 2009), though not to the same degree as Hogan. Simkin seemed to be deeply concerned about the presence of Marxian and radical leanings amongst the political economists and at various times challenged the political economists to clearly identify their exact stance in regard to Marxist thought (Simkin 1975). His methodological and ideological opposition was passionate and determined:

> Finally, I repeat a denial of the Radical Political Economist's underlying view that objectivity is an impossible, and even undesirable aim, for them or anyone else. There are plenty of examples, even in Economics, of interpersonal agreement about scientific matters – agreement between professional people with very different national, cultural, ethnic, institutional, or economic backgrounds, and with widely different ideologies. Objective science, moreover, has the independent value of providing an intellectual bridge between such people. Assertive intrusion of ideological standpoints can only weaken this bridge, just as it tends to divide teachers from some of their colleagues, teachers from some of their students, and students from some of their fellows. And, more fundamental, denial of objectivity leads, inevitably, to fostering irrational thought and action ... None of this is good, unless it can be held that conflict is a virtue and reason a vice, propositions to which I cannot subscribe.
>
> (Simkin 1975, p. 14)

This tight linking of scientific objectivity to social order can be directly linked back to Hobbes, and it has a genuinely striking affinity with a key point made by Shapin and Schaffer in Chapter 1, where it was argued that the solution to the problem of knowledge is totally enmeshed with finding solutions to the problem of social order. Just as Hobbes argued that if you 'show men what knowledge is and you will show them the grounds of assent and social order' (cited in Shapin & Schaffer 1985, p. 100), so does Simkin argue that the lack of clear and objective knowledge will lead to division, conflict and irrationality of thought and action.

On this issue of social order it is relevant to note the high status and prestige of the University of Sydney. As it is an elite university, many of its graduates became members of the ruling elite in business, government and the media. This meant that the stakes were higher than if the dispute had occurred at a less prestigious university. Various soon to be notable political figures such as Tony Abbott (a former prime minister of Australia) Malcolm Turnbull (the current prime minister of Australia) and Anthony Albanese (a very senior opposition politician) were studying at the University of Sydney during the dispute and all had some involvement in it. Furthermore, in 1975, forty-nine members of the Federal Parliament would sign a petition to query why one of the political economists, Ted Wheelwright, was passed over for promotion (Jones & Stilwell 1986).

As those from the sociology of scientific knowledge point out, 'he who has the most, and the most powerful, allies wins' (Shapin & Schaffer 1985, p. 342). Accordingly, networking and relationship-building has not been ignored by the political economists. The alumni society formed in 2005 is significant and includes a former state premier, a deputy premier, a state treasurer, ministers for housing and local government, state government parliamentarians, a leader of the federal ALP opposition, federal government ministers, a federal public service commissioner and journalists, among others (Butler, Jones & Stilwell 2009). The formation and maintenance of a powerful alumni network is probably a minimum requirement for any other political economy department, given the vicissitudes of university management, the possible backlash of the business sector and assorted other problems that could quickly arise. It should also be noted that the political economists were able to cultivate support and agreements with other social science departments that facilitated a two-way trade in students.

Marketing is also a component of the story. There have been reasonably strong and activist efforts at self-promotion. For example, in 2004 when political economy undergraduate enrolments in the first-year subject were falling the political economists created new promotional material specifically targeted at prospective first-year students and enlisted a group of both current and former political economy students to hand out brochures, put up posters and talk directly to prospective students during the university's annual open day. Putting in this additional effort restored enrolments, but from around 200 to around 400 (Rodrigo 2009; Thornton 2008). Such an active approach to marketing is reasonably rare for political economists:

> Heterodox economists mostly take a rather negative view of marketing as a discipline and profession, seeing it as providing tools that can be used to generate unnecessary wants that are wasteful of resources and make consumers socially competitive and anxious. Although the tools of marketing are indeed often used to manipulate consumer behaviour for private profit ... marketing can also be used to advance socially beneficial causes. Politicians understand the power of good marketing but heterodox economists rarely seem to reflect upon their plight from a marketing standpoint.
>
> (Earl & Peng 2012, p. 451)

We have already examined how DPE has been criticised and opposed by orthodox economists. However, it has also been criticised by other political economists. One such critic is Yanis Varoufakis, a former finance minister of Greece and a high-profile political economist and political commentator (Arnsperger & Varoufakis 2006; Hargreaves-Heap & Varoufakis 2004; Varoufakis 2009, 2010; Varoufakis, Halevi & Theocarakis 2011). Varoufakis was a lecturer in economics at the University of Sydney in the late 1980s and early 1990s, teaching in both the economics and the political economy programmes. Varoufakis's assessment of the political economy programme is ambiguous in that he praises it highly in some respects but condemns it strongly in others. Specifically, he rates it as being intellectually superior: 'political economy graduates understood the world as well as one could after dedicating three to four years of one's life to a university education' (Varoufakis 2007, p. 2). This contrasts with his assessment of the university's orthodox economics graduates, whom he sees as being 'blissfully ignorant of the important economic issues that typified the world they were about to enter. Technically excellent, they combined the philosophical background of a rather primitive computer with the historical understanding of an amnesiac' (Varoufakis 2007, p. 2). Yet he nonetheless argues that the approach pursued at DPE was an 'appallingly bad idea' (Varoufakis 2007, p. 2).

The nub of Varoufakis's concerns is his view that there is an insufficient coverage of neoclassical economics within the political economy programme. In this respect, Varoufakis's position seems quite close to that of Peter Groenewegen, a noted historian of economic thought who was part of the University of Sydney's Department of economics, and who was often directly opposed to the political economists. Groenewegen argues that one of the legacies of the split has been 'imbalances in both sets of teaching programmes' (Groenewegen 2009b, p. 87). For Varoufakis, neoclassical economics is very much a necessary evil:

> [H]owever narrow-minded and vacuous the economic education offered by the mainstream might be; however irrelevant to the understanding of capitalism neoclassical economics is, any attempt to build a curriculum which sidesteps it is bound to backfire. Mainstream economics is a well-entrenched meta-narrative, for better or for worse. Students of capitalism cannot afford to be ignorant of its twists and turns ...
>
> (Varoufakis 2007, p. 4)

An insufficient technical knowledge of neoclassical economics is said to leave DPE students with insufficient ability and confidence to debate with their neoclassical colleagues. Joan Robinson's argument that one should learn economics so as not to be deceived by economists (Robinson 1980) has some relevance to his argument. Varoufakis has put his concerns into action by developing a PhD programme at the University of Athens that sought to expose students 'to the highest forms of mainstream economics', while still claiming to have prevented orthodox economics 'taking over the spirit and direction of the curriculum' (Varoufakis 2007, p. 4).

Varoufakis's criticisms are important and they raise a really fundamental issue: how much neoclassical economics should students be taught in a department that is largely dedicated to political economy, or alternatively, in a department that is avowedly pluralist? Such questions need to be answered by first making quite a few preliminary points. First, some coverage of neoclassical economics is warranted in nearly all economics programmes, because: A. It is entirely true that it is currently the dominant discourse in economics. B. It is consistent with the intellectual pluralism that many political economist's espouse. C. It assists students to understand other competing schools of economics, as these schools are, in significant part, a reaction against the neoclassical school.

Second, it must be acknowledged that there are real opportunity costs incurred by teaching the neoclassical approach in significant detail. It is a substantial undertaking, just as learning the alternative approaches is substantial and time consuming.

Third, staff who seek a pluralist economics can easily underrate how long and difficult it may be to gain a good grasp of any school of economic thought, i.e. they can easily be afflicted by the 'curse of knowledge' – a syndrome whereby a party who is in full possession of a body of knowledge about a topic is very prone to assume that other parties either already have this knowledge, or alternatively, can quickly and easily acquire this knowledge (Heath & Heath 2006). Can the 'curse of knowledge' apply to the field of political economy? Yes it can. Consider the recollections of Potts, who, while not connected with political economy at the University of Sydney, eloquently recalls how confusing and demanding political economy is to learn if one is not introduced to it in a carefully structured and sequential way:

> The thoughtful economist will inevitably be visited by moments of doubt that will thereby admit the possibility of alternatives … Such acts will seldom usher forth immediate enlightenment; more often, the reader will find him or herself estranged within the hermetic seal of heterodox economics, where various points of theory, empiricism and critique that define each school circle impenetrably and self-referentially. Each article presumes that you have read and understood all the others. Even for self-confessed heterodox economists, this rugged aspect of the landscape carries with it in many cases an unwanted and unnecessary sense of isolation. And for students and economists with orthodox training, the absence of clear points of entry, of soft progression and navigational charts, does certainly make for tough going.
> (Potts 2000, pp. ix–x)

Teaching political economy in any depth requires a carefully constructed and sequential suite of subjects. It needs a significant amount of space in the curriculum. How then also to cover neoclassical economics in any real detail without doubling the length of the degree?

The fourth issue to consider is to do with staffing and resourcing. Most degree programmes are not willing, or do not have the resources, to employ the diversity of staff that would be needed to offer a complete suite of economics subjects across neoclassical economics and political economy. Even if a department had sufficient resources, we have already examined how neoclassical economists (if they hold the institutional power) often seek to purge or prevent the teaching of political economy and the employment of political economists.

The fifth issue to consider is that the study of neoclassical economics soon hits diminishing returns in terms of its ability to illuminate the real world. If students are *required* to undertake advanced studies in neoclassical economics, a significant proportion of these students may look back in anger if they come to conclude that their hard labour has not delivered the insights they were seeking. It is an acknowledged problem that economics courses can leave students 'unable to express an opinion of any greater insight regarding economic affairs than a member of the general public' (Sheehan, Embery & Morgan 2015, p. 215). The International Student Initiative for Pluralism in Economics also illustrates the widespread and intense disappointment many students have with the capacity of the economics curriculum to offer the insights they are seeking.

With all the five points just made, let us now answer the question: exactly how much neoclassical economics should be taught? The answer is that there is no fixed answer. The solution is to value and encourage diversity between universities on how much neoclassical economics is taught. Particular universities should be encouraged to produce particular types of graduates with different mixes of orthodox economics and political economy in their education. The outcome will be heterogeneous rather than homogeneous, graduates. This will give rise to certain strengths and weaknesses in what these graduates do and don't know. However, provided students are made aware of what their strengths and weaknesses are, and are also presented with options should they wish to pursue further study of economics in the future, then this is an acceptable situation. It is an outcome of diversity, rather than grey conformity. In fact, the development of heterogeneous, rather than homogeneous graduates is consistent with advancing economic pluralism. It is also a strategy that would appear to be the most effective approach in transferring, developing and applying *detailed* knowledge about each school of economics. The approach just outlined maximises the chances of advanced knowledge in economics and political economy being possessed *somewhere* in society. It should also produce the necessary mix of generalists and specialists to keep economic analysis and public discussion diverse. The approach would produce different kinds of graduates in political economy and economics who are suited for different lines of employment, and whom may work together to compensate for each others possible deficiences.

What would complement the approach just described would be measures to encourage increased trade in students between universities, making it easier to engage in cross-institutional studies in specialist subjects. Given the emergence of online subjects, cross-institutional study is becoming more and more practical. Online subjects should also be able to generate the necessary economies of scale to support a diversity of offerings. However, in saying this it should be emphasised that one of the most important findings that emerges from analysing political economy at the University of Sydney is the strong level of student demand for political economy. It suggests that political economists should not be too fearful of exploring the *various* options that exist for greater institutional independence and differentiation from orthodox economics.

There could also be greater degrees of trade in student enrolments within particular universities. Let us consider how this would happen in the case of the University of Sydney. Because political economy has its own institutional base, and its own cohort of students, it means that negotiations with the university's economics department can now occur between relatively equal partners. Numerous options could be explored. For example, the Department of Economics, by virtue of retaining two or three political economists, has subjects such as *ECOS3004 History of economic thought*, the Sraffian *ECOS3016 Capital and dynamics* that could be claimed as political economy subjects and could therefore become core subjects in the political economy programme. Similarly, the Department of Political Economy has numerous subjects that would broaden the learning of students doing a conventional economics degree. Encouraging more cross-departmental study is the most effective way to address an argument by Groenewegen that the creation of a separate department of political economy at the University of Sydney had resulted in 'imbalances in both sets of teaching programmes' (Groenewegen 2009b, p. 87). Even if one subscribes to the view that the programmes are 'imbalanced', such an outcome is not structurally determined by the creation of a second department: it is created by one or both departments actively deciding to restrict the trade in students across departmental boundaries.

A general model?

It is now appropriate to ponder a most fundamental question: does DPE offer a general model, perhaps *the* general model by which reformers can achieve a pluralist economics? For the political economists who established this department, the answer is clearly yes. They argue that the evidence shows that the strategy of reforming economics from within economics departments is a failed one:

> Islands of heterodoxy exist in departments of economics in a few other universities, but there is no other department that both protects and extends the traditions of political economy and assays the articulation of interdisciplinary connections with other social sciences … The strategy in some other universities of establishing one or more electives in heterodoxy and then seeking to build on these to create a major in political economy alongside other studies in mainstream economics has not worked. There has been the odd success in instituting courses in social economics with mainstream departments – that is, the use of economic concepts in considering social policy questions – but, although that is to be applauded, it does not directly confront the hegemony of neoclassical economics.
>
> (Butler, Jones & Stilwell 2009, p. 182)

Stilwell's assertion at the very beginning of this book about the 'mainstream rolling on forever' is perhaps the definitive articulation of their position. It suggests that reform from within economics department is a Sisyphean task: reformers from within are condemned for all eternity to having to roll a large and heavy boulder up a hill, only to see it then roll back.

It is easy to understand the political economists' advocacy for institutional separation and greater disciplinary differentiation. Traditional departments of economics reforming themselves to become plural, whilst clearly possible, is still very rare, and hybrid strategies (see Chapter 10) have not as yet been widely deployed. Certainly, it is completely implausible to argue that the political economists would have done better had they stayed within the department of economics (either as part of the department or in some semi-autonomous division within the department). Even if at some stage in the future the political economists were later merged back into the department of economics – something they would strongly resist – it would be hard to imagine they would end up any worse off than if they had persisted with a strategy of subservient diplomacy for the past four decades. Indeed, there is an extremely high probability they would have achieved nothing and political economy would be as absent from the University of Sydney as it is from most other universities.

However, despite the impressive results that have been achieved at the University of Sydney, it will not always be viable or desirable to pursue the strategy in every context. Notre Dame and Manitoba University clearly attest to this. Careful thought needs to be given to what is likely to succeed in each particular university. If the strategy were to be pursued, careful consideration would need to be given to establishing a plausible sequence of steps by which it might be achieved. It would generally be unlikely that it would be possible to persuade university administrators to create, from scratch, an entire department of political economy in one fell swoop. The obvious sequence would be to establish a single political economy subject in a department of politics or something similar (or within an economics department if possible), then to develop a three-year major. Alternatively, perhaps a single postgraduate offering would provide a good foundation for future offerings. Another option would be to build towards a separate institutional base via the type of hybrid strategies described in the next chapter. In general, the strategy of institutional separation and strong differentiation would often need to start via the pursuit of some more modest strategy.

Small initial steps may be required, but it is to be emphasised that the 'ambitious' form of institutional separation (separate departments of political economy) should not really be considered as being particularly ambitious because of the many precedents for it in economics and everywhere else. Universities have regularly established departments of economic history and departments of econometrics (and other departments in international relations, organic chemistry and any number of sub-disciplines). What is clear from examining such cases is that that full disciplinary differentiation is not even a required rationale for a separate department: many sub-disciplines in many universities are obviously able to acquire independent departmental status. This fact provides some flexibility in regard to how political economy might be advanced in a particular university. That said, it should still be noted that for the purposes of research there is probably less flexibility and political economy may have to be presented as an entirely separate discipline if it is to have any prospect of its research being assessed fairly. It is to be emphasised that departments can be established for many reasons: administrative considerations, tradition, convention, path-dependence, student enrolments, research income, not to mention considerations of what is likely to promote academic diversity and progress.

It is to be stressed that the the University of Sydney model is of a *general* nature and cannot function, or be followed, as a rigid and detailed template. As Stilwell, notes:

> Struggles can indeed have many twists and turns and create unforeseen dilemmas at particular strategic moments. Successful outcomes depend on staying committed, working with whoever shares the ideals and dealing with

the strategic judgments as the situation evolves. Hardly original lessons, but nonetheless learned and tested in 'the school of hard knocks'.

(Thornton 2011d, p. 1)

History can't repeat exactly, but it is of value to notice the extent to which it can sometimes rhyme.

Clearly, it is being argued here that the reform strategy of strong disciplinary differentiation and institutional separation warrants active and serious consideration. However, at this point it also probably desirable to outline some qualifications and nuances.

First, it is not argued that all political economists should give up on ever finding employment in an economics department: a few positions will continue to be offered and some individual economics departments might even be savvy enough to follow the lead taken by Kingston and Greenwich universities and harness the significant opportunities that could come from a genuine embrace of pluralism. If so, this would be a very good thing.

Second, it is not argued that even if a political economist has managed to gain some foothold in an economics department, they should automatically give up their secure position and emigrate to the social science faculty – if they can find a viable and secure base for themselves in an economics department to do the teaching and research in their area of expertise, this is a good outcome. If they can also cultivate links with other social departments then that would be all the better for political economy, and probably for them as individuals. The argument being made here is not that teaching political economy within traditional centres of economics teaching is somehow a bad thing; it is just that it is becoming more and more difficult to achieve.

Third, what is being advocated here is not intellectual apartheid: economists and political economists of all persuasions, paying due respect to differences of focus and methods employed, should maintain dialogue and seek to cooperate and collaborate wherever that can be fruitful. As was stated in the Introduction, the agenda here is not *against* economics per se, but *for* the advancement of political economy. One can be critical of the exclusionary dominance of neoclassical economics, and in particular its uncritical exposition to students, and still acknowledge that it can make some contribution to economic and social understanding – providing its strengths and weaknesses are properly understood.

Political economy at the University of Sydney presents itself as a model that many reformers might do well to consider actively as an option appropriate for their particular university. Its success in establishing a separate institutional base, then strongly defending it, has worked and brought rare levels of success in promoting a pluralist economics. If a network of similar (but not identical) departments were developed, then it seems very hard to imagine that this would not promote greater pluralism. Other strategies for pluralism can be pursued, but having this strategy somewhere within the mix seems appropriate.

References

Argyrous, G. 1996, 'Teaching Political Economy at Unsw', paper presented to Political Economy Twentieth Anniversary Conference, University of Sydney, 2 July.

Argyrous, G. 2006, 'Alternative Approaches to Teaching Introductory Economics Courses in Australian Universities', *Australasian Journal of Economics Education*, vol. 3, nos. 1 & 2, pp. 58–74.

Argyrous, G. & Thornton, T. B. 2014a, 'Disciplinary Differentiation and Institutional Independence: A Viable Template for a Pluralist Economics', *International Journal of Pluralism and Economics Education*, vol. 5, no. 2, pp. 120–32.

Argyrous, G. & Thornton, T. B. 2014b, 'Introductory Political Economy Subjects in Australian Universities: Recent Trends and Possible Futures', *Australasian Journal of Economics Education*, vol. 10, no. 2, pp. 39–59.

Arnsperger, C. & Varoufakis, Y. 2006, 'What Is Neoclassical Economics? The Three Axioms Responsible for Its Theoretical Oeuvre, Practical Irrelevance and, Thus, Discursive Power', *Post-Autistic Economics Review*, vol. July, no. 38.

Butler, G., Jones, E. & Stilwell, F. J. B. 2009, *Political Economy Now! The Struggle for Alternative Economics at the University of Sydney*, Darlington Press, Sydney.

Centre for Independent Studies 2011, *About the Centre for Independent Studies*, CIS [online] http://www.cis.org.au/about-cis [accessed 1 September 2012].

Colander, D. & Davidson, P. 2001, 'An Interview with Paul Davidson', *Eastern Economic Journal*, vol. 27, no. 1, pp. 85–114.

Department of Economics 2015, the University of Notre Dame, Department of Economics [online] http://economics.nd.edu/about/ [accessed 15 October 2015].

Donovan, G. 2004a, 'Economics Split Divides Notre Dame; Creation of Two Unequal Programs Decried by Some as Threat to Academic Freedom', *National Catholic Reporter*, Kansas City, 9 April.

Donovan, G. 2004b, 'Students Opposed Department Changes', *National Catholic Reporter*, Kansas, 9 April, pp. 1–2.

Earl, P. E. & Peng, T. C. 2012, 'Brands of Economics and the Trojan Horse of Pluralism ', *Review of Political Economy*, vol. 24, no. 3, pp. 451–67.

Fine, B. & Milonakis, D. 2009, *From Economics Imperialism to Freakonomics*, Routledge, London.

Gilling, J. 2010, 'Two Perspectives on a Long and Bitter Dispute', *Campus Review*, vol. 30, March.

Glenn, D. 2009, 'Notre Dame Plans to Dissolve the 'Heterodox' Side of Its Split Economics Department', *The Chronical of Higher Education*, Washington, 16 September, pp. 22–3.

Gresik, T. A. 2003, 'Economics Department Needs Reform', *The Observer*, Notre Dame, 11 February, p. 1.

Groenewegen, P. D. 1979, 'Radical Economics', in F. H. Gruen (ed.), *Surveys of Australian Economics*, Allen & Unwin Australia, Sydney, pp. 171–224.

Groenewegen, P. D. 2009a, '"The Book Cannot Stand on Its Own as an Accurate Portrait"', *Agenda: A Journal of Policy Analysis and Reform*, vol. 16, no. 4, p. 83.

Groenewegen, P. D. 2009b, *Educating for Business, Public Service and the Social Sciences, a History of the Faculty of Economics at the University of Sydney 1920–1999*, University of Sydney Press, Sydney.

Hallinan, M., Knight, J., Maxwell, S., McBrien, R. & Affleck-Graves, J. 2002, *Report of Blue Ribbon Committee on the Department of Economics*, University of Notre Dame South-Bend.

Hargreaves-Heap, S. P. & Varoufakis, Y. 2004, *Game Theory: A Critical Introduction*, Routledge, London.

Hawkins, J. 2009, '"By the End of the Book I Was None the Wiser"', *Agenda: A Journal of Policy Analysis and Reform*, vol. 16, no. 4, p. 101.

Heath, C. & Heath, D. 2006, 'The Curse of Knowledge', *Harvard Business Review*, December, pp. 1–4.

Hogan, W. P. 1974, *A Statement by Professor Warren P Hogan*, University of Sydney Archives, University of Sydney.

Hogan, W. P. 2007, 'Colin Simkin', in J. E. King (ed.), *A Biographical Dictionary of Australian and New Zealand Economists*, Edward Elgar, Cheltenham, pp. 87–91.

Jones, E. 1976, 'Methodology in Economics: An Introduction', in F. J. B. Stilwell & E. L. Wheelwright (eds), *Readings in Political Economy: Volume One*, Australia and New Zealand Book Company, Sydney, pp. 275–9.

Jones, E. & Stilwell, F. J. B. 1986, 'Political Economy at the University of Sydney', in B. Martin, C. M. A. Baker, M. Clyde & C. Pugh (eds), *Intellectual Suppression: Australian Case Histories, Analysis and Responses*, Angus & Robertson, Sydney, pp. 24–38.

Katzner, D. W. 2011, *At the Edge of Camelot: Debating Economics in Turbulent Times*, Oxford University Press, Oxford.

Kuhn, R. 2009, 'Recollections of Emergent Radicalism', in G. Butler, E. Jones & F. J. B. Stilwell (eds), *Political Economy Now! The Struggle for Alternative Economics at the University of Sydney*, Darlington Press, Sydney, pp. 178–80.

Lavoie, M. 2015, 'Should Heterodox Economics Be Taught in or Outside of Economics Departments?', *International Journal of Pluralism and Economics Education*, vol. 6, no. 2, pp. 134–50.

Lee, F. S. 2009, *A History of Heterodox Economics: Challenging the Mainstream in the Twentieth Century*, Routledge, London.

Lee, F. S., Grijalva, T. C. & Nowell, C. 2010, 'Ranking Economics Departments in a Contested Discipline: A Bibliometric Approach to Quality Equality between Theoretically Distinct Subdisciplines', *American Journal of Economics and Sociology*, vol. 69, no. 5, pp. 1345–75.

Lee, F. S., Pham, X. & Gu, G. 2013, 'The UK Research Assessment Exercise and the Narrowing of UK Economics', *Cambridge Journal of Economics*, vol. 37, no. 4, pp. 693–717.

Lindsey, G. & Norton, A. 1996, 'The CIS at Twenty', *Policy*, Winter, pp. 16–21.

Lodewijks, J. K. 2007, 'A Conversation with Warren Hogan', *Economic Record*, vol. 83, pp. 446–60.

Manson, A., McCallum, P. & Haiven, L. 2015, *Report of the Ad Hoc Investigatory Committee into the Department of Economics at the University of Manitoba*, Canadian Association of University Teachers, Manitoba.

O'Donnell, R. 2009, 'The Permanent Need for Political Economy', *Agenda: A Journal of Policy Analysis and Reform*, vol. 16, no. 4, pp. 89–99.

Panhans, M. 2009, 'The Homeless Heterodox', *Open Economics: economic encounters of the plural kind*, [online] http://www.openeconomicsnd.wordpress.com/2009/10/10/the-homeless-heterodox/ [accessed 6 June 2010].

Popper, K. R. 1966, *The Open Society and Its Enemies*, Routledge & Kegan Paul, London.

Porteous, P. 2009, 'Developing Skills for Social Change', in F. J. B. Stilwell, E. Jones & G. Butler (eds), *Political Economy Now! The Struggle for an Alternative Economics at the University of Sydney*, Darlington Press, Sydney, pp. 71–5.

Potts, J. 2000, *The New Evolutionary Microeconomics: Complexity, Competence, and Adaptive Behaviour*, Edward Elgar, Cheltenham.

Rakowski, J. J. 2010, 'Dissolution of Economics and Policy Studies', *The Observer*, South Bend, p. 1.

Robinson, J. 1980, *Collected Economic Papers*, MIT Press, Cambridge MA.

Rodrigo, D. 2009, 'Keeping the Political Economy Movement Flourishing', in G. Butler, E. Jones & F. J. B. Stilwell (eds), *Political Economy Now! The Struggle for Alternative Economics at the University of Sydney*, Darlington Press, Sydney, pp. 156–8.

Shapin, S. & Schaffer, S. 1985, *Leviathan and the Air-Pump: Hobbes, Boyle, and the Experimental Life: Including a Translation of Thomas Hobbes, Dialogus Physicus De Natura Aeris by Simon Schaffer*, Princeton University Press, Princeton.

Sheehan, B., Embery, J. & Morgan, J. 2015, 'Give Them Something to Think About, Don't Tell Them What to Think: A Constructive Heterodox Alternative to the Core Project', *Journal of Australian Political Economy*, no. 75, Winter, pp. 211–31.

Simkin, C. (ed.) 1975, *Political Economy Vs Economics at the University of Sydney*, the University of Sydney Archives, the University of Sydney.

Steinbaum, M. I. & Weisberger, B. A. 2015, 'Economics Was Once Radical: Then It Decided Not to Be', *HIstPhil*, [online] https://www.anticap.wordpress.com/2015/11/09/economics-looking-backward/ [accessed 15 November 2015].

Stilwell, F. J. B. 1988, 'Contemporary Political Economy: Common and Contested Terrain', *The Economic Record*, vol. 64, no. 184, pp. 14–25.

Stilwell, F. J. B. 2006, 'The Struggle for Political Economy at the University of Sydney', *Review of Radical Political Economics*, vol. 38, no. 4, pp. 539–50.

Stilwell, F. J. B. 2011, 'Teaching a Pluralist Course in Economics: the University of Sydney Experience', *International Journal of Pluralism and Economics Education*, vol. 2, no. 1, pp. 39–56.

Stilwell, F. J. B. & Wheelwright, E. L. 1976, *Readings in Political Economy: Volume 1*, Australia and New Zealand Book Company, Sydney.

Thornton, T. B. 2008, *Telephone Interview with Professor Frank Stilwell*, 29 September.

Thornton, T. B. 2009, *Correspondence with David Ruccio*, 12 March.

Thornton, T. B. 2011a, *Email Correspondence with Professor Frank Stilwell*, 3 August.

Thornton, T. B. 2011b, *Interview with Dr Stuart Rosewarne*, University of Sydney, 7 December.

Thornton, T. B. 2011c, *Interview with Professor Paul Redding*, University of Sydney, 7 December.

Thornton, T. B. 2011d, *Interview with Professor Rod O'Donnell*, Sydney, 5 December.

Thornton, T. B. 2012, *Email Correspondence with Professor David F Ruccio*, 11 December.

Thornton, T. B. 2013, *Correspondence with David Ruccio*, 30 January.

Thornton, T. B. 2015, *Email Correspondence with David Ruccio*, 8 December.

Tierney, J. 2010, 'Branch of Econ Dept. To Be Dissolved', *The Observer*, Notre Dame, 19 January, p. 1.

University, 2015, *Mission Statement*, [online] https://www.nd.edu/about/mission-statement/, accessed 4 November.

University of Sydney, 2011, *Strategic Review of the School of Social and Political Sciences Discussion Paper*, Faculty of Arts and Social Sciences, University of Sydney.

Varoufakis, Y. 2007, 'A Most Peculiar Success: Constructing Uadphilecon – a Doctoral Program in Economics at the University of Athens', paper presented to International Confederation of Associations for Pluralism in Economics, University of Utah, Salt Lake City, 1–3 June.

Varoufakis, Y. 2009, A Most Peculiar Failure: On the Dynamic Mechanism by Which the Inescapable Theoretical Failures of Neoclassical Economics Reinforce Its Dominance, Working Paper, Department of Economics, University of Athens, Athens.

Varoufakis, Y. 2010, 'A Most Peculiar Success: Constructing Uadphilecon – a Doctoral Program in Economics at the University of Athens', in R. Garnett, E. K. Olsen & M. Starr (eds), *Economic Pluralism*, Routledge, New York, pp. 278–92.

Varoufakis, Y., Halevi, J. & Theocarakis, N. 2011, *Modern Political Economics: Making Sense of the Post-2008 World*, Routledge, London.

Williams, B. R. 1943, *The Socialist Order and Freedom*, Reed and Harris, Melbourne.

Williams, B. R. 1953, 'Economic Science and Public Policy', *Sociological Review*, vol. 1, no. 1, pp. 87–109.

Williams, B. R. 2005, *Making and Breaking Universities: Memoirs of Academic Life in Australia and Britain 1936–2004*, Macleay Press, Sydney.

Williams, B. R. 2006, *Liberal Education and Useful Knowledge, a Brief History of the University of Sydney 1850–2000*, University of Sydney, Sydney.

10 Hybrid strategies

The term 'hybrid strategy' is used to describe a situation where the teaching of economics is structurally integrated in some way with other departments. For example, universities may have a political economy major where some of the subjects are taught from within the social science faculty, and other subjects are taught from the economics department. Such an approach can allow the creation of a suite of pluralist economics subjects without the challenge of having to establish and maintain all of them under the auspices of the economics department. The creation of such a major is a plausible thing to attempt if there is at least one pluralist-orientated staff member in the economics department and at least one political economist working in another department, and if the administrative systems of the university are capable of coping with a major that is cross-departmental and/or cross-faculty. In such instances there would be a strong case for calling the major a political economy major to avoid evoking any proprietorial response from orthodox economists.

Another example of a hybrid model, and the particular focus in this chapter, is offered via the development of a politics, philosophy and economics (PPE) degree. PPE degrees structurally integrate the study of economics into the two closely related disciplines of politics and philosophy, thus promoting the interdisciplinarity aspect of pluralism, as well as offering some potential to academics from other disciplines to undertake research and teaching in economics, as well as to influence decisions about what economics is taught within the degree. Hybrid approaches, being simultaneously inside *and* outside traditional centres of economics teaching, have the potential to transcend some of the problems associated with trying to push for pluralism solely from inside a traditional economics department (as was examined in the Chapter 8), or entirely from outside a traditional economics department (as was examined in Chapter 9). Hybrid strategies can succeed on their own terms, but may also function as a precursor to the 'reform from within' and 'reform from without' strategies discussed in the last two chapters.

The particular PPE degree examined is that offered by La Trobe University in Melbourne Australia. The case study provides various details of how the degree was developed in the hope that this may be a useful reference point for anybody considering establishing PPE degrees in their own university. The chapter is different from all the other chapters in this book in that it is a case study written from an insider perspective in that I currently co-convene the PPE degree at La Trobe and have been involved in its development.

The PPE degree was an innovation first established at Oxford University in the UK in the 1920s. It has gone on to have a long record of involvement in producing that country's political elite. Kelly (2010) goes so far as to say that the PPE rules public life in the UK. The strong success of Oxford's PPE degree has resulted in a fair degree of emulation with around sixty universities worldwide offering their own version of the degree. Roughly, a third of these universities are in the UK, a third are in the US and a third are elsewhere. PPE degrees are founded on the solid intellectual premise that most social and economic phenomena, and in particular public policy issues, have political, philosophical and economic dimensions. Given this, it is desirable for budding decision-makers and opinion-shapers to have a grounding in each of the three disciplines, as well as to understand the interrelationships between the three disciplines.

PPE and political economy

The PPE degree has the capacity to promote economic pluralism in general. In particular, it is quite conducive to supporting the development and maintenance of political economy in the curriculum. Political economy as an area of knowledge has always had strong and explicit philosophical and political roots. Indeed if we return again to the arguments of Chapter 4 where it was argued that because disciplinary boundaries are often fuzzy, we need not be constrained by convention and can plausibly conceive of political economy as a trans-disciplinary, or cross-disciplinary entity. Let us consider the overlaps and relationships.

In terms of the linkages with philosophy, political economy has a strong philosophical dimension. Indeed, it can be argued that both the areas of political economy and orthodox economics are, in the end, a sustained form of philosophical reasoning (Fusfeld 2002). The linkage between political economy and philosophy is clearly evident in the greater focus on methodological issues in political economy. Indeed economic methodology is in many respects just the philosophy of science as applied to economics. Stretton (1999) has argued that one of the key problems in current undergraduate economics education is lack of attention to the philosophy of science; thus a subject in the philosophy of science should be a core requirement in any PPE degree, and indeed in any economics degree. Dow has also made the point that if one really wants to get to the bottom of many disputes in economics, one has to think methodologically and philosophically (Dow 2002). Philosophy is ultimately about rigorous and clear thinking. Thus it is, or at least should be, the foundation stone of economics and political economy.

If we turn to the connection between political economy and the discipline of politics (and its central focus on analysing power), the overlaps and affinities are very strong. Most political economists would readily attest to the political dimension of the work. Joan Robinson's (1981) observation that the answer to most economic problems nearly always raises political questions is relevant to note in this regard. For political economists, power is not just market power (as it is in orthodox economics), nor is it something that just structures the costs and benefits of particular choices. It is much deeper: power changes not just what we do, but also who we are, what we want and what we believe (Bartlett 1993). The economy is not to be conceived as just a system of markets: it is a system of institutions (of which markets are just one example). Because institutions structure power, we can then conceive of the economy as a system of power (Samuels & Tool 1988).

The linkages between political economy and politics are striking. Indeed, one can again draw on the fuzzy flexibility of modern classification and the complex object that is the social sciences to argue that political economy could also be conceived as a branch of the discipline of politics (as opposed to it being a branch of the discipline of economics). In addition to the affinities and overlaps between politics and political economy just noted one can see that, in general terms, both areas of knowledge are often organised around an institutions–history–social structure nexus (as opposed to the rationality–individualism–equilibrium nexus of orthodox economics) and both tend towards a complex ontology. On this basis it could be argued that if political economy is to be considered a branch of a larger discipline, it fits just as well, if not better, under the discipline of politics than the discipline of economics. Conceiving of political economy as a branch of politics is something that warrants serious consideration, particularly if the prospects for political economists to find employment, and a fairer assessment of their research, look more promising within politics departments.

Advantages of a PPE degree

PPE degrees are an effective means for transcending a common administrative problem whereby universities impose maximum quotas on students undertaking cross-faculty subjects. This usually prevents students enrolled in economics degrees (who are often based in the business faculty) engaging in any substantive study of other social sciences. Social science students are usually similarly restricted in studying subjects offered within the economics department. The PPE breaks down this schism and avoids the need for students having to do a double-degree just to study simultaneously both economics and the arts and social sciences in any depth.

PPE degrees can also facilitate cross-faculty collaboration in teaching. While cross-faculty teaching is possible without a cross-faculty degree, a cross-faculty degree makes it more probable to occur, if only because it brings different groups of academics together in a way that would otherwise not occur. This scenario also makes such a degree easier to expedite (because the faculties are already closely involved in a partnership). Cross-faculty teaching is an important strategy to achieve greater pluralism. Obvious contenders for cross-faculty teaching include economic sociology (with sociology departments), economic history (with history departments), economic methodology (with philosophy departments) and behavioural and experimental economics (with psychology departments). Yet again, one can only remark on the fuzziness of disciplinary boundaries and the creative possibilities that come from not being constrained by traditional (and questionable) disciplinary categorisations.

There are five obvious attractive aspects to cross-faculty teaching. First, staffing and other costs can be shared between two or more departments. Second, in some universities it means that potential students can be drawn from not one, but two, faculties, thus supporting the viability of quite specialised subjects. Third, it allows academics to deepen their knowledge of other disciplines. Fourth, it is a way of economising on the shrinking pool of expertise within economics departments to teach the social-science wing of the discipline. Fifth, departments can become less proprietorial about other departments encroaching on what they might see as 'their discipline' if they have one of their staff members partly involved in teaching the subject. Sixth, cross-faculty teaching could be useful in dissipating the intellectual isolation of political economists within economics departments by bringing them into working contact with academics in other disciplines. This is important given that economics departments are increasingly staffed by 'technocratic specialists with little grounding in the broad fundamentals of enquiry in the social sciences' (Hodgson 2007, p. 20).

There are two basic PPE models. The first approach is the 'pillar model', in which the disciplines are taught largely independently of one another. The pillar model is relatively easy and inexpensive to establish, as the curriculum can be created from an already existing pool of subjects in each discipline. The second approach is the 'bridge model', in which there is an emphasis on understanding the interconnections between the disciplines. The bridge model has the intellectual edge, but it is more expensive and time-consuming to establish, as it requires the creation and maintenance of a set of inter-disciplinary subjects specifically designed for the PPE degree.

The PPE degree at La Trobe University

The idea of La Trobe University establishing a PPE degree originated in 2008 with Professor Belinda Probert, then Pro Vice-Chancellor (Education). Probert thought that a PPE degree might address what she perceived as inadequacies in social science education. Probert's view is that, currently, social science graduates are not sufficiently equipped to undertake empirical analysis, particularly statistical and quantitative analysis. This impairs the ability of social science graduates to participate fully in public policy analysis and formulation. Furthermore social science departments do not sufficiently interact with each other, particularly economics departments (Thornton 2011). Probert raised the idea of a PPE degree with professors of all three disciplines and received a positive response. From this point the three departments worked together well in putting the idea into action.

The degree was originally a cross-faculty entity. Economics was based in the Faculty of Business, Economics and Law while the Department of Politics and the Department of Philosophy were based in the Faculty of Humanities and Social Sciences. The convenorship of the degree was based in the School of Economics and Finance and was held for the first few years of the degree's existence by

Professor Don Harding. In 2015, the university was restructured into just two 'colleges'. This brought all three disciplines under the College of Arts, Social Science and Commerce. It also led to many departmental amalgamations including the School of Economics becoming the Department of Economics and Finance and the creation of the Department of Politics and Philosophy. With the creation of the Department of Politics and Philosophy there was a view that the disciplines of politics and philosophy should be more directly involved in the governance of the degree. Consequently, the degree is moving towards a co-convenorship model where responsibility is shared between the Department of Economics and Finance and the Department of Politics and Philosophy.

Moving the PPE degree from an idea to reality turned out to be an involved job that required persistence, patience and discussions with various areas and levels of the university. This was partly because of the cross-faculty nature of the degree, which was an atypical structure for the administrative structures and processes of the university to deal with. That it was not entirely straightforward is unsurprising given that large organisations typically exhibit high levels of inertia. Institutional innovations can sometimes unsettle the balance of power and control within organisations. Indeed, even when change does occur it is often channelled through existing structures of self-interest (Nelson & Winter 1982). Given all this, it was fortunate that the initiative had the imprimatur and support of senior management within the university. This fact, combined with good levels of cooperation, judgement and application by Professors Don Harding (economics) Nick Bisley (politics) and Andrew Brennan (philosophy), ultimately allowed the degree to become a reality.

How was the initiative perceived within each of the three departments? The creation of the PPE degree encountered no obstacles within economics. The lack of opposition can be largely explained by the fact that the initiative enjoyed the support of the Head of School and all the economics professors. It is notable that the degree was sold to other staff in practical rather than intellectual terms. The emphasis was placed on the potential of a PPE degree to be a new revenue stream and a source of high-calibre students (including honours students). The degree was partly sold on the basis that it was a form of risk diversification that would make the school less reliant on revenue from the Bachelor of Business degree (a degree with large enrolments, but one over which the school had diminishing levels of influence and where it feared its subjects would be increasingly marginalised). It was presented and discussed in staff meetings in terms of its usefulness to the department, rather than its intellectual merits. Concerns raised about the degree were limited to staff needing reassurance that PPE students who wanted to undertake honours in economics would need to have completed third-year micro, macro and second-year econometrics. Once this reassurance was given, the degree was accepted.

While the establishment of the degree seems to have generated no apparent controversy or resistance in the politics department, there was some discussion and debate over the degree in the philosophy department. The issue concerned the determination of what philosophy subjects would be core (compulsory) requirements and what subjects would be electives. The underlying source of the debate was between philosophers working in the analytic tradition and those working in the continental tradition. A compromise position was reached, though the analytic approach is currently more heavily represented within the core. Clearly, other disciplines can also be beset by intellectual differences that need careful management and a degree of cooperation and compromise.

La Trobe's PPE degree was largely based on the pillar model rather than the bridge model. Given the obvious cost and political challenges of establishing the bridge model, this was the practical starting point. However, from the outset some established subjects were customised to contain a bridge component. More recently, a dedicated bridge subject has been developed: *POL1PPE Politics, Philosophy and Economics*. A second-year subject *POL2PPE Political Economy* is currently awaiting final approval by the university.

In the first year, students undertake first-year micro, first-year macro, first-year philosophy and first-year politics and three elective subjects. From the second year onwards students can undertake a balanced programme that is equal parts politics, philosophy and economics. Alternatively, students, from the second year onwards, can specialise in just two disciplines: politics/philosophy, politics/ economics or philosophy/economics. Each specialisation has its own programme of compulsory and elective subjects. Depending on the programme in which a student enrols, and depending on their grade average, a student can potentially qualify for honours in any of the three disciplines. Several PPE graduates have gone on to do honours in economics both at La Trobe and elsewhere.

This ability to progress into a standard honours degree is particularly significant with regard to economics. The possession of Honours in economics is often a minimum requirement for those wishing to enter graduate programmes in government departments and agencies. Such graduate economists can go on to exercise enormous influence over public policy. Thus the PPE degree may provide a pathway by which broadly trained social science graduates have the opportunity to contribute to policy discussions that were previously the preserve of those who had a conventional economics degree. This is highly desirable given how narrow the contemporary conventional economics degree has become.

The economics component of the degree warrants specific attention. If students are undertaking the 'balanced' version of the degree, then first-year micro and macro are compulsory. Introductory statistics is also recommended but not required. At second-year level, students have to undertake either second-year microeconomics or second-year macroeconomics. They must then choose three other economics subjects. The only stipulation on electives is that they are at the second- or third-year level. Originally, it was stipulated that students needed to complete standard microeconomics and macroeconomics from years one to three, but this requirement was relaxed in early 2011, when after collegial discussion with politics and philosophy staff, it was judged that such a requirement might deter capable social science orientated students from enrolling in the degree. In other words, the need to respond to the preferences of PPE students, as well as input from staff in politics and philosophy, promoted greater levels of economic pluralism in the degree. However, microeconomics and macroeconomics, years one to three, are still required if PPE students wish to pursue honours in economics.

Currently no political economy subjects are offered within the Department of Economics and Finance, but it has been possible to establish political economy subjects within the Department of Politics and Philosophy. For example, the masters subject *POL5CPE Political Economy* is being developed as a fully online subject that will be available to any person anywhere in the world. There is also the first-year subject *POL1PPE Politics, Philosophy and Economics* (which is a subject that has a strong political economy component). Notably, *POL1PPE* gained enrolments of 154 students in its first-offering. Many of the enrolments were from students enrolled in other social sciences degrees.

For the first three years of the degree, some political economy was taught within the School of Economics, by myself primarily as a means to bolster the bridge credentials of the degree. Specifically, students doing standard subjects in microeconomics and macroeconomics undertook an additional one-hour tutorial each week. The creation of this extra hour of face-to-face teaching and discussion allowed for a political economy perspective on the content raised in that week's economics lecture and readings. The main objective was to show the inter-relationship between economics and the other disciplines and to redress some of the excessive narrowness that occurs in introductory micro and macroeconomics. Students were given a reading list or set textbook at the beginning of semester and each week a particular reading or chapter was discussed in the tutorial. Students' attendance and participation in these tutorials constituted 10 per cent of their overall mark. Given the extra in-semester work involved, the final exam was worth 10 per cent less than would otherwise have been the case. The extra tutorials were well received by students. The PPE students were grouped together for both the standard weekly tutorial (where the standard content is taught and the standard exercises were dutifully worked through) and the extra weekly tutorial (where the PPE perspective and broader discussion were fostered). That PPE students had separate tutorials for both the standard and PPE (extra) tutorials cultivated a very strong *esprit de corps* among the students. As will be seen, this turned out to be significant.

Administratively, the modified subjects existed as separate entities: separate subject codes, titles, descriptions and subject website and (slightly modified) exams. It was a structure that provided the flexibility for increasing levels of autonomy into the future. The core micro and macro subjects could, with almost complete administrative ease, have become genuinely plural subjects spanning economics and political economy. This was the long-term intention, due to the fact, already mentioned in previous chapters, that the order in which ideas are introduced is important. If key concepts in political economy are not introduced until the later years of study, students may struggle to understand them fully or accept them as legitimate; indeed, if an uncritical over-emphasis on concepts such as equilibrium and rationality is acquired early on in someone's education it can 'set up an analytical confusion that captivates the student more or less forever' (Bernstein 2004, p. 33).

The role of student activism

Many of La Trobe's PPE students have a strong interest in political economy, particularly the more senior students who had the opportunity to undertake political economy tutorials and subjects, though the type of student cohort attracted to the degree has had a general orientation towards political economy. The PPE students have also been political active. For example, the PPE Society is one of the student groups that make up the International Student Initiative for Pluralism in Economics. Indeed, a member of the PPE Society, Nicholas Pringle, travelled to Germany to participate in the inaugural ISIPE conference in Tübingen in 2014.

In April 2012, the PPE students decided, of their own volition, to advocate the extension of my fixed term contract, which had otherwise been scheduled to end on 1 July 2012, and also for the retention of pluralist subjects that I had created and taught. Students sought meetings with senior academics and administrators, where carefully compiled arguments, research and written statements by past and current students were presented. These efforts by the students eventually resulted in a six-month extension of my contract, but not in the retention of any political economy subjects or tutorials.

The School of Economics had become an increasingly difficult environment in which to be a political economist. I was originally recruited to the department in July 2007 on a three-year contract, which was then extended in twelve-month or six-month instalments. For the first few years of my time at La Trobe, the Head of Department was an economic historian who supported the department having a pluralist presence. However, once this head of school left to take up a position at another university the level of support fell away. In general, initiatives that were made with the support of the previous leadership were not sustained by subsequent leadership. The presence of pluralist staff and the existence of pluralist subjects soon ceased. By mid-2013, my run of fixed term contracts finally dried up. I was, by this time, ready to leave, given that all the political economy subjects had either already been cancelled or were being wound up. Fortunately, the opportunities to do twelve months lecturing in politics at Swinburne University presented itself – something that was assisted via the experience of teaching PPE subjects.

With the purging of the last political economist and the winding up of all political economy subjects at La Trobe one would have thought that was the end of political economy at La Trobe. Not so. The students developed their own political economy orientated subject that has run every semester since 2013. The subject has involved a weekly seminar that is led either by some of the senior PPE students or via an invited guest speaker. Leading political economists such as Therese Jefferson and Rod O'Donnell have spoken at these seminars. The PPE Society has developed into one of the most dynamic student organisations on campus. The students' PPE Society has been an impressive organisation that has played an important role in advancing political economy at La Trobe. The conclusions by Sydney University's political economists about the importance of staff and students working together has been borne out by events at La Trobe.

By mid-2014, my twelve months of work at Swinburne University had elapsed and I again needed to find employment. I found myself back at La Trobe University. A political philosopher, Dr Miriam Bankovsky from the Department of Politics at La Trobe University, offered me a two-year half-time Research Associate contract. The position was part of a large grant she had won to look at the ethical foundations of economics. I then started picking up other work within and around the department. Some of this work has included establishing a fifth-year subject in political economy, developing a first-year PPE bridge subject, and co-convening the PPE degree and Master of International Development. The main purpose of going into the details and specifics of what has occurred is simply to provide further illustration of the difficulties of working as a political economist in an economics department and the opportunities that can exist for political economists within politics departments. The details of the case also illustrate how PPE degrees can act as the vehicle for political economists to move from economics to politics departments, as well as to allow political scientists and political philosophers to engage with political economy. In particular, it was through my earlier work as coordinator of the PPE degree that I had been able initially to develop a working relationship with Dr Bankovsky and thus was able to secure the position of Research Associate in the Department of Politics and Philosophy. Furthermore, it was through Dr Bankovsky's creation and co-teaching of the PPE bridge subject *Economics and Ethics* (co-taught with the political economist Professor John King) that had allowed her to accumulate the necessary expertise to develop her successful research proposal to look at the ethical foundations of economics. That successful proposal, despite its clear 'economic' focus, was pitched in such a manner that ensured it was assessed by a panel of political philosophers (rather than economists). This greatly increased its chances for success. It was my earlier background in coordinating the PPE degree with the School of Economics that help secure my current role as co-convenor for the degree and subject coordinator for the first-year PPE subject. In summary, the PPE degree has delivered teaching and research outcomes in political economy that would not have been otherwise possible.

The story of the PPE degree at La Trobe University is a reasonably encouraging one. It presents a story that is consistent with a general argument of this book: that political economy will generally do better by establishing connections and bases for support outside the traditional economics department. The case study also shows how strong the appetite is amongst students for plurality and interdisciplinarity and how they can self-mobilise in pursuit of it.

An important strength of the type of hybrid strategy described in this chapter is its compatibility with both the 'reform from within' and the 'reform from without' strategies. Specifically, if one wants to work for change for a pluralist economics from within economics departments then the inherent interdisciplinarity of the degree offers a great means to do so. The PPE degree is also an option for those who wish to pursue a pluralist economics from outside the economics department, because such a degree fosters connections and creative partnerships with other social scientists that might not otherwise occur. It also offers the opportunity for political economists to demonstrate how political economy teaching and research can make contributions to other departments and academic disciplines. A degree such as this can lay the early groundwork for significant teaching and research programmes in political economy, either within an existing department of politics or in a dedicated department of political economy.

References

Argyrous, G. & Thornton, T. B. 2014, 'Disciplinary Differentiation and Institutional Independence: A Viable Template for a Pluralist Economics', *International Journal of Pluralism and Economics Education*, vol. 5, no. 2, pp. 120–32.

Bartlett, R. 1993, 'Power', in G. M. Hodgson, W. J. Samuels & M. R. Tool (eds), *Elgar Companion to Institutional and Evolutionary Economics*, Edward Elgar, Aldershot, pp. 119–24.

Bernstein, M. A. 2004, 'The Pitfalls of Mainstream Economic Reasoning (and Teaching)', in E. Fullbrook (ed.), *A Guide to What's Wrong with Economics*, Anthem Press, London, pp. 33–40.

Dow, S. C. 2002, *Economic Methodology: An Inquiry*, Oxford University Press, Oxford.

Fusfeld, D. R. 2002, *The Age of the Economist*, Addison-Wesley, Boston.

Hodgson, G. M. 2007, 'Evolutionary and Institutional Economics as the New Mainstream?', *Evolutionary and Institutional Economics Review*, vol. 4, no. 1, pp. 7–25.

Kelly, J. 2010, 'Why Does PPE Rule Britain?', *BBC News Magazine*, vol. 31, pp. 1–2.

Nelson, R. R. & Winter, S. G. 1982, *An Evolutionary Theory of Economic Change*, Belknap Press of Harvard University Press, Cambridge, MA.

Robinson, J 1981, *What Are the Questions? And Other Essays: Further Contributions to Modern Economics*, M. E. Sharpe, Armonk.

Samuels, W. J. & Tool, M. R. 1988, *The Economy as a System of Power*, Transaction Books, New Brunswick.

Stretton, H. 1999, *Economics: A New Introduction*, UNSW Press, Sydney.

Thornton, T. B. 2011, *Interview with Professor Belinda Probert*, Fitzroy, 14 September.

11 The market for economic knowledge

There is ever-growing interest in ensuring that education meets employer needs. It is not just employers who have this interest; groups such as politicians, university administrators and students themselves are increasingly keen to have a curriculum that meets the preferences of employers. This chapter examines what employers currently state they require from the economics and political economy curriculum. The focus is mainly on employers seeking to recruit graduates with an economics degree, though there is also some discussion of employers who want graduates with some economics education and also a look at what is required of graduates in general.

An employer backlash?

Some have asserted that both employers and society in general will one day take issue with the type of graduates that contemporary economics departments produce and thus force real reform of the curriculum. For example, Groenewegen and McFarlane speak of:

> a possible backlash among staff and students once the trivialisation of economics becomes obvious and it is realised that graduates working in business and the public service are hampered in solving concrete problems by an inadequate training and perspective. If this happens, pressure to reintroduce comprehensive instruction in aspects of the discipline such as the history of economic thought … is certain to occur.
>
> (Groenewegen & McFarlane 1990, p. 235)

A variant on this argument is that employers will increasingly demand a plural curriculum because it is the superior vehicle to develop the generic skills and graduate attributes that employers are said to value so highly (O'Donnell 2002, 2010):

> [W]ell-designed pluralist courses possess large natural advantages over orthodox courses in developing specific skills in graduates, such skills being important drivers of innovation, creativity and efficiency. These advantages

in human capital formation are maximised when pluralist courses consciously incorporate activities that synergistically interact with the pluralist content.

(O'Donnell 2007, p. 1)

Another variant on the argument is that economics departments will not so much be forced to mend their ways as simply be left behind as employers (and the world in general) turn elsewhere to gain economic knowledge:

> Government employers are themselves already disillusioned with economics, as the financial crisis has demonstrated the futility of standard economic advice and theories. Economics departments may become like departments of philosophy, theology, or ancient studies.
>
> (Lavoie 2010, p.199)

> Perhaps academic economics departments will lose mindshare and influence to others – from business schools and public policy programs to political science, psychology, and sociology departments. As university chancellors and students demand relevance and utility, perhaps these colleagues will take over teaching how the economy works and leave academic economists in a rump discipline that merely teaches the theory of logical choice.
>
> (Delong 2011, p. 2)

All these assertions are interesting, but there is a need to look at the evidence of what employers have actually stated about the skills and knowledge they seek from graduates.

There is no truly international evidence survey on employer needs in regard to economics education, but there a number of Australian-based surveys that examine what employers require of economics graduates and these provide some useful information. Abelson and Valentine (1985) argue that employers seek 'an ability to interpret economic data and events, a good knowledge of economic theory, and a good command of expression, both in writing and verbally' (Abelson & Valentine 1985, p. 15). Notably, they assert that complementary studies (interdisciplinarity) in an economics graduate are not highly valued, as 'employers place much more importance on the acquisition of sound economic skills than they do on training in complementary studies' (Abelson & Valentine 1985, p. 15). They argue that 'it is important that students be adequately trained in basic economics and not be side-tracked on to studies which are of minor value to them as potential economists' (Abelson & Valentine 1985, p. 15). Keynes's (1924) famous remarks about what is required of the 'Master Economist' obviously have little currency within the profession according to this research. In terms of what other disciplines are valued (to the extent that they are valued at all) the disciplines of accounting, business management and law feature most prominently. Such preferences, if still valid and correct, appear to express the need for a narrow, rather than plural and interdisciplinary, economics curriculum.

Somewhat more recent survey work by Hellier et al. (2004) is largely in agreement with the earlier Abelson and Valentine survey work, though they also identify some evidence that employers seek graduates with good generic skills. They define generic skills as the ability to write clearly and concisely, analyse data, present and communicate, be effective interpersonally and have a practical orientation (Hellier et al. 2004). In further contrast to the 1985 study of Abelson and Valentine, they argue that employers seek a more multi-disciplinary and business problem-solving approach from graduates. Notably, they point out problems in developing this type of multi-disciplinary economics education: it cuts across established departmental and faculty structures. They also wonder how such courses can be balanced against the substantial mathematical and quantitative prerequisites that are required for postgraduate studies in orthodox economics.

More detailed and up-to-date survey data provides further illumination. In 2011, the Economic Society of Australia conducted a general survey on the views of economists. The survey questionnaire had a total of sixty-one questions, seven of which pertained to the adequacy of the economics curriculum.[1] A total of 577 economists participated: 25 per cent from the private sector, 33.5 per cent from the public sector, 3.8 per cent from the not-for-profit sector and 37 per cent from the university sector. This wide spread of professional economists is useful for our purposes here of gauging employer expectations because the organisations these economists work for are key employers of economics graduates.

The first proposition was 'undergraduate economics degree programmes should contain more subjects that place economics in a broader context, such as economic history, history of economic thought and political economy'. This proposition gained the agreement of 75.7 per cent of all respondents. This initially suggests that there is a strong support for the very types of changes advocated in this book. Somewhat surprisingly, 75.7 per cent of academic economists were also in agreement with the proposition. Such a finding was consistent with earlier surveys that show academics wanted their students to have, among other things, a 'head for the social and political dimensions of the profession' (Anderson & Blandy 1992, p. 17).

If nothing else, such findings of majority support for a broader curriculum provide reformers with the very rare opportunity to present themselves to the orthodoxy as advocates of the stated majority will. However, the survey's results tell us nothing about the *intensity* of the preference for change or the *amount* of change that is seen as desirable or what other subjects economists might be prepared to trade-off in order to have more of these broader subjects. There are some obvious indications (to be discussed shortly) that suggest the desire for substantial change is absent, the intensity of preference for even small changes is rather small and that there would be little demand to reduce the role and presence of orthodox subjects if it was required.

A most obvious question to ask in relation to these results is that if 75.7 per cent of academic economists wanted more broadly based subjects in the curriculum, why have they not acted on their stated preferences, given that they are in a position to offer such subjects and there is worldwide student demand for broader subjects? The long-form answer to this question is in previous and forthcoming chapters, but at this point the obvious point to make is that agreeing with such statements as an undemanding abstract ideal and being willing and able to put it into practice are two quite different things. We might also note that 24.3 per cent of academic economists disagreed with the statement.

The second proposition was that the undergraduate economics degree programmes should contain more behavioural economics and experimental economics. This proposition gained the agreement of 57.8 per cent of economists. So there is majority approval within the profession for more of what was earlier termed 'modern hybrid economics'. However, a detailed breakdown of the data revealed that less than half of *academic* economists agreed with the proposition. These findings provide some encouragement for reformers, though the lack of majority support within economics departments does not exactly indicate a strong desire to integrate developments within the orthodox research frontier into the curriculum.

There was no majority preference for or against the third proposition that economics is currently taught with excessive mathematical rigour, though it should be noted that almost twice as many economists disagreed or strongly disagreed with the proposition (48.7 per cent) as agreed or strongly agreed with it (24.9 per cent). It was also notable that the sector that had the highest level of disagreement with the proposition was academic economists (56.9 per cent), followed by private sector (45.6 per cent), the public sector (44.9 per cent) and the not-for-profit sector (26.3 per cent). This may be suggestive of the not-for-profit sector requiring more broadly trained graduates.

Part of the requirement for mathematical rigour by employers may be due to signalling. Successful mastery of orthodox content can be seen as signalling determination and application and a certain type of intelligence. Indeed, even the harshest critics of standard economics acknowledge that 'it requires intellectual muscle to master' (Keen 2001, p. 20). Robert Solow picks up on the signalling issue by arguing that the ability of a graduate to master high-level orthodox theory indicates that she or he will be a more reliable practitioner of more basic orthodox theory:

> In economics I like a man to have mastered the fancy theory before I trust him with simple theory. The practical utility of economics comes not primarily from its high-powered frontier, but from fairly low-powered reasoning. But the moral is not that we can dispense with high-powered economics, if only because high-powered economics seems to be such an excellent school for the skilful use of low-powered economics.
>
> (Solow cited in Colander 2005, p. 194)

An alternative way to understand the requirement for advanced theory is that it sets up a self-reinforcing loop between self-interest and *genuine* belief. This is quite evident in Enthoven's explanation of the making of the working economist:

> The tools of analysis that we use are the simplest, most fundamental concepts of economic theory, combined with the simplest quantitative methods. The

requirements for success in this line of work are a thorough understanding of and, if you like, *belief* in the relevance of such concepts as marginal products and marginal costs, and an ability to discover the marginal products and costs in complex situations, combined with a good quantitative sense. The advanced mathematical techniques of econometrics and operations research have not proved to be particularly useful in dealing with the problems I have described. Although a good grasp of this kind of mathematics is very valuable as intellectual formation, we are not applying linear programming, formal game theory, queuing theory, multiple regression theory, nonlinear programming under uncertainty, or anything like it. The economic theory we are using is the theory most of us learned as sophomores. The reason Ph.D.s are required is that many economists do not *believe* what they have learned until they have gone through graduate school and acquired a vested interest in marginal analysis.

(Enthoven 1963, p. 422; emphasis added)

What Enthoven describes here is not just a simple case of self-interest due to sunk costs (though that is part of it); rather it is that the habitual patterns of thought acquired during an education in marginal analysis shift belief in, and preference for, marginal analysis (again, note Enthoven's use of word 'belief'). Habits are too easily seen as an optimising response to given preferences and beliefs when the reality is that habits can shape preferences and beliefs. Pierce's earlier mentioned point that the 'essence of belief is the establishment of habit' (Pierce 1878, p. 29) is relevant here.

Undergraduate degrees in most countries are usually three years in length. The survey put forward a proposition on whether an undergraduate degree in economics should be four years. There was no majority verdict either way for this proposition, and it is thus difficult to draw many firm conclusions. The most enthusiastic supporters of the proposition appear to be the not-for-profit sector. Given their expressed preference for less mathematical rigour in the curriculum, their requirement for an additional year may suggest a need for more political economy, but we cannot really know this for sure. The relatively high level of satisfaction with a three-year degree in the private sector (47.2 per cent) and the public sector (42.2 per cent) could also be read as suggesting satisfaction with current economics graduates.

The fifth proposition asked whether 'Doctoral programmes in economics generally offer high quality training'. Again, there was no majority verdict either way. The not-for-profit sector did consider doctoral programmes as being of high quality (55.6 per cent support), but they were only a small proportion of the sample. The proposition elicited an interesting response from the university sector, which in this instance is both a producer of doctoral graduates and a potential employer of such graduates. The survey found that 44.2 per cent of university economists agreed with the proposition, yet this is somewhat at odds with the ongoing trend of Australian economics departments to employ US-trained PhD graduates over Australian graduates (Millmow 2011).

The public service

A key employer of economists is the public service. To get a sense of what is required by this sector, I interviewed a senior economist with the Victorian Treasury in 2009. The economist had been closely involved in the recruitment of graduate economists and was able to provide authoritative information on what Treasury requires. It was emphasised that orthodox microeconomics and macroeconomics (years one, two and three, and preferably four) were required. These subjects are required primarily because Treasury continues to undertake cost-benefit analysis and general equilibrium modelling. This is consistent with Ackerman's point that general equilibrium remains fundamental to the theory and practice of economics (Ackerman 1999).

Public policy subjects were highly valued, particularly in areas such as labour economics, environmental economics and regional development. Applied economics subjects were much more highly valued than specialised finance, accounting or management subjects – though it was noted that first- or second-year finance could be useful. A dedicated economics degree is still seen as having a clear advantage over more general business-based degrees, though double degrees in law and economics were seen as particularly useful. Interestingly, when the economist was asked about the subjects he found most interesting and rewarding in his own economics degree, he immediately recalled subjects taught by political economists: an economic history subject and a macroeconomic course that looked at a range of competing approaches. However, while he personally recalled these subjects warmly there was no suggestion that Treasury or the State Public Service actively requires these subjects, or that graduates who have not studied these broader subjects would be seen as inadequately trained.

It was also reported that there was some interest in behavioural economics within Treasury. For example, Treasury economists had recently participated in a one-day workshop on behavioural economics run by Monash University. However, whether this interest in behavioural economics (even in its 'new' variant) will develop, or even persist, remains to be seen, given that it sits awkwardly with the type of modelling and cost-benefit analysis that is clearly still so central in economic analysis undertaken in the public service. The field of applied economics does not appear to be undergoing any type of revolution.

The private sector

The requirement for more economics graduates, rather than differently trained economics graduates, seems also to be evident in the private sector. For example, an HSBC chief economist John Edwards states that 'economics honours graduates are very employable but not enough of them are being turned out' (Edwards cited in Matchett 2009, p. 25). There continues to be demand from employers for graduates trained in economics, particularly cost-benefit analysis and econometric modelling. This preference by employers is not surprising, given that government departments and economic consultants increasingly rely on economic modelling in their analysis (Gittins 2011, p. 21). Politicians have also become more prone to almost reflexively demanding the modelling behind any figure or policy idea that an opposing politician puts forward:

> Economic modelling has, for many people ... become synonymous with the process of serious policy development. Proponents of policy change that are armed with economic modelling are often taken more seriously than those with 20 years' experience working on the same problem. The modelling result that suggests tens of thousands of jobs will be lost or created often trumps logic or experience that suggests such claims are nonsensical.
>
> (Denniss 2012, p. 1)

What should be noted in the excerpt from Denniss is the point about how modelling has 'trumped' other forms of knowledge: case studies, historical evidence or experience from the field is simply not valued anywhere near as much, yet it can clearly be at least as valuable in many instances.

Some particularly enthusiastic employers of economic modellers are big business lobby groups, paying significant amounts of money to economics consultants to produce supposedly independent and objective scientific analysis (Gittins 2012). The underlying objective of the research is less to do with the pursuit of truth, than it is with advancing the interests of the business that has commissioned the analysis:

> Any economist who can't juggle the assumptions until they get the kind of findings their client is hoping for isn't trying. If you come up with a big-sounding figure for supposed job losses, you can be reasonably sure the media will trumpet the figure in shocked tones. You can also be sure few (if any) journalists will subject your claims to examination to see how credible they are.
>
> (Gittins 2011, p. 21)

Why is this increasingly occurring? Knowledge is only a form of power over others when there is an information asymmetry (Bartlett 1993). Most people in society (including politicians) simply do not know enough about these models to understand their limitations and so this creates the capacity for such modelling to mislead as much as illuminate. Economic modelling (whether it is good, bad or otherwise) will always exclude a very large section of the public from following the detail and substance of the argument in a way that case studies or other forms of analysis do not. Modellers can thus all too easily exploit the information asymmetry for their private gain (or the larger gain of whoever has employed them to undertake the modelling). Indeed, the economics profession as a whole can all too easily utilise 'the growing information asymmetry between itself and the wider public about what it does to put 'spin' on its contributions and deny it is failing' (Earl 2010, p. 222).

Modelling also carries an additional attraction in that it is imbued with the aura of science (as the concept of science is popularly understood). This aura of science comes by virtue of the fact that it is characterised by the use of mathematics and statistics; these things are associated with rigour, precision and objectivity.

What is the remedy for the overuse and misuse of modelling and econometrics? That the abuse of econometrics will somehow completely resolve itself is unlikely, given that 'bad economic modelling is preferred by many advocacy and industry groups to good economic modelling for three main reasons: it is cheaper, it is quicker, and it is far more likely to yield the result preferred by the client' (Denniss 2012, p. 1). Part of the solution relies on producing better-trained economists and political economics as well as a more economically literate populace. Towards this end Denniss (2012) has produced a practical guide for anybody (politicians, the media, the general public) that will help them to identify poor-quality, and/or intentionally mischievous, economic modelling. Denniss provides a list of straightforward questions, such as: does the model rest on structural or technological changes that are yet to occur? What linkages between variables are assumed? Do problems of circularity exist (does the model assume the very conclusions it supposed to prove)? Is the type of model used employed outside its normal domain of applicability? If the modeller cannot, or will not, answer such questions, then this in itself, argues Denniss, should raise immediate questions about the quality of the modelling.

It is useful to think of economic modelling in terms of the distinction that some institutional economists make between instrumental versus ceremonial institutions. Economic modelling can be an instrumental institution in that can be a source of knowledge and is of social benefit when used honestly, intelligently and with regard to its strengths and limitations. However, the fact that it *can* make this positive contribution and that it necessarily *will* make a positive contribution are of course two different things (Denniss 2012). As Binmore notes, it is a time-honoured game for professional philosophers 'to gain popular acceptance by telling people what they want to hear and papering over the inconsistencies that this entails with various obscurantist devices' (Binmore 1998, p. ix). Because of issues of information asymmetry and the aura of science as popularly understood, economic modelling is particularly prone to being used as a ceremonial institution that exists to support established hierarchies of status, wealth and power.

What then can we say about employer needs and economic pluralism? There is evidence that employers in general require the type of graduate skills, knowledge and attributes that a plural curriculum is best placed to supply. However, the evidence on whether employers of economists are likely to demand, or at least value, a more plural curriculum appears rather mixed and ambiguous in the survey results examined here. The evidence examined in this chapter appears to indicate that employers of graduate economists (or of graduates with some economics training) are not currently calling for significant change to economics. Indeed, the evidence in the latter part of this chapter indicates that there is a significant appetite for more of the same from economics departments. If we accept that a pluralist approach to economics would make for better graduates (including economics graduates), political economists have got a task in front of them to persuade more employers (and society in general) that what they say they want may not be the thing that they actually need (presuming that such employers are not in the business of producing intentionally misleading analysis). This task of persuasion will be a long-term process, but continuing to produce research and disseminate existing research (see in particular O'Donnell 2002, 2007, 2010) is worthwhile and is capable of making a difference.

Note

1 For a detailed presentation and analysis of the survey findings see Thornton (2013).

References

Abelson, P. W. & Valentine, T. J. 1985, 'The Market for Economists in Australia', *Economic Papers*, vol. 4, no. 4, pp. 1–16.

Ackerman, F. 1999, Still Dead after All These Years: Interpreting the Failure of General Equilibrium Theory, Working Paper 00–01, Tufts University, Global Development and Environment Institute.

Anderson, M. & Blandy, R. 1992, 'What Australian Economic Professors Think', *Australian Economic Review*, vol. 100, pp. 17–40.

Bartlett, R. 1993, 'Power', in Geoffrey M. Hodgson, Warren J. Samuels & Marc R. Tool (eds), *Elgar Companion to Institutional and Evolutionary Economics*, Edward Elgar, Aldershot, pp. 119–24.

Binmore, K. 1998, *Game Theory and the Social Contract: Just Playing* Massachussetts Institute of Technology, Cambridge, MA.

Colander, D. C. 2005, 'The Making of an Economist Redux', *Journal of Economic Perspectives*, vol. 19, no. 1, pp. 175–98.

Delong, J B 2011, 'The Crisis in Economics', *The Economist's Voice*, May, pp. 1–2.

Denniss, R. 2012, *The Use and Abuse of Economic Modelling in Australia*, The Australia Institute, Canberra.

Earl, P. E. 2010, 'Economics Fit for the Queen: A Pessimistic Assessment of Its Prospects', *Prometheus*, vol. 28, no. 3, pp. 209–25.

Enthoven, A. C. 1963, 'Economic Analysis in the Department of Defense', *The American Economic Review*, vol. 53, no. 2, pp. 413–23.

Gittins, R. 2011, 'It's a Load of Hot Air: The Coal Lobby Is Mining for Favourable Treatment', *The Age*, Melbourne, June 20, pp. 20–1.

Gittins, R. 2012, 'The Very Model of a Future Based on Guesswork ', *The Age*, 4 February, pp. 3–4.

Groenewegen, P. D. & McFarlane, B. J. 1990, *A History of Australian Economic Thought*, Routledge, London.

Hellier, P., Keneley, M., Carr, R. & Lynch, B. 2004, 'Towards a Market Oriented Approach: Employer Requirements and Implications for Undergraduate Economics Programs', *Economic Papers*, vol. 23, no. 3, pp. 213–21.

Keen, S. 2001, *Debunking Economics: The Naked Emperor of the Social Sciences*, Pluto Press, Annandale.

Keynes, J. M. 1924, 'Alfred Marshall, 1842–1924', *The Economic Journal*, vol. 34, no. 135, pp. 311–72.

Lavoie, M. 2010, 'Are We All Keynesians?', *Brazilian Journal of Political Economy*, vol. 30, no. 2, pp. 189–200.

Matchett, S. 2009, 'Dismal Science of Economics Faces Dilemma', *The Australian*, Sydney, 25 March, p. 1.

Millmow, A. 2011, 'Economists All Dressed up with Nowhere to Go', *Australian Financial Review*, Sydney, 28 February, p. 29.

O'Donnell, R. 2002, What Kind of Economics Graduates Do We Want? A Constructive Critique of Hansen's Proficiencies Approach, Working Paper, Department of Economics, Macquarie University Sydney.

O'Donnell, R. 2007, 'Teaching Economic Pluralism: Adding Value to Students, Economies and Societies', paper presented to Second International Conference for International Confederation of Associations for Pluralism in Economics, University of Utah, 1–3 June.

O'Donnell, R. 2010, 'Economic Pluralism and Skill Formation: Adding Value to Students, Economies, and Societies', in R. Garnett, E. K. Olsen & M. Starr (eds), *Economic Pluralism*, Routledge, New York, pp. 262–77.

Pierce, C. S. 1878, 'How to Make Our Ideas Clear', *Popular Science Monthly*, no. 12, January, pp. 286–302.

Thornton, T. B. 2013, 'The Possibility of a Pluralist Economics Curriculum in Australian Universities: Historical Forces and Contemporary Strategies', PhD thesis, La Trobe University.

12 The three purposes of economics

This chapter offers some general conclusions about economics as a discipline. It is not focused on evaluating particular strategies by which political economy may be advanced, but is instead focused on better explaining why political economy has struggled to maintain itself against the dominance of orthodox economics. The chapter weaves together various arguments from previous chapters by reflecting on the functions economics, particularly orthodox economics, performs in society. This chapter owes much to an unduly neglected argument of Warren Samuels, who by drawing on the work of Robinson, Shackle and others, argues that there are three (inter-related) purposes of economics: scientific explanation, social control and psychological balm (Samuels 1989). These three purposes exert a powerful influence on the nature of economics and an understanding of them, including an understanding of the circular and cumulative interrelationship between them, captures something important. Explaining the nature of economics via three interrelated and self-reinforcing purposes is admittedly both reductionist and ambitious. It does not explain everything. However, it draws together various arguments in a way that is not otherwise possible.

Economics as science

The idea that economics exists to provide us with scientific explanation has already been examined in the latter part of Chapter 3, and need not be extensively restated at this point. However, some central points warrant further reflection.

The purpose of supplying scientific explanation is the most obvious aspect of economics. Many people (particularly orthodox economists) might see it as the *only* purpose of economics. Certainly, it is the case that many orthodox economists often pride themselves on being the only true scientists in the social sciences (Lazear 2000; Mankiw, Gans & King 2009; Samuelson 1970). A particular conception of what constitutes a true science is at work here. For economists a properly scientific economics is characterised by the building (and perhaps statistical testing) of closed-system deductivist mathematical models:

> For most mainstream economists, of course, there is only one way to do economics. It requires the construction of a model, collection of relevant data

and subsequent testing. The model itself must be consistent with the fundamental principle of methodological individualism: that is to say, it must be based on the assumption of optimising behaviour by rational agents. The tests must employ the most advanced econometric techniques rather than – or at least in addition to – descriptive statistics. For the defenders of mainstream economics these simple rules are what make it a science, which is envied and increasingly imitated by the practitioners of less favoured disciplines in the areas of management and social studies.

(King 2011, p. 64)

This view of science has its roots in the logical positivism of the Vienna Circle, the falsificationism of Karl Popper, and the instrumentalism of Milton Friedman. It has been referred to as the 'received view' of science and of economic methodology. It is a rule-based methodology that posits that the single best theory can be found. It is therefore a philosophy of science that is antithetical to the idea of intellectual pluralism.

The problem with the received view, from a modern philosophy of science perspective, is that science is not practised like this, and to an extent, it *cannot* be practiced like this: under-determination, theory-ladenness, the social nature of science, relativism, anti-foundationalism and naturalism all make the old rules-based approach to science and economic methodology more problematic (Boumans et al. 2010; Hands 2001a, 2001b).

Modern philosophies of science provide much more intellectual support for pluralism, because in the absence of a decisive rule-based methodology to decide between theories, we should be open to consideration of multiple theories and to a degree of eclecticism and even of synthesis. This is not to argue that 'anything goes' or that evidence and testing do not matter (these things remain central). Rather, it is arguing that a modern philosophy of science suggests that we should not pretend that things are simpler than they are, and that all we need to do in our work is to apply a limited and consistent set of rules that will clearly adjudicate between knowledge and error.

There is an ongoing inability within orthodox economics to come to terms with the modern philosophy of science. Remedying this situation is a challenge, given that the orthodoxy has little appetite for methodological discussion (Lawson 1997); if one assumes that one has already clearly arrived at the pinnacle of scientific practice, what would there be to discuss?

To summarise, supplying scientific explanation is a valid fundamental purpose (or at least aim) of economics. But the merit of pursuing this purpose is contingent on economics acquiring a more developed understanding of the history and philosophy of science to comprehend better that 'real science is pluralist' (Fullbrook 2001).

Economics as social control

The idea that economics needs to be understood, in part, as a means of social control is consistent with a general argument about knowledge and social order that is recurrent across multiple disciplines and literature. Within philosophy, Nietzsche went so far as to argue that all things are subject to interpretation and that whichever interpretation prevails at a given time is a function of power and not truth (Kaufmann 1954). Radical political economists have also asserted a relationship between social order and knowledge, particularly with regard to social order and economic knowledge (Marx 1946). Beliefs about the system are seen as being produced by the system:

> Dynamic societies built their success on two production processes unfolding in parallel: manufacturing surplus and manufacturing consent regarding its distribution. The 'mind-forg'd manacles', as William Blake called them, are as real as the hand forged ones.
>
> (Varoufakis, Halevi & Theocarakis 2011, p. 22)

Institutionalists have also long argued that beliefs about economic and social systems are working parts of these systems (Stretton 1999) and that the economy itself should be regarded as a system of power (Samuels & Tool 1988). The Post-Keynesian Joan Robinson stressed the role of the education system in obscuring these realities:

> What is characteristic of the private enterprise system is that it condemns the wealthiest nation the world has ever seen to keeping an appreciable proportion of its population in perpetual ignorance and misery. The professional economist keeps up a smoke screen of 'theorems', and 'laws' and 'pay-offs' that prevent questions such as that from being asked. This situation is, I think, inevitable. In every country, educated institutions in general, and universities in particular, are supported directly or indirectly by the established authorities and whether in Chicago or in Moscow, their first duty is to save their pupils from contact with dangerous thoughts.
>
> (Robinson 1980, p. 98)

Even Keynes, not normally considered a radical political economist, also emphasises the social control aspects of economics:

> The completeness of the Ricardian victory is something of a curiosity and a mystery. It must have been due to a complex of suitabilities in the doctrine to the environment into which it was projected. That it reached conclusions quite different from what the ordinary uninstructed person would expect, added, I suppose, to its intellectual prestige. That its teaching, translated into practice, was austere and often unpalatable, lent it virtue. That it was adapted to carry a vast and consistent logical superstructure, gave it beauty.

That it could explain much social injustice and apparent cruelty as an inevitable incident in the scheme of progress, and the attempt to change such things as likely on the whole to do more harm than good, commended it to authority. That it afforded a measure of justification to the free activities of the individual capitalist, attracted to it the support of the dominant social force behind authority.

(Keynes 1936, p. 33)

We should not be surprised that in a capitalist economic system, the currently dominant approach to economic analysis is particularly adept at being applied in a manner where it legitimises the essential features of the capitalist economy. Whilst neoclassical economics does have a certain plasticity to it (for example, it was used as a framework by socialists in the socialist calculation debates of the 1930s), its core features adapt easily to legitimising a certain type of capitalism. For example, the emphasis on self-interest, the self-correcting nature of markets, the idea that one is rewarded in accordance with one's contribution, that we have perfect rationality and that market agents have the ability to see into the future probabilistically. It also directs us from examining the type of institutional structures that delineate more satisfactory versions of capitalism from less desirable ones, via its inability to analyse and recognise institutions in a satisfactory way. It has an obvious enduring appeal for any party interested in believing, or at least maintaining, the status quo in economic and social arrangements.

The case study of the political economy dispute at Sydney University regularly illustrated that the economists were deeply concerned that political economy would challenge the social order. Hogan recognised that there was a dimension of 'political and ideological confrontation' (Hogan cited in Lodewijks 2007, pp. 450–1). Simkin was deeply concerned about the political economists' embrace of Kuhnian paradigms, and in particular, their scepticism towards the existence of objective truth. He feared their teaching of a 'holistic method that both predicts and facilitates wholesale change' and that 'promotes both sympathy and activism in conflicts' (Simkin 1975, p. 5). Simkin's analysis of the dispute links directly to Hobbes's argument: 'show men what knowledge is and you will show them the grounds of assent and social order' (Shapin & Schaffer 1985, p. 100). It all underlies Shapin and Shaeffer's argument that 'the problem of generating and protecting knowledge is a problem in politics, and, conversely, that the problem of political order always involves solutions to the problem of knowledge' (Shapin & Schaffer 1985, p. 21).

Economics as psychological balm

Economics also supplies psychological comfort (what Samuels called 'psychic balm'). This is the least obvious of the three purposes, and the one most easily subsumed under the other two purposes. It is nonetheless distinct and important as an explanatory variable. Economics does assist in meeting psychological needs. That it should be called upon to do so should not be very surprising, as it is really just a reflection of a more general and deep-seated psychological (and practical) appetite for order, control and predictability. Geuss has noted:

> For most of human history, human life has been a terribly dangerous and unpredictable activity; disease struck people down unexpectedly, and so it's not at all surprising that as human beings we have a deep-seated need for regularity and predictability in our lives, and a desire to have a sense of having control over the world, and one of the ways in which we get control over the world is by having predictive mechanisms and having reliable instruments for dealing with situations is a perfectly understandably human desire. And of course it isn't just understandable, it's a good thing we have that desire.
>
> (Geuss 2009, p. 1)

Given that it is both understandable and beneficial to desire a degree of order, control and prediction, what, then, is the problem? Problems emerge when it is not possible to see or impose much order, or to have much predictability and control. Instead of recognising this uncomfortable reality (i.e. that what we want is incompatible with the reality that confronts us), we either pretend to have this desired predictability and control or pretend that we could have it (Geuss 2009). At this point good judgement is necessary, for without good judgement our analysis stops being constructive and helpful and degenerates into becoming delusional and harmful. We should not overrate our chances of exercising good judgement, given that 'staring into chaos and seeing in it significant patterns is not only the job of the scientist, but the hallmark of the mad person' (Varoufakis, Halevi & Theocarakis 2011, p. 17) and that 'nothing is so difficult as not deceiving oneself' (Wittgenstein 1980, p. 34).

Working out when our pursuit for order, predictability and control is helpful, rather than delusional, has been a particular challenge for economics. In particular the allure of the elegant can so easily take us away from the relevant. Adam Smith, for example, spoke of how our minds crave 'the beauty of systematic arrangement of different observations connected by a few common principles', and compared the pleasure of a grand system of thought to that of listening to a well-composed piece of instrumental music (cited in Skinner 1986, p. 33):

> Philosophy is the science of the connecting principles of nature. Nature, after the largest experience that common observation can acquire, seems to abound with events which appear solitary and incoherent with all that go before them, which therefore disturb the easy movement of the imagination ... Philosophy, by representing the invisible chains which bind together all these disjointed objects, endeavours to introduce order into this chaos of jarring and discordant appearances, to allay the tumult of the imagination, and to restore it, when it surveys the great revolutions of the universe, to that tone of tranquillity and composure, which is both most agreeable in itself, and most suitable to its nature.
>
> (Smith 1776 [1982], p. 47)

It gives us a pleasure to see the phenomena which we reckoned the most unaccountable, all deduced from some principle (commonly a well known one) and all united in one chain.

(Smith 1795 [1982], p. 134)

Smith appreciated how we crave order, beauty and systematic arrangement from a few common principles, but he was also wise enough to realise the dangers that can result when we uncritically pursue what we crave. For example, he points out that 'the learned doth ignore the evidence of their senses to preserve the coherence of the ideas of their imagination' (cited in Skinner 1986, p. 33); originally he made this observation in regard to the conduct of astronomers, though it is hard to imagine that he would not hesitate to apply it to the economics profession of today.

In a way that is very similar to Smith, Shackle has also written very perceptively on how our need for order, predictability and control (psychological balm) is very much at the heart of economic theory:

The chief service rendered by a theory is the setting of minds at rest ... Theory serves deep needs of the human spirit: it subordinates nature to man, imposes a beautiful simplicity on the unbearable multiplicity of fact, gives comfort in the face of the unknown and unexperienced, stops the teasing of mystery and doubt which, though salutary and life preserving, is uncomfortable, so that we seek by theory to sort out the justified from the unjustified fear. Theories by their nature and purpose, their role of administering to a 'good state of mind,' are things to be held and cherished. Theories are altered or discarded only when they fail us.

(Shackle 1967, pp. 288-9)

All we can seek is consistency, coherence, order. The question for the scientist is what thought-scheme will best provided him with a sense of that order and coherence, a sense of some permanence, repetitiveness and universality in the structure or texture of the scheme of things, a sense even of that one-ness and simplicity which, if he can assure himself of its presence, will carry consistency and order to their highest expression. Religion, science and art have all of them this aim in common. The difference between them lies in the different emphases in their modes of search.

(Shackle 1967, p. 286)[1]

There is abundant evidence of ongoing desire for psychological balm in economics. For example, Hal Varian, the author of the world's leading intermediate neoclassical microeconomics textbook, is entirely candid that most economists do the work that they do for reasons of aesthetic beauty and psychological enjoyment:

Why is economic theory a worthwhile thing to do? There can be many answers to this question. One obvious answer is that it is a challenging intellectual exercise and interesting on its own merits. No one complains about poetry and music, number theory or astronomy being 'useless', but one often hears complaints about economic theory being overly esoteric. I think that one could argue a reasonable case for economic theory on purely aesthetic grounds. Indeed, when pressed, most economic theorists admit they do economics because it is fun.

(Varian 1997, p. 108)

This recalls Adam Smith's point that many study 'for its own sake, as an original pleasure or good in itself, without regarding its tendency to procure them the means of many other pleasures' (Smith 1800 [2005], p. 340).

The economic historian Alexander Gerschenkron also touches on our desire for psychological balm as being a deep-seated yearning to possess a single approach that can unlock the puzzles of any place or time, though he implores us to outgrow this nomothetic objective that he sees as a false chase:

There is a deep-seated yearning in the social sciences for the discovery of one general approach, one general law valid for all times and all climes. But these attitudes must be outgrown. They overestimate both the degree of simplicity of economic reality and the quality of the scientific tools. As the economic historian organises and interprets his material, all he can hope for is the discovery of limited patterns of uniformity which may possess explanatory value for some places and periods but may be utterly inapplicable to others.

(Gerschenkron 1962, p. 67)

Loasby (1991, p. 20) also points to psychological balm's centrality in sustaining Kuhnian paradigms or Lakatosian research programmes, for they provide the means 'to put our minds at rest'. Note that this is a different concern from pursuing social acceptance for one's work within the community of scientists: it is a more internally focused motivation (notwithstanding the interrelationship between gaining external acceptance and feeling psychologically at ease). Loasby goes on to explain that having embraced a particular paradigm or research programme:

[T]hereafter we expect to increase our ability to predict and control by incremental experimentation. We expect that any changes in the theories which we hold will take the form of modifications, primarily extensions; and we may decide in advance that no message from our environment will be allowed to displace any major elements.

(Loasby 1991, p. 20)

Our need for predictability, order and control is also evident in the capacity within economics to come to terms with Knightian or Keynesian uncertainty and the consequent seeking out of psychological refuge in the ergodic axiom (that the past is essentially a facsimile of the future). This delusional retreat from perhaps the most central aspect of economic reality (the fact that we can't see into the future) is not seen as a bizarre and harmful conceit, but as something that needed to be done for economics to be a true science (Samuelson 1970). This is a very clear illustration that, just as we cannot separate economics as science from economics as social control, neither can we separate economics as science from economics as psychological balm. There are interdependencies of a circular and cumulative nature.

The concept of equilibrium is another example of psychological balm. Consider its properties: essentially blind to historical process and thus nomothetic, precise and ordered and offering a soothing picture of stability. It is also a fundamentally teleological concept:[2] it assumes the very future that it seeks to explain, for it is fully determined by its foundations. While Post-Keynesians such as Robinson and Kaldor long ago exhorted the profession to break with equilibrium, it remains an overly dominant organising concept that is often deployed with little sense of its inherent limitations as a means to understand economic and social processes.

Psychological balm often works its seduction on economists insidiously. Much economic theory starts off as *knowingly* simplistic and reductionist, but along the way this knowingness behind the reductionism and abstraction falls away and the analysis becomes perceived as truth. Blaug picks up on this problem when he talks about the general tendency for neoclassical economists to 'read more significance into the analysis than is inherent in the procedure' (Blaug 1997, p. 692). Notably, he describes how the tendency to do this has been 'irresistible' and that it was a 'temptation' that most neoclassical economists could not help but 'succumb' to (Blaug 1997, p. 692). Whitehead argued that we should seek simplicity, yet distrust it once we find it (Whitehead 1920). While the former part of Whitehead's directive comes easily, the latter part is far more challenging. Pierce provides part of the explanation for this in his argument that a state of doubt is an irritant to the human mind, but that a state of belief resolves this irritation (Pierce 1878).

Perhaps the best example of the economics profession's inability to follow Whitehead's dictum is general equilibrium theory. Frank Hahn, one of the architects of modern general equilibrium theory, has always stressed that, because the precise nature of the theory required such an exacting statement of the highly unrealistic assumptions involved, its 'application to the 'real world' could be at best provisional' (Hahn 1994, pp. 245–6). Yet, general equilibrium remains fundamental to *both* the theory *and* the practice of economics. One can explain this in terms of economists' conception of science (the building of mathematical models) and also the social control aspect of economics (by its presentation of a market economy as being self-correcting and stable), yet psychological balm is evidently a factor here as well. Hahn himself talks about the 'pleasures of the theorem and proof' and laments how this 'pleasure' will be largely denied to those economists who are forced towards 'the uncertain embrace of history and sociology and biology' (Hahn 1991, p. 48).

What all this suggests is that mathematics in economics, in addition to its clear practical capacity, has a psychological appeal that is seductive to economists. Mathematics has, almost from the very beginning, a special ability to engender a quasi-religious, or even fully religious, devotion; the most dramatic example of the latter was Pythagoras, who invented a religion based on numbers. Notably, Pythagoras is said to have either murdered (or at least exiled) his student Hippasus, who tried to leak the concept of irrational numbers; perhaps the world's earliest example of the upholding of Kuhnian normal science. For Pythagoras, the impetus to reduce all phenomena to mathematical relationships was spiritual or psychological in nature.

One need not look back to the ancient Greeks to see a link between mathematics and the divine. Herbert Gintis – a former Marxist and one of Colander's 'cutting edge' economists (Colander, Rosser & Holt 2004) – in the preface to his textbook *Game Theory Evolving* not only thanks his friends and family, but also 'the creator who gave us consciousness, filled the world with love and joy, and made it understandable in terms of mathematical models' (Gintis 2008, p. i). What is particularly distinctive here is not that he chooses to feel thankful to a creator, or even thankful that the world can be understood; rather it is his gratitude for the *manner* in which it can understood – via mathematical models. This seems to be a rather Pythagorean take on mathematics: could one not be simply grateful that the world around us can be understood?

Gintis's colleague Samuel Bowles argues that a more problem-driven and less tool-driven approach within economics will involve developing more sophisticated tools and more complex mathematics (Bowles 2005). More complex mathematics and sophisticated tools may well yield more insights into economic phenomena. But surely other ways of knowing also remain legitimate and promising. For example, perhaps advances in psychology, or anthropology, or sociology, might be more useful to economics than the application of more powerful mathematics. Indeed, some of Bowles and Gintis's most interesting work since making these statements above has drawn upon the work of other social sciences, particularly anthropology (see in particular Bowles & Gintis 2013).

The most obvious danger of the *a priori* commitment to mathematics at the level of method is that it puts that cart in front of the horse methodologically: if one commits to a certain method, this then drives many of the subsequent commitments at the theoretical, epistemological and ontological level. It would seem more sensible to consider the nature of reality one is confronted with and then let *that* shape the subsequent decisions in matters of epistemology and theory.

The obsession that mathematics is somehow a higher form of knowledge can transcend even lines of analysis that are supportive of one's own ideological position. Ward recalls how a subject that had content very much in line with the right-wing ideological orientation of his department was still seen as being inferior and lacking in rigour:

> Courtenay Wright and I proposed a third-year subject about ideology. It was a sophisticated subject. The head of department said it couldn't be called ideology, so I said 'we'll call it capitalism: contrasting views'. We will have a lot of Hayek and Stigler, which he thought was good. But he said we won't have it in a third-year course because he said 'its not real economics, you can

have that sort of crap at second year, we want rigorous stuff in third-year.' I
wouldn't call Hayek crap.

(Ward cited in Thornton & Millmow 2008, p. 9)

Notably, the two academics persisted with trying to get the subject established at
a third-year level, putting the matter to a vote and gaining a majority of votes (six
votes to five). However, the Head of Department's response to the majority verdict
was to say that he was 'not interested in majority rule, it was the truth that matters,
what he was arguing was true and what they were arguing for was false' (Ward in
Thornton & Millmow 2008, p. 9).

The problem of excessive devotion to formalism is not limited to economics.
McCalman, Muir and Soeterboek (2008) argue that universities continue to be
divided between those who adopt formalism and those who eschew it. This divide
was recognised by Snow in his classic essay on the 'Two cultures' (Snow 1964).
Unfortunately, the problem Snow identified has endured all too well and 'the
shifting boundaries between disciplines within the sciences, the humanities and
the social sciences, have made little impact on the fundamental divide between the
way humans see, interpret, analyse and explain the world, i.e. between words and
mathematics' (McCalman, Muir & Soeterboek 2008, p. 17). The relationship
between the two sides remains one of incomprehension tinged with hostility
(Kimball 1994).

Why has economics come down so strongly on one side of Snow's divide?
Backhouse and Fontaine (2010) argue that 'the Second World War brought
economists together with mathematicians, statisticians, engineers, and more
generally, natural scientists in a way that had profound consequences for the way
the discipline was conceived' (Backhouse & Fontaine 2010, p. 6). This led to a
strong identity of economics as being a 'rigorous, dispassionate and apolitical
discipline' (Bernstein in Backhouse & Fontaine 2010, p. 6). Such a definition is a
long way from Keynes's view of economics as being an art, based on common
sense, subject to the principles of reason (Lodewijks 2002). The Second World
War and other factors that Backhouse and Fontaine mention are relevant to
explaining the nature of contemporary economics, but in addition to these the
variable of psychological balm appears to be significant.

The rejection of pluralism also needs to be understood as being partly to do
with the need for economics to provide psychological balm. Because pluralism is
inherently tentative it denies, or at least heavily attenuates, the psychological
pay-off that many economists are used to receiving from the analysis that they
undertake. The greater scope for doubt and self-scepticism inherent in the pluralist
approach is just not as appealing in many respects. As previously mentioned, the
pragmatist philosopher William Peirce emphasised that human beings seek to free
themselves from doubt because it causes us to feel ill at ease and dissatisfied.
Doubt 'stimulates us to action until it is destroyed' (Pierce 1992, p. 114). We long
not for doubt but to 'pass into a state of belief where our minds can be at rest'
(Pierce 1992, p. 114). If we accept Pierce's argument, then it makes sense that we
might not only presuppose a closed system for the purposes of theorising, but also

presuppose it as an actual reality. However, if we opt to do this, it becomes less a process of scientific inquiry and more a flight from a reality that we cannot face. Nietzsche's point that 'the will to a system is a lack of integrity' (Nietzsche cited in Kaufmann 1954, p. 470) is apposite here, particularly if he is understood to be referring to a closed system, as is Hegel's point that 'the search for certainty reveals itself as a fear of the truth' (cited in Nightingale 2003, p. 149).

It is not just professional economists who are prone to be misled by their need for psychological balm. Consumers of economic analysis (politicians, public servants, the media and society at large) are also easily seduced by analysis that promises order, prediction and control. One can see this clearly in the premium put on economic analysis that provides exact forecasts and precise figures and that elides more descriptive or nuanced analysis. Precision and exactitude suggest that the phenomena under investigation are ordered, predictable and thus potentially controllable.

Students, while often being open to new ideas, are also prone to be avid seekers of psychological balm. It takes careful management to bring out their open and critical predilections. Consider Earl's recollection of teaching a microeconomics class in a pluralist manner:

> [N]othing had prepared me for the resistance I encountered from the students, who had no expectation of being taught in a pluralistic manner.[3] They were used to multiple choice exercises and short answer types of problems and lacked experience in essay writing and open-ended problem solving. To them, economics was a matter of moving lines on graphs and the invitation 'discuss' meant 'describe'.

> (Earl 2002, p. 2)

Earl then goes on to recall another experience of 'brutal' resistance to a pluralist course, including a 'petition and a steady stream of e-mail complaints about virtually every aspect of the course, which grew into an organized campaign' (Earl 2002, p. 1). Earl asserts that a pluralist course 'looks far harder and more threatening than a typical one-eyed mainstream offering' (Earl 2002, p. 1) and goes on to explain how the work of Perry (1970) can be helpful in understanding and managing these types of rebellions against plurality and criticality. Notably, the intellectual development from a dualistic conception of the world to 'a kind of committed relativism' is 'painful' without careful and proper guidance throughout every stage of the process (Earl 2002, p. 3).

Feminist economics, and in particular feminist philosophers of science, provide further contributions to the understanding of economics as psychological balm. It is argued that the excessive and uncritical pursuit of order, predictability and control is a reflection of a deeper masculinist bias in standard conceptions of science. The masculinist conception of science is understood to have emerged during the Enlightenment, where both the natural and social world came to be viewed as clockwork-like and mechanical and thus well suited to being understood via mathematical modelling (Nelson 2002). For feminist scholars this 'epistemology reflects a fantasy of achieving solid security through the control of nature by our minds, and a denial of all connection, embodiment, vulnerability, or flux' (Nelson 2001, p. 2). Notably, the over-emphasis on mathematical elegance is understood to have its origins in a 'misguided attempt to achieve certainty and absolute control' (Nelson 2002, p. 1). Note how psychological security and comfort (psychological balm) has an interdependent relationship with such a conception of science.

The feminist critique of the history of science offers considerable insights into why it is that the economic orthodoxy was never able, and still is unable, to understand properly the central message of Keynes's *General Theory*: that we face a fundamentally uncertain future. It was an insufficiently masculinist text; indeed, William K. Tabb argues that it exhibits feminist characteristics (Tabb 1999). On the topic of the fantasy of total control via rigorous and precise methods, consider Robert Lucas's view of how we understand economic growth (or indeed, understand anything at all):

> If we understand the process of economic growth – or of anything else – we ought to be capable of demonstrating this knowledge by creating it in these pen and paper (and computer-equipped) laboratories of ours. If we know what an economic miracle is, we ought to be able to make one.
>
> (Lucas 1993, p. 271)

Note that in Lucas's view the model maker is not just the one who understands, but is the *creator* of miracles. It should also be noted that it is not 'some understanding' or a 'partial understanding' but simply 'understanding'. It is a preposterous claim given how complex and contingent the process of economic growth is. As the institutional economist and economic historian Hugh Stretton notes:

> The fact is that 'growth' is a misleading metaphor. Economic development is history: complex, inventive, conflict-ridden, partly repetitive but partly different every time. And 'differently different' – you can't always foresee which elements of the process will continue as before, and which will vary next time.
>
> In more than two thousand years since Greek historians and philosophers began the search, historians have not discovered any reliably regular models or paths of historical change. Instead of simple or rigid theories of change, what the best historians have in their heads as they research the relevant facts are very complicated explanations, alternative possibilities, and lessons of experience.
>
> Think for yourself. Suppose you want to understand the history of England. Or the history of war. Or the history of childhood. Or the history of some other complex human activities and institutions. You don't reach for some mechanical, single-cause theory of growth, or some predetermined path of growth. You know better.
>
> (Stretton 1999, p. 85)

Stretton's political-economy perspective on the complex, contingent and ever-changing nature of economic growth is at odds with the reductionistic and mechanistic conception of growth within neoclassical economics.

Further evidence of how neoclassical economists can exhibit unwarranted levels of confidence in their own capacity to understand and control is provided Robert Solow's and Olivier Blanchard's claims in relation to neoclassical macroeconomics:

> Most economists feel [now] that short-run macroeconomic theory is pretty well in hand ... The basic outlines of the dominant theory have not changed in years. All that is left is the trivial job of filling in the empty boxes, and that will not take more than 50 years of concentrated effort at maximum.
>
> (Solow cited in Garnett 2004, p. 231)

> For a long while after the explosion of macroeconomics in the 1970s, the field looked like a battlefield. Over time however, largely because facts do not go away, a largely shared vision both of fluctuations and of methodology has emerged. Not everything is fine. Like all revolutions, this one has come with the destruction of some knowledge, and suffers from extremism and herding. None of this is deadly however. The state of macro is good.
>
> (Blanchard 2009, p. 1)

The message coming from Solow and Blanchard sits in contrast to that of the political economist Joan Robinson, who exhibits no delusions of power and control in her estimation of what any economic or political economic theory provides us with, or is likely to provide us with:

> It is often said that one theory can be driven out only by another; the neoclassicals have a complete theory (though I maintain that it is nothing but a circular argument) and we need a better theory to supplant them. I do not agree. I think any other 'complete theory' would be only another box of tricks. What we need is a different habit of mind – to eschew fudging, to respect facts and to admit ignorance of what we do not know.
>
> (Robinson 1980, p. 119)

The need for absolute control and the denial of vulnerability also helps explain Haldane's four usual stages of scientific advance: '(i) this is worthless nonsense; (ii) this is an interesting, but perverse, point of view; (iii) this is true, but quite unimportant; (iv) I always said so' (Haldane 1963, pp. 463-4). Note how the scientist protects that fantasy of total control at every stage of the process.

Feminist economists provide some of the explanation of why economists are often so rigid in their views. They emphasise that changing one's view is not just subject to the forces of habit or path-dependency: it can also be genuinely psychologically threatening and confronting. Adherence to a paradigm has a strong emotional basis and to abandon it in any real way endangers ties to colleagues and mentors (Nelson 2001). Learning involves not only the joy of realisation, but also involves the loss of certainty and of there being an altered sense of self (Perry cited in Garnett 2009). Nelson emphasises that it can be confronting and threatening:

> [W]henever we call for more connection to social problems, whenever we call for more concreteness, for more flexibility, or for more embodiment, we are asking a lot. We may think we are shaking a disciplinary branch, but in reality we are rattling a very big emotional and socio-cultural tree. We should not be surprised when defenders of the status quo often fail to engage with us at an intellectual level. The fact that we are, in fact, generally much more reasonable than they are (in the broad sense of human wisdom) is almost beside the point. Our calls for change will often be perceived as calls for the emasculation of economics, for making economics soft, for making economics impotent. Our calls for change demand that our listeners 'think outside the box' in a radical way that will, at the least, feel unfamiliar and uncomfortable to many, and be perceived as profoundly threatening by some.
>
> (Nelson 2001, p. 1)

What this suggests is that the intolerance that many political economists complain of – the 'persistent inquisition of heretics' who question holy writ (Butler, Jones & Stilwell 2009, p. 186) – has its basis in fear. Indeed, it has been stressed that fear and intolerance go hand in hand:

> Intolerance is a psychologically interesting phenomenon because it is symptomatic of insecurity and fear. Zealots who would, if they could, persecute you into conforming with their way of thinking, might claim to be trying to save your soul despite yourself; but they are really doing it because they feel threatened.
>
> (Grayling 2001, p. 8)

While feminist economists and philosophers of science do not use the terminology of psychological balm, their analysis integrates well with the idea that it is a fundamental purpose of economics. As already mentioned, there are obvious linkages between the concept of 'economics as psychological balm' and the masculinist bias in science. Feminists also offer a deeper and richer way to understand Kuhn's observation that science is largely a conservative entity. All these lines of analysis offer a deeper grounding for much of the analysis and observation of previous chapters. The current state of the curriculum cannot simply be seen as just the result of factors such as institutional inertia, cognitive path-dependence, particular conceptions of science, and that certain ideas serve certain interests. A role needs to be ascribed to psychological balm.

It is to be emphasised again that it is not just the presence of the three purposes that is significant; it is also their circular and cumulative interrelationship. Consider Pullen's (1997) argument that so-called economic laws have little empirical basis as laws and thus are more ideological than scientific (in the terms used in this chapter, they are more for the purposes of social control than science). He then goes on to note that the laws themselves are 'therapeutic': they reduce 'anxiety' and 'suffering' and make the phenomena seem natural and comprehensible and ordered (Pullen 1997, pp. 33–4) – in the terms of this chapter, they also supply psychological balm. In addition to this, it can be pointed out that the psychological balm thus provided then assists economics to provide both scientific explanation and social control. To summarise the various relationships: enhancing the scientific credentials of economics boosts its effectiveness as a means of social control. Enhancing the scientific credentials of economics also increases the capacity of economics to supply psychological balm. If economics can supply increased psychological balm then it increases its capacity to function as a means of social control. Science itself is fuelled by the thirst for psychological balm. The need for psychological balm drives the need to achieve social order.

Notes

1 It is appropriate to note that I originally encountered these two excerpts from Shackle in Samuels (1989).
2 The fact that the teleological nature of equilibrium is so seldom recognised or admitted reflects Haldane's point that 'teleology is like a mistress to the theorist – they cannot live without her but they are unwilling to be seen with her in public' (cited in Mayr 1974, p. 91).
3 The avid embrace of psychological balm would appear to be also partly to do with constituency: Earl notes that 'they had no intrinsic interest in economics as a subject for making sense of the world; it was taken merely as a hurdle en route to a degree that would provide better job opportunities' (Earl 2002, p. 1). By contrast, and significantly, he recalls a much happier experience in teaching a first-year subject (albeit at a different university) in pluralist political economy. In this instance the subject 'was taken mainly by Arts students, with Commerce and Economics students sticking to orthodox micro and macro papers' (Earl 2002, p. 2). This suggests that the main constituency for political economy may be with social science students. It also suggests that introducing pluralism at a first-year level may be much easier than at a second-year level.

References

Backhouse, R. & Fontaine, P. 2010, *The History of the Social Sciences since 1945*, Cambridge University Press, New York.
Blanchard, O. 2009, The State of Macro, Working Paper 14259, National Bureau of Economic Research Cambridge MA.
Blaug, M. 1997, *Economic Theory in Retrospect*, Cambridge University Press, Cambridge.
Boumans, M., Davis, J. B., Blaug, M., Maas, H. & Svorencik, A. 2010, *Economic Methodology: Understanding Economics as a Science*, Palgrave Macmillan, Basingstoke.
Bowles, S. 2005, *Microeconomics: Behavior, Institutions, and Evolution*, Princeton University Press, Princeton.
Bowles, S. & Gintis, H. 2013, *A Cooperative Species: Human Reciprocity and Its Evolution*, Princeton University Press, Princeton.
Butler, G., Jones, E. & Stilwell, F. J. B. 2009, *Political Economy Now! The Struggle for Alternative Economics at the University of Sydney*, Darlington Press, Sydney.

Colander, D. C., Rosser, B. J. & Holt, R. P. F. 2004, *The Changing Face of Economics: Conversations with Cutting Edge Economists*, University of Michigan Press, Ann Arbor.

Earl, P. E. 2002, 'The Perils of Pluralistic Teaching and How to Reduce Them', *Post-Autistic Economics Review*, vol. 11, January.

Fullbrook, E. 2001, 'Real Science in Pluralist', *Post-Autistic Economics Review*, March.

Garnett, R. F., Jr. 2004, 'Rhetoric and Postmodernism in Economics', in J. B. Davis, A. Marciano & J. Runde (eds), *The Elgar Companion to Economics and Philosophy*, Edward Elgar, Cheltenham, pp. 231–59.

Garnett, R. F., Jr. 2009, 'Rethinking the Pluralist Agenda in Economics Education', *International Review of Economics Education*, vol. 8, no. 2.

Gerschenkron, A. 1962, *Economic Backwardness in Historical Perspective*, Belknap Press, Cambridge.

Geuss, R. 2009, *Getting Down to Reality*, The Philosophers Zone, Radio National [online] http://www.abc.net.au/rn/philosopherszone/stories/2009/2536997.htm [accessed 6 October 2011].

Gintis, H. 2008, *Game Theory Evolving: A Problem-Centered Introduction to Modeling Strategic Interaction*, Princeton University Press, Princeton.

Grayling, A. C. 2001, *The Meaning of Things: Applying Philosophy to Life*, Weidenfeld and Nicolson, London.

Hahn, F. 1991, 'The Next Hundred Years', *Economic Journal*, vol. 101, no. 4, pp. 47–50.

Hahn, F. 1994, 'An Intellectual Retrospect.', *Banca Nazionale del Lavoro Quarterly Review*, vol. 48, no. 190, pp. 245–58.

Haldane, J. B. S. 1963, 'Book Review – the Truth About Death', *Journal of Genetics*, vol. 58, no. 3, pp. 463–4.

Hands, D. W. 2001a, 'Economic Methodology Is Dead – Long Live Economic Methodology: Thirteen Theses on the New Economic Methodology', *Journal of Economic Methodology*, vol. 8, no. 1, pp. 49–63.

Hands, D. W. 2001b, *Reflection without Rules: Economic Methodology and Contemporary Science Theory*, Cambridge University Press, Cambridge.

Kaufmann, W. 1954, *The Portable Nietzsche*, Viking Press, New York.

Keynes, J. M. 1936, *The General Theory of Employment, Interest and Money*, Macmillan, London.

Kimball, R. 1994, 'The Two Cultures' Today: On the C. P. Snow–F. R. Leavis Controversy', *The New Criterion*, vol. 12, February, p. 10.

King, J. E. 2011, 'Arguments for Pluralism in Economics', in F. J. B. Stilwell & G. Argyrous (eds), *Readings in Political Economy: Economics as a Social Science*, Tilde University Press, Melbourne, pp. 54–6.

Lawson, T. 1997, *Economics and Reality* Routledge, London.

Lazear, E. P. 2000, 'Economic Imperialism', *Quarterly Journal of Economics*, vol. 115, no. 1, pp. 99–146.

Loasby, B. J. 1991, *Equilibrium and Evolution: An Exploration of Connecting Principles in Economics*, Manchester University Press, Manchester.

Lodewijks, J. K. 2002, 'The History of Economic Thought in Australia and New Zealand', *History of Political Economy*, vol. 34, Annual Supplement, pp. 154–64.

Lodewijks, J. K. 2007, 'A Conversation with Warren Hogan', *Economic Record*, vol. 83, pp. 446–60.

Lucas, R. E., Jr. 1993, 'Making a Miracle', *Econometrica*, vol. 61, no. 2, pp. 251–72.

Mankiw, N. G., Gans, J. & King, S. 2009, *Principles of Microeconomics*, Cengage Learning Australia, South Melbourne.

Marx, K. 1946, *Capital: A Critical Analysis of Capitalist Production*, Allen & Unwin, London.

Mayr, E. 1974, 'Teleological and Teleonomic: A New Analysis', *Boston Studies in the Philosophy of Science*, vol. 14, pp. 91–117.

McCalman, J., Muir, L. & Soeterboek, C. 2008, *Adventures with Breadth a Story of Interdisciplinary Innovation*, Melbourne University, Melbourne.

Nelson, J. A. 2001, 'Why the P.A.E. Movement Needs Feminism', *Post-Autistic Economics Review*, no. 9, October, pp. 2–3.

Nelson, J. A. 2002, 'What Should Be Retained from Standard Microeconomics?', *Post-Autistic Economics Review*, vol. 14, no. 9, June.

Nightingale, P. 2003, 'If Nelson and Winter and Are Half Right About Tacit Knowledge, Which Half? A Searlean Critique of 'Codification'', *Industrial and Corporate Change*, vol. 12, no. 2, pp. 149–83.

Perry, W. G. 1970, *Forms of Ethical and Intellectual Development in the College Years: A Scheme*, Holt, Rinehart and Winston, New York.

Pierce, C. S. 1878, 'How to Make Our Ideas Clear', *Popular Science Monthly*, no. 12, January, pp. 286–302.

Pierce, C. S. 1992, *The Essential Pierce: Selected Philosophical Writings*, Indiana University Press, Bloomington.

Pullen, J. 1997, 'The Teaching of Economics: The Art of Paradigm Protection and Suppression', *Journal of Economic and Social Policy*, vol. 2, no. 1, pp. 28–40.

Robinson, J. 1980, *Collected Economic Papers*, MIT Press, Cambridge MA.

Samuels, W. J. 1989, 'In Praise of Joan Robinson: Economics as Social Control', *Society*, vol. 26, no. 2, pp. 73–6.

Samuels, W. J. & Tool, M. R. 1988, *The Economy as a System of Power*, Transaction Books, New Brunswick.

Samuelson, P. A. 1970, 'Classical and Neoclassical Theory', in R. W. Clower (ed.), *Monetary Theory*, Penguin Books, Baltimore, pp. 1–25.

Shackle, G. L. S. 1967, *The Years of High Theory: Invention and Tradition in Economic Thought, 1926–1939*, Cambridge University Press, Cambridge.

Shapin, S. & Schaffer, S. 1985, *Leviathan and the Air-Pump: Hobbes, Boyle, and the Experimental Life: Including a Translation of Thomas Hobbes, Dialogus Physicus De Natura Aeris by Simon Schaffer*, Princeton University Press, Princeton.

Simkin, C. (ed.) 1975, *Political Economy Vs Economics at the University of Sydney*, Sydney University Archives, Sydney University.

Skinner, A. S. 1986, 'Adam Smith: Then and Now', in R. D. C. Black (ed.), *Ideas in Economics*, Macmillan, Basingstoke, pp. 16–42.

Smith, A. 1776 [1982], *The Wealth of Nations*, Penguin, Harmondsworth.

Smith, A. 1795 [1982], 'Essays on Philosophical Subjects', in W. P. D. Wightman, J. C. Bryce, I. S. Ross & D. Stewart (eds), *The Glasgow Edition of the Works and Correspondence of Adam Smith*, Liberty Classics, Indianapolis.

Smith, A. 1800 [2005], *Essays, Philosophical and Literary*, Kessinger, Whitefish.

Snow, C. P. 1964, *The Two Cultures, and a Second Look: An Expanded Version of the Two Cultures and the Scientific Revolution*, University Press, Cambridge.

Stretton, H. 1999, *Economics: A New Introduction*, UNSW Press, Sydney.

Tabb, W. K. 1999, *Reconstructing Political Economy: The Great Divide in Economic Thought*, Routledge, London.

Thornton, T. B. & Millmow, A. 2008, *Interview with Assoc Prof Ian Ward* La Trobe University, 23 May.

Varian, H. 1997, 'What Use Is Economic Theory?', in A. d'Autume & J. Cartelier (eds), *Is Economics Becoming a Hard Science?*, Edward Elgar, Cheltenham, pp. 108–19.

Varoufakis, Y., Halevi, J. & Theocarakis, N. 2011, *Modern Political Economics: Making Sense of the Post-2008 World*, Routledge, London.

Whitehead, A. N. 1920, *The Concept of Nature: The Tarner Lectures Delivered in Trinity College, November 1919*, University Press, Cambridge.

Wittgenstein, L. 1980, *Vermischte Bemerkungen – Culture and Value*, Blackwell, Oxford.

Index